The Best Guide to

Success

The Best Guide to Success

Barbara A. Somervill

Series Editor Richard F. X. O'Connor

RENAISSANCE BOOKS
Los Angeles

Library of Congress Cataloging-in-Publication Data
Somervill, Barbara.
    The best guide to success / Barbara Somervill.
        p. cm.
    Includes bibliographical references and index.
    ISBN 1-58063-065-0 (trade paper : alk. paper)
    1. Success in business. 2. Career development. I. Title.
HF5386.S737   1999
650.1—dc21   99-34112
                                             CIP

10 9 8 7 6 5 4 3 2 1

Design by Lisa-Theresa Lenthall
Typesetting by Jesus Arellano

Distributed by St. Martin's Press
Manufactured in the United States of America
First Edition

For Chuck and Harold

Acknowledgments

The author thanks Richard Klesius, Margaret Vickery, Ed Duncan, Anne Dessert, Kate Kiley, Betty and Bill Ellis, and countless other friends and colleagues for providing interesting anecdotes from their treks toward success. The author notes that while names have been changed and some details altered, case studies supporting material in this book represent real situations involving real people.

Contents

The Keys to Success Are Already in Your Pocket

There are three words people hoping for career advancement should immediately drop from their vocabularies: can't, won't, and never. If you truly believe you *can't*, you *won't—never* in a million years.

Success, whether in career or in life, comes from within. It is motivated by self, nurtured by desire, evaluated on personal criteria and achieved in our own minds. To become a success, you must develop what we call SuccessThink—a method of planning, programming, and promoting yourself via a positive mindset.

Once, I interviewed for a position as editor of a food service magazine. The current edition was on the table between me and the executive vice-president of the corporation. It was black-and-white (never a plus for food photography), printed on cheap, yellow-tinged stock, and unappealing to the eye. The VP asked me if I could make it look better.

"Absolutely," I answered. I've always found confidence to be the best seller in an interview.

Could I do it cheaper than their current agency? "Absolutely."

Experience is a valuable tool too often used to limit horizons rather than expand them.

Could I upgrade the writing? Add color? Develop better ads to promote the corporate image? "Absolutely!"

The one question he never asked was whether I had ever edited or worked for any magazine in the past. I would have had to say "No," but that wouldn't have meant I couldn't do the job. My mind was made up—I was determined to meet the criteria set by my supervisor. Within eighteen months, the magazine was a full-color book printed on glossy stock—and making a $300,000 profit.

It was less important that I had no experience than that I was willing to apply what I did know to the task: writing, print buying, an eye for good photography, and the ability to keep production costs under control.

Experience is a valuable tool too often used to limit horizons rather than expand them. If you are a purchasing agent, buying office supplies for six departments, you possess the buying and negotiating skills to become a purchasing agent for a hardware store or the purchasing manager for an electronics distributor.

Consider the skills, talents, and techniques you already possess and work to discover how to use them to grow your position, put you in line for a promotion, add satisfaction to your work, or further develop your life.

The keys to success are already in your pocket. Pull them out, rev up the engine, and put your foot on the gas. Only you can accelerate your career growth—although a quality mentor and a good boss can help. Only you can set and meet your expectations. Only you can determine what success means to you.

This book is a guide to success in the broadest sense of the word. If you hope to be the editor of a magazine, the CEO of a major company, the owner of a plumbing shop, or the curator of a museum, this book is for you. It's also for you if you want to grow in the job you have now or change that job for a better one—and better is from your viewpoint, not from your paycheck.

If you want to leave corporate life and start your own business; if you want to become a better manager, negotiator, salesperson, or contributor to society, you can.

The one thing you must accept in all enterprises, regardless of size, is change. Embracing change, and making it work for you, will be key means for career advancement. Your adaptability will affect how you manage your department, your workload, layoffs, mergers, team building and changes in your workforce.

Part of the "change" that's happening in business today is a growing need for employees, regardless of level, to take responsibility for their own futures. Companies no longer play the role of "Big Brother," overseeing your finances, training, promotion, and even pay increases. You have to do that for yourself.

Each chapter of *The Best Guide to Success in Your Career* stands on its own. You can read the entire book or just a chapter or two that meet your current career needs. Put it on your reference shelf, take it out again next year, or the year after, and read another section. In two or three years your career perspective will change—guaranteed. And your career interests and motivations will change as well. This is all part of career growth.

The Best Guide to Success delves into the tried-and-true wisdom of dozens of success mavens. It will help you establish a personal plan for your future, as well as offer techniques you can use in your business life today.

The one thing you must accept in all enterprises, regardless of size, is change. Embracing change, and making it work for you, will be key means for career advancement.

Think Success—
Plan Ahead

*I*n part 1, you will learn what success is, and what elements are necessary to achieve it. Success isn't an out-of-reach, indescribable goal. It is something tangible and concrete. Remember that success is rarely instantaneous—planning is an essential ingredient. However, there isn't one single form of success. You can succeed no matter what you do or how much money you have in the bank. Getting on the road to success can be as simple as listing the events you want to achieve in your life. Believe in those events, think about them regularly, and work toward attaining those goals. As you read through part 1 the changes you need to make and the steps you need to take will become apparent.

The Essence of
Success Think

W e all watch movies or read books in which a rags-to-riches hero performs a magical transformation from the mailroom to the board room in the space of two short hours or 264 pages. Does it happen? It's possible—but don't bet your life or your success on a magic wand.

Without a prosperity spell, you'll need to set a course toward success. You must understand the critical factors that help you reach your goals. We'll examine the advice of success gurus like Napoleon Hill, Tom Peters, Og Mandino, and Tony Robbins, to discover how their business mastery applies to your current skills and future expectations.

IN THIS CHAPTER:

- *How to recognize success*
- *Developing a success-oriented thought process*
- *Adjusting to levels of success*
- *Knowing your own value*

RECOGNIZING SUCCESS

Success, regardless of who achieves it, is rarely an instantaneous event. It's not a title on the door. It's not a six-figure paycheck. It's not a company car or traveling first class. It's not even being listed in the Forbes Four Hundred Richest People in America, although that's one list where most of us wouldn't mind finding our names.

Success is a process of planning, taking action, and achieving results, regardless of the task at hand. You don't have to be the CEO of a high-tech corporation, an award-winning actor, or a guest on 60 Minutes. You can be a success no matter what you do or how much money you have in the bank.

Martin Luther King Jr. said, "If a man is called to be a streetsweeper, he should sweep streets even as Michelangelo painted, or Beethoven composed music, or Shakespeare wrote poetry. He should sweep streets so well that all the hosts of heaven and earth will pause to say, here lived a great streetsweeper who did his job well." Dr. King had a good fix on success.

Success is fire in the belly. Discipline and determination. Burning desire. It is personal, private, driving, and satisfying. And it is yours if you want it badly enough.

Disciples of Napoleon Hill, a student of business practices of the rich and famous, follow the concept of cosmic habitforce to reach a level of success. To achieve success, make a list of events you want to achieve in your life, at home and at work. Believe in those events, think about them regularly, and work toward attaining those elements of success. This will put you on the road to success.

"Too many people focus on the trappings of success—without understanding what really brings peace and happiness."

—*Jim Murphy, president and CEO, ENFO Research Group*

EXERCISE   *What's Success?*

How do you decide what is successful and what isn't? Make five columns on a page of legal paper and head the columns as follows: name, age, years of experience in job/occupation, three signs of success, three signs of failure. In the first column list the names of three people you consider successful, leaving plenty of space between each name. Complete the next two columns for each person.

The fourth column is a bit harder. You must choose only three things that show each person is successful. Your choices

EVALUATING SUCCESS

Name	Age	Years of Experience in Job	3 Signs of Success	3 Signs of Failure
Jack Snow	37	7—sales representative 6—director, marketing	1. BMW 2. $500K house 3. heads "dept. of the year" at Waffler & Co.	1. divorced twice 2. passed over for V.P. 3. rejected for golf club membership
Lisa Frost	28	1—sales representative 2—district sales manager 2—regional sales manager	1. two major promotions in 5 years 2. mentored by CEO 3. top sales district—2 years	1. no family life 2. no friends outside work 3. disliked by subordinates
Elmer Raines	54	retired at 43	1. citizen of the year 2. volunteers for SCORE 3. financially stable enough to retire at 43	1. laid off twice in his career 2. wrote book that bombed 3. children unmotivated, unemployable

can be material holdings (house, car, boat, vacation home in the Bahamas) or intangibles (respect, self-confidence, talent). Next, consider three things in this person's life that could be considered failures. Again, this is difficult because often we are unaware of other people's failures. However, you might choose divorce, job loss, obnoxious children, or something similar.

Review your chart. How did you define success? Failure? Are your signs of success financial or consumer goods? Are they signs of character, service, or respect? What did you consider failure?

You need to decide what success means for you in order to achieve it. If it's owning a BMW, you can get a second job and reach your goal within a year. If it's peer recognition, it may take considerably more time and effort.

Now, to the point of this exercise: Is your name on the top of your list? Is it even on the list? If you didn't include yourself, why not? To attain success, you have to develop SuccessThink—a mindset in which you consider success a daily part of your thought processes and actions.

You don't do things right once in a while. You do them right all the time. Winning is a habit. Unfortunately, so is losing.

SuccessThink

Legendary coach Vince Lombardi believed, "Winning is not a sometime thing; it's an all-the-time thing. You don't win once in a while. You don't do things right once in a while. You do them right all the time. Winning is a habit. Unfortunately, so is losing."

What mental habits have you formed to promote your own success? Creating a positive, proactive mindset is the essence of SuccessThink. It's a process of planning small successes each day, taking action to make those successes happen, and recognizing the achievement of results. It's looking at every project and finding all of its positive aspects—even in failure. It's learning from mistakes, analyzing where you went wrong, taking a better path, producing better results.

To relate this concept to daily life, consider two well-known groups that help people overcome problematic habits: Alcoholics Anonymous and WeightWatchers®. Neither of these groups tells its members to develop large, impossible plans for the distant future.

AA members take one day at a time. Their daily ritual begins with "just for today," and wisely so. No one addicted to alcohol can fathom staying sober for ten years, but one day is doable.

A new participant at WeightWatchers is never encouraged to set a goal of losing 150 pounds. That's like planning to climb Mount Everest barefoot. A sound weight plan breaks up a lengthy weight-loss program into small, attainable goals. In this case, two-pounds-a-week becomes doable.

These two groups actively work to . . .

- break long-standing, defeating habits

- develop a pattern of small successes

- recognize milestones

- create new, life-fulfilling habits

In knowing its destination, you can break the journey into small, manageable segments.

One warning that should be issued along with every formula for success is this: Remember the Golden Rule. At the pinnacle of your career you should still maintain a positive, ethical approach to your work. This includes dealings with vendors, colleagues, and subordinates.

Be forthright and honest, and respect will automatically come to you. Your work environment will be positive, relaxed, and nurturing, and your subordinates will willingly tell you about problems because they trust your good judgment and fairness. Isn't that what you want?

> **At the pinnacle of your career you should still maintain a positive, ethical approach to your work.**

HOW DO YOU SET UP A PLAN FOR SUCCESS?

- *Know what you want.*
- *Set a goal to obtain it.*
- *Investigate your goal. Know what it requires and what you must do to achieve it.*
- *Stop only when you're satisfied.*

What Is Your Word Worth?

Business ethics, should be—although they rarely are—part of career success. No matter how large the paycheck, the bonus, or the Jacuzzi, if you can't look at yourself in the mirror each morning, think twice about your actions.

Honesty, integrity, and decency do not have to be casualties of daily business. Make integrity a part of your success package. You'll sleep better at night, earn the respect of colleagues, and achieve meaningful success.

Make integrity a part of your success package.

Periods of Adjustment

As you develop your goals, remember few people use the same measure of success throughout their lives. At twenty, success might be a paying job, your own apartment and a car that runs. At thirty, it might be a house in the suburbs, 2.4 healthy children, and a happy marriage. At sixty, you might want the respect of your peers, an education for your grandchildren, and a retirement home in Maui.

EXERCISE   *Reflecting on Achievements*

What did you want way back when? This is a three-column exercise, and you'll need plenty of space for filling in the blanks.

List three ages of your lifetime. They can be childhood, teenage years, novice employee, middle age—it's your choice. Next to each one, write down three things that were important to you then. In the third column, add whether or not you achieved those goals.

Did you always achieve 100 percent success in everything you wanted? If so, then you were unusually lucky. Most of us settle for partial success and recognize even failure isn't tragic. No, there was no date for the prom, but straight As got you into a good college, a great career, and the chance to show off a charming spouse at your high school reunion ten years later.

Just as dreams and ambitions change by the decade, they also change year to year. Consider the external forces that affect your criteria for success: marriage and divorce, moving or transfers, mergers and acquisitions, loss or addition of colleagues,

STAGES OF ACHIEVEMENT

Age	3 Things that Seemed Important	Achieved?
Junior in H.S.	1. becoming a cheerleader 2. date for the prom 3. straight *As*	1. yes 2. no 3. yes
Novice Employee	1. keeping the job 2. buying a car that worked 3. paying bills	1. yes 2. no 3. most of the time
Department Managers	1. reaching target projections 2. staying within budget 3. promoting key personnel	1. for the most part 2. yes 3. only one out of three

births and deaths in the family, changes in health, acts of God, the list goes on. If you wish to be successful, your idea of success must be flexible enough to adjust for outside influences.

KNOW YOUR OWN VALUE

The first step toward success is knowing your own value. At the start, your perceived value will be small. You have limited experience, few unique skills, and lack expertise. It's up to you to create a reputation that singles you out from the crowd. Once you've done that, your reputation becomes part of your success and actually feeds it.

Engineering genius Charles P. Steinmetz was hired by General Electric to solve a baffling mechanical problem. Steinmetz walked around the machinery, considered the problem and drew a chalk X on the spot where he believed the trouble originated. As the story goes, Steinmetz hit the target, and the problem was fixed.

As a hired consultant, Steinmetz sent GE a bill for his fee: $10,000. GE's financial department was in an uproar.

It's up to you to create a reputation that singles you out from the crowd.

They demanded an itemized invoice. Steinmetz's response was as quick and to the point as his diagnosis:

- Making one chalk mark: $1.

- Knowing where to place it: $9,999.

There is nothing like knowledge to add value to a person. And it needn't have been gained in a classroom.

Clearly, Steinmetz knew his own worth. But do you? If you fall under the category "six of one—half dozen of the other," you must do some careful evaluation. Answer these questions:

- *What will make me more valuable to my company?* More valuable to those outside the company? Employees who do what they're asked and little extra aren't considered valuable—they're considered replaceable. You must be productive: do more, achieve more, and reach beyond expectations to be noticed.

- *What do I need to know to become more valuable?* There is nothing like knowledge to add value to a person. And it needn't have been gained in a classroom. Keep current with trends in your industry and parallel industries. Read, watch business-oriented programs on TV, attend seminars on your own, and ask people considered tops in your field for their advice. When the opportunity arises, offer your knowledge to make a project more successful.

- *What talents do I have that are not being fully used?* Only you can answer that question, but some talents that might be worth cultivating are creativity, resourcefulness, problem-solving, long-range planning, and leadership.

- *How can I put myself in a position to use these talents?* Offer them. When a project arises you feel would showcase your talent, tell your boss or the project leader. Be sure to explain why you want to be part of the project and what talent or know-how you can offer.

- *What in my past record shows I can stand out?* What results can I use to foster my reputation as a success? Keep a record of each project you work on and its perform-ance. As the file fills up, you'll see a pattern of success. Use this material to doc-ument requests for raises or promotions.

> ### SUCCESSTHOUGHTS
>
> *Today's the day to start your "future" file. Write down the answers to the preceding questions and put them in the file. As you achieve results, no matter how small, write them down and put them in the file too. Review the file monthly. Add whatever and whenever you can. There is great strength in knowing you are developing your reputation for success—one step at a time.*

- *What things do I want in my future record to add perceived value to my position?* If you receive an "atta-boy" from a col-league or superior, make a copy and send it to your boss with a comment like, "Thought you'd like to see the XYZ project worked out well." Ask your supervisor to put a copy in your personnel file.

- *How do I let my boss, colleagues and others in on my value?* Be patient. If you are regularly answering all the above questions in a practical manner, people will notice.

Be patient . . .

people will notice.

Never Underestimate Hard Work

Tycoon Andrew Carnegie once said, "The average person puts only 25percent of his energy and ability into his work. The world takes off its hat to those who put in more than fifty percent of their capacity, and stands on its head for those few and far between souls who devote one hundred percent.

Once called the "work ethic," a quiet devotion to hard work is scoffed at today by those who happily slide by with two-hour lunches and hourly chats around the coffee pot. Don't let them fool you; success is hard work.

In his book *Self-Made in America,* entrepreneur John McCormack gives several laws for success. The top two laws concern hard work—because, in McCormack's own words, "Hard work works."

If you don't like your job or career, change it . . . [otherwise] you won't be a success, you'll just collect a paycheck.

—*McCormack and Legge,*
Self-Made in America

Love It or Leave It

Two hundred years ago, people were born into their careers. If your father was a stablehand, you were destined for the stables. Grab a shovel and get busy.

One hundred years ago, your job was influenced by your social status, family history and, frequently, ethnic heritage.

Fifty years ago employees retired from the same company they were employed by when they finished school. Here's your gold watch. Come back and see us some time. Moving to Sun City? Enjoy your retirement.

Today career choice is yours. If you don't like your job or career, change it—everyone else is doing the same thing. The reason is simple: Don't spend your life in a job that makes you miserable. You won't be a success, you'll just collect a paycheck.

"History has shown that the majority of people who achieve massive success love what they do. Think about it—can you name one success who didn't have a passion for his or her work? One of the keys to success is making a successful marriage between what you do and what you love," suggest Anthony Robbins and Joseph McClendon, III, in *Unlimited Power, A Black Choice.*

ROLE MODELS

If you don't know how to get to your goal, follow the path of someone who has been where you want to go. Choose

a role model—carefully. This decision, while not permanent, largely determines what kind of life you work
towards. Your role should be someone whose values and
lifestyle you respect and admire. Be selective in whom you
emulate, and don't blindly follow where your role model
leads. Be sure you know why you are following them—
what is it about them that you like. Many of today's role models have character flaws that are not worth admiring or copying.

> ### SUCCESSTHOUGHTS
>
> *Read, learn, investigate, and devour information about success in the same way you would investigate investing $1,000,000—because that's exactly what you're doing! The difference between your lifetime earnings as a mediocre player and as an industry star will be $1,000,000 or more.*

You might select someone in your own industry or a community leader. Or you might want to investigate success gurus who are nationally and internationally known.
Most have written extensively on their theories and prac-
tices—and these vary widely—only you can decide if their
description of success matches your needs. At the head of
the guru list you will find such notables as:

- *Tom Peters*—author of the *Excellence* series of books

- *Napoleon Hill*—one of the founders of the personal
  success movement

- *Stephen Covey*—known for his *Seven Habits of
  Highly Effective People*

- *Anthony Robbins*—an internationally known
  motivational speaker and author

- *Og Mandino*—an inspiring sales representative
  and author

The list gets longer every day. Take a methodical, thorough approach to learning about success theories. After
all, it's your future.

Picture Your Future

Let's go back to the chart you created at the beginning of this chapter. Once you've defined your destination you're ready to go. From today on, put yourself at the head of your list of successful people, and mean it.

E X E R C I S E	*Thinking Ahead*

Turn the paper over and start a new chart with four columns; Me, Job/Occupation, Signs of Success, and Road Map. In the

CAREER PATH

Me	*Job/Occupation*	*Signs of Success*	*Road Map*
Me Today	purchasing agent	1. house 2. healthy children 3. happy marriage	1. loyalty to my company 2. taking on extra work 3. balancing work and home
Me Next Year	senior purchasing agent	1. new car 2. family vacation to Hawaii 3. reach 30% bonus target	1. renegotiate pricing on products 2. replace XYZ and DDD vendors 3. exceed this year's targets by 25% 4. top sales district-2 years
Me in Five Years	director, purchasing	1. promotion to director 2. all department members meet or exceed targets 3. $300,000 house on golf course	1. work with colleagues to achieve better purchasing ROI 2. improve relationship with current director 3. acquire mentor

first column down, list Me Today, Me Next Year, and Me in Five Years. Leave plenty of space between entries.

What will be your job or career path five years from today? What you aim for requires effort and results to get there.

Write three signs of success you expect to achieve at each point in your life. Then, write the path (efforts/results) you need to take to get there.

The next step—your first big step—is up to you. Use SuccessThink for every step, every project, every meeting. Become the guide to your own success.

"Determination + Goal-Setting + Concentration = Success."

—Harvey Mackay,
Swim with the
Sharks without
Being Eaten Alive

CHAPTER RECAP

- Success is your perception, not the preconceived notions of others

- To become successful, you must establish success goals

- It is necessary to understand your value to your company and your colleagues

- Your perception of success changes as you mature

Recommended Reading

Mackay, Harvey. *Swim with the Sharks without Being Eaten Alive.* New York: William Morrow and Company, 1988.

Mandino, Og. *The Return of the Ragpicker.* New York: Bantam, 1992.

Peters, Tom, and Nancy Austin. *A Passion for Excellence.* New York: Random House, 1985.

Powell, Colin, with Joseph E. Persico. *My American Journey.* New York: Random House, Inc., 1995.

Self-Assessment

*W*hen creating a long-range growth plan, you must do a thorough self-assessment. Evaluate your strengths, talents, and skills. And, to get a well-rounded picture, don't forget those weaknesses! Despite all your strengths, it may well be those pesky flaws or gaps in your profile that keep you from moving forward.

The first step is to look at each item in your personal inventory. We all have assets worth cultivating: quirks, eccentricities, and peculiarities that define our personalities. To reach your goals, consider how your assets assist you in work situations and determine how they can contribute toward your advancement.

Your personality influences your promotability. Are you easygoing? Quick to anger? Avoid confrontation at all costs? You need to look at these aspects of your personality and consider how they fit with the position you wish to attain.

Decide which skills and talents, what business know-how you have and how they translate into a higher performance level, either in your current or next job.

IN THIS CHAPTER:

• *Two exercises to identify personal characteristics*

• *Tips on comparing yourself to others*

• *Recognizing your type— A or B?*

• *Assessing skills v. talents*

Next, what work and lifestyle situations make you happy? Do you prefer working in a small office with limited personal interaction or would you rather be in a "pool" surrounded by others? Finding your niche is essential for on-the-job happiness.

Finally, discover ways to minimize the effects of weaknesses on job performance and discover ways to turn negatives into positives.

Ready to take a close look in the mirror? Then, let's go.

> *"The key to success is to do things with an unlimited upside potential and a downside that is limited to the use of your time."*
>
> —*Scott Adams, creator of Dilbert*

Ask Yourself

Joe Girard, salesman extraordinaire, in *Mastering Your Way to the Top* suggests we ask ourselves some important questions:

- Have I clearly defined my goal?

- Is my goal a long-range one, a short-range one?

- Is it an achievable goal for me?

- Is my goal flexible so it can change when my needs change?

As you ask these questions, consider your strengths. One of the most significant strengths you might have is the ability to ask yourself the right questions and answer them honestly. This probably sounds a bit silly, but too many people gloss over their problems.

EXERCISE   *Know Your Job-Oriented Characteristics*

Here is a list of job-oriented characteristics. Place a check next to each of the strengths you believe you possess.

Go back over each item you checked. Circle the five you consider most important. Then, re-evaluate the same list from your supervisor's perspective. Which characteristics would she

MY CHARACTERISTICS

persistent	solid work ethic	shrewd
team player	team leader	long-range planner
strategic planner	inventive	progressive thinker
short-range planner	sharp-witted	solid speaking skills
solid writing skills	self-motivated	effective
results directed	goal directed	people directed
pragmatic	logical	sociable
efficient	organized	multi-tasking
time directed	effective time use	visionary
trustworthy	confident	high earning potential
tenacious	convincing	solid negotiator
solid sales technique	scrupulous	detail directed
problem solving	resourceful	structured
reasonable	demanding	fair minded
sense of integrity	sense of loyalty	community directed

If you know someone who is currently in your ideal job, go back over the list and determine which strengths have helped him succeed.

think are important? Remember, these are your strengths, honestly evaluated. You may consider creativity a plus—but not for an accountant. In many cases, creative accounting equals a trip to the unemployment office. On the other hand, if your future is in advertising or entertainment, creativity is a real plus. Do your strengths match the job you have now? The one you are aiming for in the future? If you know someone who is currently in your ideal job, go back over the list and determine which strengths have helped him succeed.

What Is Possible?

"After you decide what you want to do, assess the possibility. This is not intended to lower your sights, but rather to serve as a reality check. You can't fly. You can't make yourself invisible. Don't spend your time on those issues; they won't happen even if you really want them to," advises J. Robert Parkinson in *How to Get People to Do Things Your Way*.

Don't spend time spinning your wheels wishing to be something you're not. Instead, invest your energy in who you are. In the long run, you'll be happier and more successful. As a nation, we disparage achievement that is less than perfect. When an Olympian gets a bronze medal, we groan that she's only came in third. Hold on a minute! Third best in the world is not failure. How many of us can say we are thc third best in what we do?

CULTIVATING STRENGTHS

Certain strengths are especially well worth cultivating if you have not fully developed them. They are: visionary, strategic planner, and team leader. A visionary sees where the company could go, a strategic planner sees how to get there, and a team leader motivates others to make it happen.

Once a goal—vision—is identified, the plan necessary to achieve it is needed. Strategic planning enables a vision to come to fruition. What exactly does a strategic planner do? He considers the goal from all angles:

- What personnel, materials, manufacturing capabilities are needed?

- What assets are available to use toward achieving the goal?

- What assets are lacking? Is there funding available to fill the gaps? If so, where does it come from? Will it deplete resources needed elsewhere?

- What people and departments will play key roles in the success of the plan? Who does what? Who will take charge?

- What are the financial, physical, and emotional impacts of achieving the plan?

- What is the up side? What is the down side?

- How can the competition affect the goal?

- What is the market potential from achieving the plan?

- When does everything happen (creating the schedule)?

- What glitches can occur during implementation? Roll out? Long range?

You get the picture, and you can probably see how critical this style of thinking is for a company on the brink of expansion.

Finally, leadership is crucial. A leader may be a manager, or not; *leadership* and *management* are not the same thing. There is more to leadership than organization and delegation. A leader motivates others, generates excitement, cultivates talents—characteristics that will be of increasing significance in the new millennium.

The combination of these characteristics—vision, strategic planning, and leadership—are unbeatable. Bill Gates, Ross Perot, Cornelius Vanderbilt, Oprah Winfrey, and Steven Spielberg all possess this triple-winner combination. Do you?

How can you access these strengths? First, take seminars or classes to build your know-how on the planning end. Many communities have leadership programs, coaching classes and opportunities to become a community leader. Work with people who have vision and investigate the creative process.

It's true you can't be Bill Gates or Steven Spielberg, but you can maximize the strengths you have through practice, assertive action, experience, and learning.

A or B?

A great deal has been studied, written, and regurgitated about Type A v. Type B personalities. Where did this idea come from? In 1958, Drs. Friedman and Rosenman, medical researchers, identified a behavioral profile most prone to heart attack: Type A.

The Type A person tends to be anchored to work, spends long hours at the office, and micro-manages every project because no one else can do anything as well as she can. Type As measure life by the numbers: how many hours they work, the number of people working under them, the productivity (in dollars) of those workers, their own salaries, houses, cars, vacation homes.

> **SUCCESSTHOUGHTS**
>
> *Type A? Type B? Which is best? Probably a combination of both. Most of us are more one type than the other, but we all have tendencies toward both. Balance, perspective, and moderation smooth the rough edges of A, while ambition, pressure, and stress light a fire under B. If you have too many Type A traits, develop stress reduction habits. If you are too B-oriented, develop self-motivation if you intend to reach the top.*

Type As play to win in every arena: at work, at home, on the golf course, at the Little League field, in the classroom. You can drive to work every morning watching the Type As pass you left and right, while they talk on their cell phones, apply their makeup or shave, read the *Wall Street Journal,* and drop their kids off at private schools—all at the same time.

Type Bs, on the other hand, are more relaxed and less stressed. They maintain a perspective on life that allows them to take vacations without guilt, drive to work with their hands on the wheel, eat lunch away from their desk, and get home in time to help Ken or Christie with algebra homework. Type Bs are not the last to leave every night, nor are they the first to arrive every morning. They tend to handle pressure without exploding, don't chop subordinates heads off for making minor mistakes, and leave at 3:15 on Thursday because Wendy's in a ballet recital or Will's championship soccer match starts at 3:30. Type B would never miss an event like that.

Personality Plus

Being elected Miss Congeniality is wonderful. Not being elected Miss Congeniality is also wonderful. Your job should suit your personality. Some jobs require outgoing, fun-loving, extroverted personalities; others require a more serious, contemplative bent.

Know Your Personality Traits	E X E R C I S E

Put a check next to the personality traits you possess.

PERSONALITY TRAITS

gregarious	insensitive	hostile
introverted	rude	broad-minded
happy	cooperative	radical
sad	helpful	chauvinistic
serious	understanding	humorous
light hearted	sympathetic	whining
relaxed	nervous	flexible
stressed	easygoing	moody
friendly	bigoted	honest
competitive	touchy	enthusiastic
deceitful	selfless	reclusive
open	selfish	shy
sincere	indulgent	kind
generous	crafty	arrogant

Go back over the list. Which are your best personality traits? How can they be helpful in your job? Which are your worst character traits? How do they detract from your success? Can you do anything to change them?

What would your boss consider your best traits? If you don't know, ask! Be sure to ask what negatives your boss sees and take the news calmly. If your boss says you are temperamental and cranky at times, you'll only prove his point if you explode in his face and complain he doesn't treat you fairly.

Here's an example: Jackie's best trait is her honesty. You can always depend on Jackie to tell the truth. Most of us would consider this a blessing because when we work with Jackie we can trust her. However, what happens at a meeting where Jackie's boss tells the CEO that the department is too jammed with work to take on the BrandEX new product introduction? The CEO asks Jackie's opinion. She says that the department is not too busy. In this case her truthfulness becomes a liability. Look at your own personality traits from your personal standpoint and that of others. If you have trouble assessing your qualities, ask your spouse—especially if his best quality is diplomacy.

Now, consider which traits you have that will help in your next position—the promotion you've been working for. Are there traits that hold you back? If so, can behavior modification smooth your rough edges? When you come up for review, mention those traits that will help advance your personal goals. Don't assume your boss already knows your virtues—put them down on paper!

Last, if you checked only positive traits, review the list again. We all have faults, and if you can't acknowledge yours, that's a fault in itself. Besides, how can you overcome a negative you won't admit exists?

SKILLS V. TALENTS

Skills are bits of business know-how that help you do your job. Here are some examples: planning a budget, printing a brochure, utilizing computer software, running a copier or fax machine, making a decent cup of coffee, or putting someone on hold without disconnecting the call.

Skills are, for the most part, buildable commodities. If you don't know how to do something, you can learn. Talents, on the other hand, are innate; you're born with them. No classes, seminars, private tutors, or mentors can turn you into a pianist, a gymnast, a professional athlete, or a musician, particularly if you have no talent along those lines.

Talents, luckily, don't all fall in the arts or sports areas. Number crunchers have a talent for seeing figures as information. A graphic designer has a talent for taking those numbers and presenting them in pictorial form. A talented speaker shows the graphs and charts to an audience and explains what it all means.

SKILLS V. TALENTS

Skills	*Talents*
hiring photographers, journalists	gifted writer
planning an editorial calendar	strategic planner
purchasing paper stock and print	organizational skills
purchasing art	good negotiator and salesperson
computer graphics (PageMaker, Quark, Photoshop, Illustrator)	artistic, creative
computer word processing (Microsoft Word, Word Perfect)	interpersonal skills: working with artists, writers, advertisers
degree in English, minor in Graphic Arts	developing and implementing a budget
editing, journalism experience	managing others
budgeting	visionary
page design	excellent personal presentation

We drag substantial baggage into every decision, and it affects both our personal and public lives.

Here's an example of how skills and talents blend to enhance success. Kevin is editor of a small, local newspaper with an annual budget of less than $400,000. A publisher in a neighboring city is looking for an editor for a new food magazine, annual budget of roughly $3.5 million dollars. If you think Kevin doesn't have what it takes for this job, think again. Kevin can do budgeting, knows publishing, and is a self-starter.

Yes, this is a step up for Kevin and will expand his knowledge and challenge his talents. It's a stretch. However, there is nothing the food magazine editor needs that Kevin doesn't have.

How about you? Do your talents and skills match the job you're shooting for? Make a written comparison and see if you fall short. If so, do what you can to fill in the gaps through self-help, formal education, or on-the-job training.

IMPORTANT WORK-RELATED ITEMS

Concept/Value	Irrelevant	So-So	Vital
advancement to a better position			
adventure/travel			
benefits			
daily challenge			
community orientation			
corporate culture			
creative opportunities			
decision making			
education or training opportunities			
family time			
fast track advancement			
flexibility			
friendships			
group associations			
helping others			

helping society			
independent work			
job stability			
location of home or work			
money			
moral or ethical standards			
new ideas/things			
personal safety			
physical challenge			
recognition			
routine tasks			
relaxed work atmosphere			
rewards other than money			
self-employment			
self-reliance			
size of company			
skill building			
status symbols			
supervision of your work			
supervisory responsibility			
working for a specific company			

"There are two kinds of men who never amount to much: those who cannot do what they are told, and those who can do nothing else."

—*Cyrus H. Curtis*

WHAT DO YOU WANT?

What things complete your life: business or career, family, health, marriage, friends, community, spirituality, physical appearance? Which can you do something about? What can you do? How important is any change in the overall scheme of things?

Go through the following list and determine which work-related items are most important to you. Then, determine which lifestyle items are most important. Ask your spouse to mark his or her choices, and compare the results.

How do your choices tally with your self-assessment to this point? As you look at the whole picture, you should see yourself as a person whose personality, skills, and talents are equal to those areas that you value.

A Reality Check

Despite the calmest personality, the most easygoing disposition, the know-how to douse the worst corporate fire, other factors can work against us when pressure, stress, decision-making, or other crises-related situations are involved.

Those pressures could include: the timeliness of the situation (its urgency), the opinions of others, our personal value system, social status or expectations, basic needs and desires, family events occurring at the same time, our self-understanding, the needs of the many as opposed to the few (common in corporate decisions), and our past history of decision making.

We drag substantial baggage into every decision, and it affects both our personal and public lives. It is important to keep baggage under control. You can't avoid it; but you can take charge of how it affects your actions. In other words, you can determine whether outside influences cause you to be reactive or proactive.

In general, reactive people are influenced by what goes on around them. Proactive people create their own atmosphere; they build their emotional lives around areas within their control. Choose a proactive means of describing your accomplishments, whether it is in conversation, business meetings, or applying for a new job. Wouldn't you prefer to hire someone who asserts that she...

- authored a program on HR benefit access

- presented corporate benefits programs to all personnel

- reduced benefit spending while increasing overall benefits coverage

- consolidated benefit providers

- implemented programs for well-baby care, dental health, and substance abuse care

- trained three new human resources employees in benefits administration

When talking about yourself and your work, do so in a positive way. Choose from this list, or find specific active verbs of your own to describe your accomplishments:

ACTIVE VERBS

accelerate	edit	organize	streamline
analyze	expedite	perform	supervise
attend	formulate	preside	track
broaden	head	promote	train
control	hire	propose	translate
create	implement	recruit	triple
develop	improve	reduce	unify
design	increase	research	utilize
dominate	monitor	strategize	verify

> *"Too many people focus on the trappings of success—without understanding what really brings peace and happiness."*
> —*Jim Murphy*

Evaluate your day or week—how did your projects work out? What did you accomplish? Did you fulfill obligations and personal needs? Did you build strengths? Did you control your weaknesses? Did you address priorities in a timely fashion? Did you complete urgent business? Did you follow patterns leading to personal, economic, or spiritual success?

This all sounds like a lot to do, but self-evaluation, on a daily, weekly, and yearly basis, is part of the pattern that makes up SuccessThink.

"It took me fifteen years to discover that I had no talent for writing, but I couldn't give it up because by that time I was too famous."

—*Robert Benchley*

CHAPTER RECAP

- Assess your personality, abilities, and skills from both your viewpoint and that of others.

- Cultivate your strengths and minimize your weaknesses.

- Identify your personality type to understand how you approach work.

- Be realistic, but pursue your dreams in a positive, assertive manner.

Recommended Reading

Barrett, Jim, and Geoff Williams. *Test Your Own Job Aptitude: Exploring Your Career Potential.* New York: Penguin, 1995.

Edman, David. *Your Weaknesses Are Your Strengths: Transformation of the Self Through Analysis of Personal Weaknesses.* Chicago: Loyola Press, 1994.

Gale, Barry, and Linda Gale. *Discover What You're Best At: The National Career Aptitude System and Career Directory.* New York: Fireside, 1990.

Johnston, Susan M. *The Career Adventure: Your Guide to Personal Assessment, Career Exploration, and Decision Making.* Englewood Cliffs, NJ: Prentice Hall, 1998.

Sturman, Gerald. *The Career Discovery Project.* New York: Main Street Books, 1993.

Move Ahead with Change

Y ou're cool. You're calm. You're unflappable. When change hits you, you just go on smiling and move forward. Nonsense! Change—both good and bad—is always with us, affecting our lives, our moods, our accomplishments, and our paychecks.

Most people react to change with stress. If you are one of those people, you're in good company. It's important to understand that not all stress is bad. We all live with stress, and a certain amount is necessary for us to function in our daily lives.

However, change-induced stress can influence you adversely. How much is too much? We all have different coping abilities, different sirens sounding the alarms on our stress-o-meters. Consider the top stressors affecting our lives:

- *change in the family structure*—aging, divorce, marriage, birth, or death

- *change in the workplace*—occupation, position, responsibility

- *change in financial status*—both less money and more money

- *change in personal well-being*—illness or health

All these stressors are connected to change—that one constant factor we deal with every day.

A marriage or birth is supposed to be a happy event, but how many times have you seen a bride burst into tears, or a new mother flustered caring for her baby? Additions to a family bring change that, welcome as it may be, adds to our stress levels.

Workplace changes are so frequent we hardly take notice anymore. Again, major and minor work changes influence our daily lives. The addition of new people throws off the equilibrium of a department as does the loss of an employee, regardless of why the employee leaves. Promotions, while actively sought, add pressure and responsibility to daily burdens.

Oddly enough, having more money can create as much stress as having less money. And the effects of physical wellness/illness are significant.

If change is a constant, what can we do about it? What aspects of change can we influence? And, how can we cope with change—that one factor in our lives that just keeps on ticking like a Timex watch?

FACTORS THAT EFFECT CHANGE

First, change in the workplace is created by both internal and external forces. While you may be able to influence internal factors, most external factors are beyond your reach.

Among those elements that effect internal change are: profit margins, acquisitions and mergers, increased debt load, promotions, relocations, restructuring within the company, and even relocation to a new facility. Those are the "biggies." But just as important are the small, daily

"In a time of turbulence and change, it is more true than ever that knowledge is power."

—*John F. Kennedy*

changes affecting productivity: work hours, flex time or space, illness, absence, attitude, vacations, work loads, interruptions, power outages, computer bombs, and even surprise birthday parties. Anything that demands a reorganization of your daily plan is a change—even an unplanned lunch with the boss.

External forces promote change, including technological advances, development of global markets, decrease in existing markets, loosening or tightening of government regulations, and trade agreements such as NAFTA.

In *Unlimited Power, A Black Choice,* Anthony Robbins and Joseph McClendon urge, "As soon as something happens to you, whether good or bad, your job is to start looking immediately for the benefit. Sometimes it's hard, but if you keep looking, you will find it, and that's when your life will change for the better."

Let's look at the external forces promoting change and see how a potential negative can be perceived as a benefit:

> ### SUCCESSTHOUGHTS
> *Take time to identify and evaluate changes occurring in your workplace. Are these changes major? minor? Recognize which changes cause you stress and work to keep it under control.*

- How many of us still have an 8-track stereo cartridge system? A record player? A non–self-cleaning oven? As technology advances, a company's share of the current market changes. What can your department or your company do to be on the cutting edge? Is there current technology that can make you more efficient? Can you create a new product, revise a process, and utilize a product differently to give your company an edge? Technological advances are positive influences, as long as your company keeps up with the times.

- When most of us think "global," we automatically think Japanese. Wake up! There is a whole world out there beyond Japan, and those other countries welcome American products and American know-how. Many exportable skills and services available in the U.S. are bankable in other countries: infrastructure, heavy construction, technology, health and dental care, communications, retail products. Perhaps your company could venture into the global marketplace. As changes go—that could be the most exciting. Investigate the potential of South America, Southeast Asia, Australia, and become a "global" asset.

• *Economic factors* may signal a decrease in your company's existing market. If so, discover new opportunities, products you currently market that can be sold elsewhere or marketed in a different way. Or, there may be technology your company has which can be applied to another industry. Look for alternative markets and put economic factors into perspective.

• *Governmental regulations* affect a company's profit. An increase in the minimum wage, mandated parental leave, mandated levels of health care, and safety requirements can make a major impact on the bottom line. Notification is given well in advance, and companies should begin implementation of rules and regulations as soon as they are known. Volunteer to be part of the team to develop a swift, efficient implementation plan. It's experience that will serve you well in the future.

• *Political factors*—like trade agreements or tariffs—change how we do business as a nation. NAFTA, a trade agreement with Canada and Mexico, directly influences manufacturing practices of many American corporations. Do you speak

Spanish or French? Could you become a liaison between your company and Mexican or French-speaking Canadian suppliers?

What You Can't Plan On

There are many change-inducing factors that can't be anticipated. Among these are inventions or developments that are yet to be completed, or ideas which are yet to be implemented. Your company may suffer financial setbacks relating to cash flow, liquid assets, or the purchase of goods and services. You can't anticipate mergers and acquisitions by competitors, nor can you develop a scheme to prevent acts of God, like hurricanes, tornadoes, droughts, and floods.

Despite your inability to anticipate it, you can always turn a disaster into triumph. Suppose your company was consolidating three locations into one mega-distribution facility. Three months before the planned consolidation, a hurricane strikes, demolishing a warehouse, and putting millions of dollars of product at risk. How do you handle a situation like that? Here's what one Southern-based distributor did.

When Hurricane Hugo struck, it tore the roof off a large distribution facility scheduled to close in a few months. The warehouse was filled to capacity with a salable product at risk of being destroyed. What did the company do?

Because the new distribution facility was finished, they were able to implement an emergency consolidation plan. All truck drivers reported for duty. Warehouse personnel at both sites worked round the clock to move the remaining product into the new facility and store it properly.

Yes, the hurricane was a disaster and a good deal of product was lost. However, there were benefits even the best planner couldn't have arranged. The personnel from both facilities became an instant "team," supporting each

> *Despite your inability to anticipate it, you can always turn a disaster into triumph.*

other, working together, and triumphing against enormous odds. No planned activities could have created the team effort established by one natural disaster.

When disaster strikes your company, be part of the "team" finding the benefit—not the liability.

WHY COMPANIES MAKE CHANGES

There are dozens of goals corporations have in mind when making major changes. Some of these changes are planned, like moving to another state or building branch locations. Some changes are out of local control, like a hostile takeover or the sale of your division by the parent corporation. For the most part, changes are made to effect one of the following:

- *Reduced or reorganized layers of management.* Many companies find that after years of growth and change, they have developed a management tree that is in desperate need of pruning. If your company has more than two or three layers of middle management, don't be surprised that some of those extra layers are facing the ax.

- *A new management system.* As a less flexible company leader retires or moves to another job, new management may want to bring in a different system. It might be team-oriented, project-oriented, or decision-oriented. Whenever there is a change at the top, expect change to filter down.

- *Team building.* In a quest for a more employee-friendly system, some companies are again pursuing team building as their dominant strategy. Teams have leaders, not bosses, and layers of middle management are no longer needed once a true team structure is in place.

- *Outsourcing.* Outsourcing is a popular program for reducing overhead. Surprisingly, there are few areas in which outsourcing cannot take place. Some typical areas in which outsourcing is popular are payables and receivables, accounting, purchasing, human resources, marketing, legal, and transportation. Your company may decide to outsource all or part of your department, in which case you should sign on with the service provider and basically keep your job by doing it for someone else.

- *Long range supply contracts.* Companies today don't want to maintain large supply inventories. It is cheaper and more efficient to develop long-range contracts with materials suppliers who deliver just-in-time inventories as needed. Major manufacturers are developing to just-in-time inventories, which will require inventory management personnel. If your role is eliminated at the company end, see if you can fit in at the supplier end.

- *Low-cost production.* Many large corporations have decided to add efficient production at all locations. This requires doing more with less—less materials on hand, less materials cost, and less employee overhead. Profits are the ultimate goal of corporations, and low-cost, quality production adds to the bottom line.

Dealing with Change

You'd think that with all the change occurring in business, dealing with change would be as easy as sending out monthly statements. Not so. Not even close.

John Kotter, in *Leading Change,* explains that companies in a state of flux tend to make these major errors in their efforts to bring about change:

- Allowing too much complacency.

- Failing to create a sufficiently powerful guiding coalition.

- Permitting obstacles to block the new vision.

- Declaring victory too soon.

- Neglecting to anchor changes firmly in the corporate culture.

What does this all mean? Simply this: change comes about as part of a plan (vision) with specific goals at the end. Those goals are usually greater profits, greater efficiency, and a more competitive position in the marketplace. To achieve these goals, it's important all employees understand where the company is going and why, how it will affect them, and what their roles are in achieving success.

Change and You

Renowned African American scholar Booker T. Washington said, "I have learned that success is to be measured not so much by the position that one has reached in life as by the obstacles which one has overcome while trying to succeed." What obstacles do you face on the path to success? How does change affect you? The answers depend on your personality and your position in the company.

On the path to success there is no room for negative reactions. Thus, you will want to accept whatever changes come along. More than that, you will want to actively implement the changes with the least amount of disruption to your company and/or department. Be flexible. Adapt yourself to new policies and procedures. Identify obstacles to success brought about by the changes being made and find possible solutions before the obstacles thwart progress.

If you are an employee or associate, ask your supervisor about the changes and how they will affect your work. Suggest how your department can adapt to new scenarios. Show management you can work within the new parameters dictated by change.

If you are a manager, communication is your most effective weapon in dealing with change. Your employees may be frightened, stubborn, defensive, and/or hostile. Layoffs, outsourcing, loss of middle management levels and budget cuts affect people in different ways. Uncover the answers your people need—then communicate about changes as quickly and clearly as possible. This eliminates the negative rumor-mongering that generally accompanies major changes. Encourage your people to ask questions and give them honest answers. If you don't know, admit it—and commit yourself to finding the answer.

As a member of upper management, you may find yourself distanced from the average employee and unable or unwilling to understand the concerns of your employees. Never underestimate the magnitude of the problems change can cause in your company. Make sure department heads communicate fully the scope of the problem, the need for change, and the end results expected from change.

Most of all, point out that change generates opportunity. Then, weigh it with your own actions. Promote from within, expand training, and give your people a chance to reach your highest expectations.

If you are a manager, communication is your most effective weapon in dealing with change. Encourage your people to ask questions and give them honest answers.

The Value of Communication

When Fieldcrest-Cannon purchased Bigelow-Sanford in the mid-eighties, the purchase involved assumption of a huge debt load. In an effort to bring Bigelow in line with other Fieldcrest Cannon companies, hourly personnel were put on salary equivalent to their normal hourly pay per week. On the surface, this seemed a positive change, as hourly employees would no longer lose paid time for doctor, dentist, or other personal appointments.

Shortly thereafter, another change was made: business hours at Bigelow headquarters changed from 8:30–5:00 to 8:00–5:00. Ostensibly, this change was made to instill a sense of urgency in headquarters personnel. The impact on formerly hourly workers was significant. Many had children in elementary school or daycare, and the change meant increased hours at work and increased daycare costs, but no pay increase. Employee grumbling could be heard for miles.

How could this situation have been avoided? First, top management should have met with department heads and explained the rationale for all changes. Second, department heads should have met with their people, explained the goals and vision of the changes, and motivated their personnel toward accepting change with a positive attitude.

Embracing Change

"To some people, change feels good. It rids their lives of boredom, stimulates them, and sparks their creative juices. They may purposely get involved in risky, unpredictable ventures because they like living on the edge, seeking out change, challenging it, and getting the best of it on their own terms," says Robert M. Hochheiser in his insightful book, *If You Want Guarantees, Buy a Toaster.*

For most of us, though, change is a large bear, growling, threatening, and liable to chew our collective heads off. Embracing the bear is beyond us. Or is it?

Think of changes happening in your company today, this week, this month. Are there new projects you can volunteer for? New employees you can assist with settling in? New support personnel who need guidance? Are you changing from one accounting system to another, one software program to another? Is your budget undergoing a stringent reduction?

"Business people are not just managers; they are also human. They have emotions, and a lot of their emotions are tied up in the identity and well-being of their business."

—*Andrew S. Grove,*
Only the Paranoid
Survive

Determine what small changes are taking place in your scope of action, then get busy. Offer to represent your department on a major project or take on the orientation of new people in your department (with your boss' permission, please). Learn the ins and outs of a new software program so you can assist your supervisor and/or colleagues in using the new materials successfully. Figure out ways to reduce department spending or pare down project budgets. All these are examples of embracing change on a small scale.

When larger changes are in the works—mergers, acquisitions, layoffs, expansions, plant closings, new market involvement—address broader opportunities with the same interested, proactive attitude.

If you do, success will be one change you won't be able to avoid!

"Change for change's sake is wrong. But when it's due and when it's right, it is the lifeblood of growth and success in business."

—*Barry Gibbons,*
This Indecision
Is Final

CHAPTER RECAP

- Change is all around you.

- You must accept change or it will defeat you.

- Most change is beyond your control.

- You can take advantage of change if you plan ahead.

Recommended Reading

Drucker, Peter F. *Managing for the Future.* New York: Truman Talley Books, 1992.

Frost, Ted S. *The Second Coming of the Woolly Mammoth.* Berkeley, CA: Ten Speed Press, 1991.

Hochheiser, Robert M. *If You Want Guarantees, Buy a Toaster.* New York: William Morrow, 1991.

Kotter, John P. *Leading Change.* Boston: Harvard Business School Press, 1996.

Building Your Future

*I*t's time for you to develop a personal "game plan." Where do you want to go? What are the steps involved? Which steps are most important? Which steps need attention right away? Which ones can wait? How long should it take? What things can you do to achieve the desired result?

Let's begin by evaluating where you stand today and where you want to go. Don't be surprised if you don't have all the answers right now. You'll have to think for a while before some parts of your plan become clear. Developing a plan takes time. It may take hours—or it may take weeks. And the plan must be flexible—you'll change it frequently during the next few years.

IN THIS CHAPTER:

• *Developing a personal game plan*

• *Applying a positive attitude to problem solving*

• *Avoiding negative influences*

Assessing Your Position

EXERCISE

On a blank sheet of paper, make three columns and five rows. Along the top of the columns, write Needs, Today's Position, and Tomorrow's Position. Divide each column into five levels: Experience, Education, Skills, Additional Changes, Personal. Here's how one person filled out her chart. Jane currently has entry-level skills, experience, and education. In order to expand her horizons she needs more experience. How can she get it?

JANE'S SKILLS, EXPERIENCE, AND EDUCATION

Needs	*Today: Purchasing Agent*	*Tomorrow: Purchasing Director*
Experience		
• more years in current position • marketing and merchandising experience	• 3 years line purchasing • exposure to marketing • exposure to merchandising	• 5–8 years line purchasing • merchandising • marketing
Education		
• MBA? • individual courses in marketing, merchandising, management, research?	• college degree	• college degree +
Skills		
• improve computer skills • expand interpersonal skills • communications • budgeting	• interpersonal skills	• computer direct order entry, spreadsheet, Web information • interpersonal, management • business communications • budget planning, management
Additional Changes		
• wardrobe • increased responsibility • lateral move • new company	• mixed professional and non-professional appearance	• management level appearance and attitude
Personal		
• more stable relationships • home • hobby	• dating • apartment	• marriage and child • house • interior design

Jane can improve her situation in two ways: increasing time and responsibility in her current job or moving into a lateral position using similar know-how but gaining increased exposure to different purchasing opportunities.

For example, Jane currently purchases a line of baby wear for a retail chain. If she accepts a position as merchandising manager at a company retail outlet, she expands her purchasing skills, and also gains on-site merchandising skills, inventory maintenance skills, and even customer service experience.

Jane has the minimum acceptable education for her position as stated by her employer. If she wants to move up, she'll have to gain knowledge of three kinds: book learning, practical knowledge, and self-help knowledge.

Book learning requires attending courses at a local college or university, or attending business/career seminars and conferences. Hopefully, these will be toward an advanced degree. Practical knowledge is gained through daily work experience, by becoming involved with a mentor, and/or by volunteering for projects at the limit of one's expertise. Self-help requires valuing new concepts, technology, and/or advances pertaining to your field. One way or another, Jane must increase her current knowledge base to prove she can handle a more complex position.

Skills are basic tools needed to perform a job. Jane is not a good business communicator; she should take a course in business writing or speaking. She quickly absorbs computer skills; she can teach herself to use spreadsheet software. Jane makes personal friends easily; however, she's never managed other people, only worked with them. She might want to take a career-building seminar on managing people.

Finally, Jane lacks the appearance or manner of management. Wardrobe is a serious consideration, as most businesses are fairly conservative when it comes to dress. In her current job, Jane meets few people outside the office. In the job she's aiming for, she would be attending regular meetings with executives from many other companies. Jane has two "trendy" business suits that will likely be out of style next year. She tends to wear clothes better suited for dating than business.

SUCCESSTHOUGHTS

Dress for your next job. Begin purchasing your management wardrobe long before you get that promotion, and, literally, dress for success. What do the executives in your company wear? That's what you should be buying for your wardrobe.

Basics for men: two to three classically tailored suits (navy, charcoal, gray, or navy pinstripe), three pairs solid-color dress slacks and a navy blazer, white and/or blue shirts, black dress shoes, black executive length socks, and a selection of ties (your choice), black belt.

Basics for women: two to three classic business suits (not trendy—in navy, gray, black, dark brown), two to three one-piece conservative business dresses, silk blouses to match the suits, two to three skirts with jackets in contrasting colors, nude and/or taupe and/or gray hose, two pairs low-heeled pumps (one black, one navy), matching handbags, silk scarves to accent your clothes, and conservative jewelry.

Jane should also seek increased levels of responsibility to demonstrate her ability to handle a heavier workload, delegate responsibility, and bring a large project to fruition.

All this may take three years. It may take ten years. However, there is something Jane should consider very early on: Does her company have a record of promoting from within? Do promotions go primarily to men, or are women and minorities regularly promoted? Will she be passed over because of the department she works in or the boss she works for? Is nepotism the key to success in her company?

While loyalty to a company is admirable, it will seem like idiocy if, fifteen years from now, Jane is still in the same position, still waiting for her big chance. Your company's first loyalty is to the bottom line. Yours should be to your bottom line, i.e., your position and paycheck.

Don't allow yourself to become a contented frog in a stagnant pond. As you develop your game plan, leave room for making changes, either laterally within your present company or to a different one. Keep your eyes and ears open to opportunities—it's the way to turn SuccessThink into reality.

FORMAL EDUCATION

Learning costs big bucks, even if you only take a couple of courses at a time. Your company may have a tuition-reimbursement plan or a training/education budget. Ask your supervisor what assistance is available for you to pursue your education. If the answer is none, don't despair. Ask if a tuition-reimbursement plan could be considered. Your higher education benefits your company. Still no? Move on to an alternative.

Ask the public library's reference librarian to help you find information on graduate grants, conference/seminar grants and assisted tuition plans. Search the Internet for scholarships, grants, tuition or education loans. Pursue tuition dollars aggressively to ensure your opportunity.

The increase you see in your paycheck down the road will more than compensate you for what you spend in time and money to get an advanced degree.

Never say you're too old. Ben, in his early fifties, was an advertising executive with a multi-national tire manufacturer. When his company underwent restructuring, Ben was downsized. He made several well-considered decisions concerning where he wanted to live and the lifestyle he and his wife wanted. There was little opportunity for him to step into another executive position in corporate advertising where he and his wife wanted to relocate. Using his severance and the profits from the sale of his Ohio house, he went back to school to get a CPA degree.

Ben's decision had several marked effects on his and his wife's lifestyle. Yes, money was tight, but what they sacrificed in "things," they gained in a more contented, happier lifestyle. The plusses far outweighed the minuses. Ben found the CPA program exhilarating, rejuvenating. It

Keep your eyes and ears open to opportunities—it's the way to turn SuccessThink into reality.

was the cliché "new lease on life." He was also offered an excellent job months before he completed his degree—which more than made up for any sacrifices Ben made to re-educate himself.

Seminars and Conferences

Several nationwide groups offer short seminars on management and business practices. Local university business departments offer similar courses. Your HR department should know what's available in your area. These courses are the Campbell's soup of business learning: condensed, packed with interest, and surprisingly satisfying.

Your company may willingly pop for the several hundred dollars it costs for you to attend. If so, do a quick write up after you've been to the session to let your boss know what you learned. This is one way to ensure the dollars will be there the next time something interesting comes along.

However, be aware that training and education dollars are shrinking in most corporations. Along with marketing money, training is one budget category that goes under the ax whenever budget dollars get tight. Professional meetings also offer seminars, papers, and information, as do trade shows, professional luncheons, and networking groups. Don't discount any source of learning.

In addition, don't limit yourself to "business only" seminars. There are plenty of free talks about retirement planning, financial planning and investing, and motivational meetings—all of which will help you in the long run. Remember: SuccessThink means you look out for yourself, your career, and your retirement.

LESSONS IN EVERYDAY LIFE

We are a country full of opportunities to learn. Yet, we often have trouble seeing them in front of us and using them in our daily lives. There are situations in family life, sports, friendships, hobbies, even at the supermarket, that teach savvy business thinking.

Consider this: Fred watches pro football throughout the fall. He loves the games, the reactions of the fans, and the different coaching methods. Here are a few simple facts he knows about football:

- Not every play is successful.

- You get more than one chance to make a first down.

- Sometimes you make points through passing, other times running, and other times kicking field goals. Success is not limited to a single avenue.

- If the offensive line doesn't do its job, your team won't score many points.

- If the defensive line doesn't do its job, no matter how many points your team scores, you probably won't win. You need good work from both to win the game.

- Every coach has a management style. Some yell, some simmer, others take mistakes, fouls, and penalties in stride. Some yell at one player, but not another.

Okay, Fred, it's Monday morning. Back to work and the weekly departmental meeting. The team's in trouble. The competition stole a bid out from under Sam's nose. Sandy is taking too long to bring a contract to fruition. Our biggest customer is making moving noises. The support staff helps Joe but avoids working with Olga.

What does Fred do? He forgets everything he saw work effectively in Sunday's game and drops a universal H-bomb. Everyone is stupid, everyone is inefficient,

"I challenged myself to do whatever job assigned to me with intense commitment and a good cheerfulness."

—*Maya Angelou*

everyone is a failure. The results? Tempers flare, mistakes abound, people avoid Fred, and, by the end of the week, the situation is worse.

Fred should consider the progress being made, the players on his team (we all have different strengths, paces, abilities), and ways to use what he has to score some points. Sure, maybe this week is only a field goal—next week, let's throw the long bomb and score a touchdown.

Look for lessons in daily life that you can take to the office. After all, what you'll find outside the office is the same thing you'll find inside: people.

SELF-HELP AND SKILL BUILDING

When was the last time you scoured your local bookstore for self-help tapes, books, and videos? Have you tried the public library? Your local tech school resource center? Your business friends?

You should not only investigate "business" self-help opportunities, but also develop interests to make your conversation sparkle and to make yourself a more accomplished person.

Don't know where to start? Can you answer any of these questions with a "no"?

- Do you know how to meditate? Ever tried meditation?

- Have you ever been to a planetarium? An aquarium?

- Do you ever watch The Learning Channel? Discovery Channel? PBS? The History Channel? The Food Channel?

- Do you know how to surf the Net?

- Have you visited a museum in the past year?

- Have you attended a play, concert, or sporting event recently?

- Have you read a book this year? Any poetry? A biography?

- Can you find NPR (National Public Radio) on your radio dial? (Hint: It's usually in the high 80s to low 90s on FM.)

- Have you attended professional meetings of any kind?

- Do you do something daily for your body, your spirit, and your soul?

Uh-oh. Six "no" answers! Well, think of all the opportunities for self-improvement. While you're at it, take a computer software class that might come in handy at work, learn about the current technology in your field, and discover who is on the cutting edge in your area of expertise. Next, take the bread baking class you always wanted to—kneading bread releases frustration as nothing else can!

You and Your Community

Your place in the community is a factor in your success. If there are professional organizations in your field or generic professional business organizations, join and become an active member.

Investigate the Chamber of Commerce in your town, the Better Business Bureau, and other nationally based associations that offer you both learning and networking opportunities.

Most importantly, don't isolate yourself within your company. Reach out to provide a stable base for yourself if, or when, you are no longer part of the company.

Become a Communicator

What kind of communicator are you? Oral? Written? Do people fall asleep reading your memos?

One of the oddest—and most poorly constructed—memos to ever cross my desk announced the promotion of Kevin to General Manager of a branch location. The memo went something like this:

- *Paragraph 1.* The importance of the position to the company and the promoter himself. No word about Kevin.

- *Paragraphs 2 and 3.* The industrious efforts made by the promoter to find the right candidate. Still nothing about Kevin.

- *Paragraph 4.* The undying pleasure it gave the promoter to offer a promotion from within the ranks. Who's getting promoted?

- *Paragraph 5.* Self-praise by the promoter for choosing the right candidate. Who's the candidate?

- *Last Paragraph.* Oh, yeah! A short sentence saying the promotion goes to Kevin, followed by a series of superlatives about how lucky he is to follow the promoter's footsteps.

Incredible! This memo was highly effective in that everyone talked about it. Unfortunately, Kevin's promotion wasn't the topic under discussion—only the promoter's bloated ego!

Business writing is a learned skill. You can do better with practice. Most vocational or technical schools offer classes in business communications.

> **SUCCESSTHOUGHTS**
>
> *A few quick tips for clearer memos: On scratch paper write down the answers to who, when, where, what, and why for the content of your communication. As you write the memo, stick to those details, and don't go off on tangents. Head your memo with a subject line, such as, Re: QuickEx Brand Intro Meeting. Don't use fifty-cent words; clarity is the key.*

Just as you can improve your business writing, you can learn to make more interesting presentations. Again, your local vocational-tech school has classes in speech that will help. The first thing you need to know in making presentations is people learn in different ways. This is basic learning theory taught in every education class, but rarely included in business classes.

> ### SUCCESSTHOUGHTS
>
> *Consider how you learn and apply that knowledge to your work habits. If you need to take notes, don't be caught without a pen and paper. Let your supervisor know your learning methods; it will make his instructions to you more effective and your learning easier.*

There are three learning modes: auditory, kinesthetic, and visual. Auditory learners absorb what they hear. Kinesthetic learners learn by using their hands, taking notes, or through a hands-on demo. Visual learners must see it or read it to understand it. To reach the most people, use all three methods.

How? Make sure everyone has paper and pen for taking notes. Use a flip chart (prepared in advance) to give the basic elements of your discussion. Discuss each aspect clearly, thoroughly, using simple vocabulary. Move around in front of the group, making eye contact with as many people as possible. And, finally, never provide all the reading material before you're finished giving your presentation. If they can read it at their seats, why should they listen to you?

FOCUS ON SOLUTIONS

As you learn, grow, and progress toward your goals, apply what you know to daily situations. One way to do this is to become problem-aware and solution-oriented. Here are a few ideas:

- *Evaluate what's working and what's not.* Work to strengthen what's working and make it better.

- *Keep your eye on the goal.* If you know where you are going, you can find ways past obstacles. Every obstacle overcome is another step toward your goal.

- *Develop a positive, energetic outlook.* "Can do" motivates more than "can't do." It will also help you avoid anything that is adversely affecting your work.

"Your vision will become clear only when you can look into your own heart. Who looks outside, dreams; who looks inside, awakes."

—Carl Jung

While negative influences can be serious and debilitating, the way you handle them signifies your growth as a person and a manager. These include:

- *Loss or illness of a significant person.* Loss can be through moving, death, divorce, or even marriage. Don't discount the loss of a close friend as insignificant.

- *Loss of income, job, self-esteem, or status.* When life goes in the dumpster, so do your spirits. Give yourself a chance to adjust.

- *Failure.* Find success in your failures. We all fail; the only real failure is the failure to learn from your mistakes.

- *Personal illness.* Illness requires so many personal changes, there is no possibility that work will be unaffected.

- *Family problems.* Nothing strikes harder than difficulties in the family. When you have problems with a spouse, parent, or children, let your supervisor know—things will be easier for everyone involved. Don't go into all the particulars, but an informed boss is more likely to be a compassionate boss.

- *Financial burdens.* Particularly if they're unexpected. Everything from a blown transmission to legal fees for that problem child in the preceding item add weight on your shoulders. Short of winning the lottery, the best you can do is keep a reserve for unexpected financial needs.

By creating a long-term vision of success, a personal game plan, you can put negative influences in perspective.

Plan the Life—Live the Plan

The process of creating your personal mission statement is as vital as what you write. It is a time of self-evaluation, prioritizing the elements in your life, assessing in new ways.

Here's a list of things to consider when creating a personal game plan or mission statement: self, family, spouse, colleagues, superiors, friends; home, community; learning, growing; body, soul, spirit; recreation, work; saying v. listening, thinking v. reacting, considering other points of view; personal hopes and dreams. This is your personal mission statement. It can be wordy or terse, idealistic or practical. It's up to you. Think—set priorities—write.

> **PERSONAL MISSION STATEMENT**
>
> *Every day I will do at least one thing to enhance my body, my mind, and my spirit. I will learn something new, create something exciting, work on my personal plan. I will offer help to my subordinates, develop relationships with my colleagues, provide for my family, and recognize the efforts of others. I will give something of myself to others.*

Now ask yourself these questions:

- What's really important to me?

- Why is it important?

- What can I do to influence the outcome or attainment of these goals?

You've set your priorities; your next step is to write your plan, then condense it into your personal mission statement. This is your long-term vision. Plan the work and work the plan. Plan the life and live the plan. Take setbacks in stride. As you encounter the bumps, ditches, and potholes on your road to success, keep in mind Walt Disney's advice: "All our dreams can come true—if we have the courage to pursue them."

BIBLIOTHERAPY

In *Toxic Work,* Barbara Bailey Reinhold notes that we seem to be a people who like to read about how to do things better. Career-related books and articles come in four quite different categories:

- *Self-assessment.* Books that help you get an honest reading on your interests, skills, values, and passions.

- *Career information.* An inside look at various fields and functional areas.

- *Job search.* The nuts and bolts of cover letters, resumés, interviews, networking, and marketing yourself.

- *Career management.* How to play the game in different fields, positioning yourself for advancement, and so on.

CHAPTER RECAP

- A personal game plan will help you achieve your goals in life.

- Education, regardless of the source, has value in your job and your life.

- If your company will not help you further your skills, do it yourself.

- Look for lessons in everyday life.

- Become a problem solver in all areas of life.

Recommended Reading

Angelou, Maya. *All God's Children Need Traveling Shoes.* New York: Random House, Inc., 1986.

Brown, Les. *It's Not Over Until You Win!* New York: Simon & Schuster, 1997.

Fulghum, Robert. *All I Really Need to Know I Learned in Kindergarten.* New York: Villard Books, 1986.

People Skills

*O*ne hundred percent of everything that happens in a business involves people: employees, managers, family, friends, customers, potential customers, irate customers, suppliers. The list is endless, but important.

No product is created, developed, manufactured, marketed, purchased, or used without people. Understanding people and developing people skills are business imperatives.

No matter what your occupation, your position, or your personal inclinations, you have daily contact with people. Robert Fulghum, author of *All I Really Need To Know I Learned in Kindergarten*, hit the nail on the head with these points from the "sand pile at Sunday School":

- share everything

- play fair

- don't hit people

- put things back where you found them

- clean up your own mess

How many of these describe the people around you? Your supervisor? Your subordinates? And, most of all, yourself?

Sharing in the business world means offering ideas to make projects and people successful, promoting better business practices, and giving credit where credit is due. Do you fit this description?

Do you hoard your ideas like Scrooge or do you share them freely? Are you a plagerist—stealing the ideas of others and passing them off as your own? Remember, credit is easily taken and rarely given.

> ### SUCCESSTHOUGHTS
>
> *Always give credit to the originator of any idea you present. You will be recognized for valuing the idea and being a "big enough" person to give others credit.*
>
> *Play fair. Being honest and ethical in your business practices is unquestionably a valuable asset. When you deal honestly and fairly with others, they are encouraged to treat you the same way.*

HONESTY IN BUSINESS

Here are five quick rules for honest business dealings:

- *Be honest with your customers.* If you can't provide a product or service, if you can't meet a deadline, if your work is less than promised—tell the truth.

- *Be honest with your vendors.* We all have deadlines, pressures, demands placed on us. If you make unreasonable and untruthful demands on your suppliers, they will soon find business elsewhere.

- *Be honest with your colleagues.* A solid working relationship is based on trust, and no one trusts a liar.

- *Be honest with your subordinates.* The truth, even when painful, is still more palatable than lies. Plus, when you are "found out," you lose the respect of those whose respect you dearly need.

- *Be honest with yourself.* Shakespeare had it right when he said, "This above all, to thine own self be true." You're the one who's putting on makeup, or shaving off yesterday's beard. Whom do you see when you look in the mirror? If you openly admit weaknesses and failings as well as strengths, you'll find it easier to look in the mirror each morning.

By treating others as they treat you, you will promote positive interpersonal skills—a key element of success.

RECOGNIZING EMOTIONS

Whoever said emotions have no place in a work environment must have been working with robots. There is no way to check your emotional life at the door and work only on an even keel. We don't work in a void, and, yes, the fight with your spouse, disappointment with Johnny's Biology grades, excitement over Susie's acceptance to Vassar, and even pride in that new grandchild can come into play in your daily work.

Tune in to emotions by recognizing how they play a major role in our lives. Napoleon Hill in *Keys to Success* lists seven negative and seven positive emotions that effect us on a regular basis.

The positive emotions are love, sex, hope, faith, sympathy, optimism, and loyalty. The negative emotions are fear, hatred, anger, greed, jealousy, revenge, and superstition.

> "I am in the 'people business.' All industries are operated by human beings, and I have dedicated my life to a study of people and to trying to help them as persons."
>
> —*Norman Vincent Peale,*
> The True Joy of
> Positive Living

Measuring Your Emotional Awareness   E X E R C I S E

Let's measure your emotional awareness. Draw a table with five columns and fifteen rows. Along the top, label the columns as follows: Emotion, Me at home, Family at home,

Me at work, Colleagues at work. Under the Emotion column, list seven positive and seven negative emotions. You can use Napoleon Hill's choices—or your own. Remember what we said about being honest with yourself? This is the first step towards honesty in all of your relationships. Here's your first chance to really be honest. Go through the "Me at home" column and determine whether or not you have felt each emotion during the past three days. Check the box if you've felt the emotion. Now, see what you observed in your family. If you have no family, consider your friends. Next, do the same for your work environment.

POSITIVE AND NEGATIVE EMOTIONS

Emotion	Me at home	Family at home	Me at work	Colleagues at work
love				
joy				
compassion				
patience				
sympathy				
optimism				
charity				
sorrow				
hatred				
anger				
greed				
envy				
revenge				
deceit				

Do you see patterns? Are you more positive at work than at home? Does any particular emotion predominate?

ASSESSING TALENTS AND SKILLS

Somewhere along the line, you will have to use your people skills to make some personnel decisions. Oh, right, you hoped HR would do that for you? Poor soul, you are sadly mistaken. Human Resources departments are so busy in establishing policies and policing them, they have little time to do more than screen applicants for new positions. After that, it's up to you.

And that's how it should be, because only you can tell if that "chemistry" or what '60s aficionados call "vibes" exists between you and the quivering candidate across the table.

Assessing talents is not an easy task. How a person appears in a resumé can be a different matter altogether from whether that person will fit in and work comfortably with other department members.

In addition, there are laws prohibiting discrimination in hiring because of age, sex, marital status, race, religion, disability—this is one list your HR department will go over with you.

Base your hiring decisions on solid information:

• Does the person have the experience needed to do the job?

• Does the person have the necessary skills?

• Are the skills and experience commensurate with the salary being offered?

• Is the person willing to do the job required? (Don't think this is a "given." Many a supermarket manager can tell you about the packer or stocker who refuses to clean up a mess because "it's not my job.")

And finally, consider your gut reactions:

• Do you feel comfortable with the person? Is he or she comfortable with you?

- Do you think other department members will feel comfortable with the candidate?

- If you have no comfort level today, how will you survive working with this person for the next five years?

Ted Frost in *The Second Coming of the Woolly Mammoth* offers sage advice on the hiring of new employees: "The secret to good hiring is good firing. Competent, conscientious employees are hard to find. Most of the time, you'll have to try several people before finding the right one."

Ouch! You mean we might not find a Bill Gates on our first attempt? What's worse, we'll have to go through the dreadful hiring process again? Maybe more than once! Many companies avoid the time consuming problem of hiring the wrong person by going through a temporary agency. Temps come in all flavors now, not just secretary/clerk. You can hire temp engineers, temp marketers, temp planners, even temp CEOs. That way, you can give the candidate a legitimate "try out" without getting into the hire/fire scenario.

> **SUCCESSTHOUGHTS**
>
> *Keep in mind these basic tenets of interpersonal relationships:*
> - *Understand how your actions and behavior appear to others.*
> - *Recognize behaviors that may need adjustment or toning down, and also those behaviors to enhance.*
> - *See yourself as others see you.*
> - *View the actions of others with patience and generosity.*
> - *Take responsibility for your attitudes, actions, and behavior. Only you can change yourself.*

Finding Solutions

How many times have you sat at a conference table and heard people talk about creating win-win scenarios? This is no joke. You should be seeking out ways to enable each person to leave the table with something of value. And it should not be that you are a hard-nosed, stubborn louse.

The win-win scenario should always be your goal. Much like the Oriental concept of saving face, in which everyone is allowed to leave the table with some sense of victory. No one ever enjoys feeling like a loser, and you'll foster difficult relationships if you make people feel inferior.

Look for solutions to interpersonal problems in an intelligent, non-belligerent, objective manner. No one is perfect, don't expect yourself to be. And always remember basic courtesy.

WHO IS YOUR CUSTOMER?

Some of the best advice a manager can give to her staff is, "Treat every caller and visitor as a customer." Typically, this advice is followed by a few hours of zealous customer regard. Then the employee in a retail store waits ten minutes while the clerk discusses his dating plans over the phone. Next, the employee is told "you're in the wrong line," sent to another wrong place, and ends up wondering, "Why should we treat our customers so well?"

> ### THE VALUE OF CUSTOMERS
>
> *This poster is found throughout the company:*
>   *What Is a Customer?*
>   *A customer is the most important person ever in this office . . .*
>   *in person or by mail.*
>   *A customer is not dependent on us . . . we are dependent on him.*
>   *A customer is not an interruption of our work . . . he is the purpose*
>   *of it.*
>
> *—L. L. Bean, Freeport, ME*

Your customer is every person who has ever bought your product or service, who is buying it today, who might buy it in the future, or who knows someone who might buy it. Your customer is all the other people in your company who depend on your work to make their work easier or more efficient. Your customer is the guy in the next office, the woman in accounts payable, the security guard who walks you to your car at night.

When you are ready to blast someone—and that does happen occasionally—just stop and think: If you were a customer in a store, how would you react to someone talking to you that way?

Chauvinism, Bigotry, Racism

There is no room in any business for chauvinism, bigotry, or racism. Yes, you hear comments, jokes, and stories all the time, but you don't have to buy into what's being said.

When people make ill-judged comments in your presence, try one of these techniques:

- Say, "Thank you, but I don't enjoy that type of joke."

- Tell them there is no room for such inappropriate remarks in your company, department, or project group.

- Don't become a link in a chain of insensitive remarks. Don't pass along tasteless or offensive jokes.

- Treat everyone as your equal.

When confrontations do occur, handle them calmly. Try to uncover any underlying causes of the problem and ease tension caused by hard feelings.

Bad Vibes

No matter how hard you try, there will always be frayed tempers, minor explosions, and confrontations. Mark those situations "Handle With Care." Ted Frost recommends that we "be aware of employees' egos. The biggest cause of dissatisfaction isn't low pay or poor working conditions. It's feeling insignificant, thinking what they are doing is piddling and unimportant."

When confrontations do occur, handle them calmly. Have your discussion behind closed doors. Keep your cool. Be understanding; work through and beyond the problem at hand. Try to uncover any underlying causes of the problem and ease tension caused by hard feelings.

If all this fails, find some neutral ground, either a conference room or off-premises site, where you can discuss the problem with the help of a neutral party or mediator. If you are the cause or an exacerbating factor in the situation, step out of it. You won't be able to mediate with the offended party.

At all costs: Keep comments and solutions confidential.

Constructive Criticism

At some point, you will have to criticize someone else's work, work habits, or actions. This is uncomfortable for both of you. Here are a few tips on giving productive, rather than destructive, criticism:

- *Don't generalize, specify.* It doesn't help to say, "You don't get along well with others." If you want a person to change specific behavior, you'll have to say what the behavior is and give an example: "Yesterday, when giving Felix instructions, you lost your temper. This happens frequently, and you need to work on getting your temper under control. Is there any way I can help you do that?"

- *Can the problem be solved?* Look at the problem objectively. Can the person change? Will he need seminars, medical help, or constant supervision in order to change? Or is it just that he is so much taller than other people he's intimidating? Height can't be changed.

- *Easy does it.* Do speak calmly, be friendly, smile, and offer your assistance. Don't be insulting, badgering, or belittling. If you treat a person with respect, you can criticize behavior without damaging the ego. If you don't show respect, you won't get positive results.

"I recall the story of the farmer who, when asked by his neighbor why he was working his sons so hard just to grow corn, replied, 'I'm not just growing corn, I'm growing sons!' "

—*Kenneth Blanchard,*
The One Minute Manager Meets the Monkey.

- *This is not the time for punishment.* Too many managers use criticism as a way to keep people in their places. If you beat someone up, you lose the opportunity to get decent work from them.

- *Pick the right moment.* Never criticize anyone in public, only behind closed doors. Don't pick a time when deadlines are looming, the person is sick or under extreme stress, or when you are in a hurry. This meeting should be a moment when you can both be relaxed, honest, and communicative.

- *Address problems as they arise.* If there is a problem at hand, take care of it. Then let it go. Give the person a chance to fix what is wrong. Look for an opportunity to praise her in front of others. If performance improves, be sure the person knows you have noticed her efforts. Once you voice your criticism, look for positive changes. Let the person know you support his efforts. Remind him that he is valued by you and by others.

"I do not know anyone who has got to the top without hard work. That is the recipe. It will not always get you to the top, but it should get you pretty near."

—*Margaret Thatcher,*
London Daily
Telegraph, *1986*

Your Rights as a Human Being

We all have rights as individuals, and it's up to you to assert your rights and safeguard the rights of others. You have the right to say "no" to a request, particularly if it goes against your religious or ethical beliefs. You have a right to voice your point of view on a topic, and the listener has the right to agree or disagree with you.

You can change your mind and act on that change. You can be with others—or not, depending on your wishes. In the same way you want to be respected and to be treated with dignity, offer respect and dignity to others.

Balance your life with work and play, learn about the world around you and how others enjoy their world, and you will find a success of great value.

CHAPTER RECAP

- Honesty in business is an admirable quality.

- It is impossible to be at work all day without showing emotion.

- Always give people a way to feel successful.

- There is no place in the workplace for bigotry, chauvinism, or racism.

- Criticize with caution, allowing the other person to maintain their dignity.

Recommended Reading

Anderson, Walter. *The Confidence Course.* New York: HarperCollins, 1997.

Bick, Julie. *All I Really Need to Know in Business I Learned at Microsoft.* New York: Pocket Books, 1997.

Brinkman, Dr. Rick, and Dr. Rick Kirschner. *Dealing with People You Can't Stand.* New York: McGraw-Hill, Inc., 1994.

Fulghum, Robert. *All I Really Need to Know I Learned in Kindergarten.* New York: Villard Books, 1986.

Kaplan, Burton. *Winning People Over.* Englewood Cliffs, NJ: Prentice Hall, 1996.

Is Your Net Working?

No network? Then, get busy! Networking is the way to get a current job done better, the means for hiring new employees and consultants, the access to new customers and suppliers, and—most significantly—the way to keep in touch with the outside world.

When you network, you meet people, initiate conversations, find out about possible business ventures, and listen to business gossip—the kind that might prove valuable in job searches or improving your current job status. Network colleagues offer solid information about your market, major changes in the business arena and about people moving to new positions.

Why should you care? Here are three common scenarios in which networking could enhance your current situation:

- Your electrical supply company is considering hiring a software company to develop an on-line ordering system for distributing electrical components. A key element in the system will be automatic substitution

IN THIS CHAPTER:

- *Networking aids in every area of your life*

- *Looking for sources and contacts*

- *Identifying and employing networking skills*

- *Practicing builds positive contacts*

of like products for out-of-stock items. At a Chamber of Commerce luncheon you meet a food-service distributor who has a similar program already up and running. You get the name of their software developer and save your company time and money.

"Networking is not a favor bank."

—*Gilda Carle*

- Your company wants to outsource human resources benefits administration. There are more than two dozen firms providing that service in your area. You have been given the task of selecting the best one and it is daunting. The following morning you read in the paper that Acme Corporation has restructured, outsourcing benefits administration and accounting functions. Your son's soccer coach works at Acme—a quick call gets you a contact to call in Acme's HR department. You call and ask how they narrowed down the field. The answer gives you four firms worth investigating, saves you time, and helps you make the correct decision for your company.

- You've been in the same dead-end position for six years. Any thoughts of promotion are slim, since the boss' son, niece, and second-cousin-twice-removed are in line ahead of you. AAA Corporation has a write-up in the business section—they're doubling their staff. Now, if you only knew someone at AAA! The three people you know who know the most people in town are Uncle Dave, your next door neighbor, and your rabbi. You call each and Bingo! Trust Rabbi Green to know the right people in the right places!

NETWORK YOUR WAY TO MENTAL HEALTH

In addition to smoothing out the speed bumps in daily corporate life, networking can ease job stress, provide an "outsiders" view, and give you a reprieve from office politics. There is nothing quite like a respected, impartial opinion to put your woes back in perspective. If your molehills are assuming mountain-like proportions, go to lunch with someone whose sense of humor makes you laugh. Not all networking has to be serious, and laughter reduces pressure and stress.

One more reason to keep a network thriving: There is an 85% probability that your next job will come to you via someone in your network. I know, you like your job and have no interest in taking a position elsewhere. Fine—for today. But you're developing a SuccessThink mentality, and when your plumber's Aunt Sophie calls and says she's got a director's job open that would suit you to a T, you're going to think about it, aren't you?

That job offers a $10,000 bump in salary, a private office with carpeting and a window, and a 35% potential bonus. That job offer also came via your well-manicured network.

> ### SUCCESSTHOUGHTS
>
> *Make networking a regular addition to your planner—whether it's a desk calendar, a day-timer, or on your computer. At the beginning of each month, look for one or two meetings you can attend, add five people you haven't talked to for awhile to your phone call list, and make an effort to meet five new contacts. At the end of the month, do a two-minute review of your networking efforts—then, repeat or increase those calls next month.*

Everyone Needs to Network

Many people think networking is a "corporate only" phenomenon, but that's not true. Networking works in large and small businesses, in academics and sports, for men and women. Here are two specific examples:

Charlie was a middle school principal in a district outside Philadelphia. When hard times hit his district, two out of five principals' jobs were eliminated, including Charlie's. He and his wife wanted to return to Long Island, but Charlie knew finding a principal's job would be difficult—particularly since he had lost contact with his education network.

Charlie took a proactive approach, taking a non-educational job in the Long Island area. He joined an active, thriving network that enabled him to identify top administrative jobs coming across his desk. The network got him back in touch with colleagues, fellow graduate-school alums, and friends from the area. When the right job came up—Chief Financial Officer of a large Long Island district—Charlie tossed his name in the ring.

Here's an example from the small business arena. Ellie returned to her hometown after several years. When she left, Ellie was a multilingual administrative assistant in a corporate environment. During the years she lived in Akron, Ellie went back to school and earned a master's degree in journalism. However, her return to South Carolina put her in a bind. The only journalism jobs available were entry-level positions on the local paper—she was looking for a more challenging job.

Ellie needed to create a new network—people with whom she had no previous contact—and fast. She took a well-organized, two-pronged approach to creating a vital network.

First, Ellie combined her journalism degree with her administrative skills and contacted the local technical school. There she began teaching several courses in business etiquette and office management. However, that was only a part-time opportunity, so Ellie began working with the local chapter of the Association of Women in Communications—where she found an interesting and challenging part-time job with a growing public relations company.

In Ellie's case, two halves developed into more than a whole. Her contacts through both positions enabled her to start her own company, a fledgling business that goes on-site to teach general business skills.

Networking—Do it Right the First Time

Just like everything else in life, networking has a specific protocol you must follow. Here are some tips on what you should do—and not do:

- *Always attend meetings with your business cards and a pencil.* If you don't have business cards, get some at a quick print shop. The cost is minimal. When you get information from a new contact, note it on the back of her business card.

- *Use networking opportunities* to arrange future meetings in a more personal arena, like over lunch, dinner, golf, or a beer. Think of this as a "first date." If you meet ten new people, select at least one to ask out to lunch during the next week or two. Look for common areas of interest, like sports, children, or music. You won't really get to know this person until your second or third "date." By then, you'll know whether or not you have the rapport to develop a win/win relationship.

- *Meet at least three people of the opposite sex out of every ten new contacts you make.* Often men stick with other men, women with other women. It's the fifth grade dance all over again.

- *"Work the room" at social events.* Meet as many people as you can, giving each your business card. Put their business cards in your left-hand pocket. Keep your cards in your right-hand pocket, so you don't mix up cards and mistakenly give someone else's away. Hint: Never go networking without two pockets and a supply of cards.

- *Give people specific information about yourself.* If they're asking, they're interested. Tell them you are new to the area, or this is your first meeting with the Chamber of Commerce. Explain what you do—briefly and accurately. "I'm a salesperson" doesn't cut it. What do you sell? To whom? Are you looking to expand your market? Your product offerings?

- *Develop a "60-second sound bite"* which you practice in front of the mirror. This is a terse summary of who you are and what you do, including a few personal bits to interest the listener. No one likes a conversation hog. Learn how to talk about yourself succinctly. Then be prepared to listen to your new contact.

- *Be upbeat.* If you met a person who related every miserable event from the past five years, would you want to spend more time with him? When you are making contact with a person, remember to project a positive image. First impressions count. Smile.

- *Develop good listening skills.* Use the person's name again later in the conversation so she knows you remember it. Ask questions in response to the information offered by the other person. Make a connection between your experiences and those of the speaker. "Your son plays soccer? What team? Oh, my daughter's team is playing them next Saturday. I'll see you there!"

- *Don't be a "job-stalker."* If you are in the market for a job, you can say so, but make it part of a larger conversation. Otherwise, people will hide in the restroom when they see you coming.

PRACTICE, PRACTICE, PRACTICE

Not everyone can be a networking star on his first attempt. Most people need to practice in the same way you might practice a piano solo or shooting nature photos. In "The Big Hurdle: Contacts and Referrals," Kay Green suggests starting with people you already know, regardless of the closeness of the relationship." Here are some tips about making cold calls—those dreaded first contacts that make cold chills run up and down your spine:

- *Work at a desk or table where there's nothing to distract you.* Make sure the radio, TV, or other distractions are eliminated so you can pay attention to the conversation.

- *Be confident.* The worst this person can say is that he can't or won't help. So, what have you lost if he does? Less than ten minutes of your time. On the other hand, you just might find someone who can give you real help.

- *Have paper, pencil, and an appointment calendar* on your desk. Take notes during the conversation, including the person's response to your call, their position and company, and any follow up you should make. If the person says, "Call me next Tuesday. I'll have more time to talk then," ask if there is a best time, note the time, and add "I'll call you Tuesday at 9:00." Whatever you do, don't miss making that call.

- *Offer remedies.* This person already knows you— calling shouldn't be so difficult. If the relationship is distant or only recently acquired, remind the person where you met. Make a comment that will jog his memory. "Bill, it was great to meet you at the Lion's Club last Thursday."

- *If you are networking for a job, don't ask for one.* Instead, have a short chat, then ask for an appointment with the goal of getting advice.

"I don't care who you are; you cannot succeed alone in this world. It is impossible. Especially now, as the world becomes more and more complex, and as the threats to our survival become great, we are all dependent on an increasingly large and varied network of others."

—David Mahoney

• *Put the appointment in your calendar.* Call a couple of days in advance to see if the time and place are still convenient. Business schedules change quickly, and you may have to make a new date.

I Don't Know Anyone Who Can Help Me

Sure you do. You just don't realize the value of the people you know. There are people available to help you everywhere you go—if you have the right attitude and approach.

EXERCISE   *Making Contacts*

Go through this list and put a check next to each category in which you can name a contact.

POTENTIAL CONTACTS

	immediate family		neighbors		relatives
	friends		employers		business friends
	doctor/dentist		lawyer		banker
	schoolmates		fraternity/sorority		sports team
	church		Lions/Rotary/Junior League		teachers
	college alumni		high school alumni		military friends
	local shop owners		tradespeople		car salespeople
	local Better Business Bureau or Chamber of Commerce		local news writers		library

Now, all you have to do is a bit of simple arithmetic. You know at least 3 people in 10 categories, or 30 people. Contact each one of those people and ask for a referral to two, three, or four other people. Quick multiplication shows you now have a network of between 60 and 120 people.

Don't limit yourself to building your network with contacts from others. "The easiest way to start networking is to join an organization. Most groups go out of their way to help new members and show them 'the ropes.' Look for groups that have meetings and group gatherings on a regular basis," suggests Joan Sotkin in *Starting Your Own Business.*

Make your own new contacts by joining an association, club, or team. Check off the groups you currently belong to. Mark with an *X* those you want to target.

GROUPS TO JOIN

	Better Business Bureau		Chamber of Commerce		Small Business Association
	bowling league		softball team		other sports group
	scouting		sports coach for kids		neighborhood association
	professional society		charitable organization		church
	Internet chat group		service club (Lions, Rotary, Kiwanis)		P.T.A.

Again, some quick math. You join a professional society, the Lions Club, and a local church and become an active member of each. You will meet about 75–100 people from each group, or roughly 300 people. Add that to your original 60–120, and you've got a sizable network.

THINK LINKS

You have a home business. You network through your local BBB, Chamber of Commerce, and the PTA, but it isn't enough. You're going high tech—your own Web site. Now's the time to think links and spiders and e-mail. It sounds like lions and tigers and bears, oh my!—but it's not really so scary.

What are links? They are direct connections between your site and others with similar or parallel interests. Here's an example of how links work: A tree surgeon develops a site and gets hits, but not enough to generate sufficient business. A landscaping business in the same area also has a site. Both the tree surgeon and the land-scaper add links (connectors) to each other's site. Voilà! Networking over the network.

Spiders are target words that draw unsuspecting web surfers into your Web site. For a dentist, spiders might include the terms "teeth, dentistry, cosmetic dentistry, crowns, dental, and so on."

E-mail allows people to contact you for information, advice, or to offer you a job. It's quick, easy, and non-threatening, even for the computer neophyte. Just fill in the blanks and send.

The Internet is the network of the future. Don't be afraid to use this valuable tool to create an electronic net-working arena for your career and personal advancement.

Care and Feeding

Like a family Bible, your Rolodex should be protected and revered . . .

Networks, like pets, are starved for attention. They need grooming, exercise, a loving pat on the head, and a healthy dose of interest. The classic, and probably the best, way to keep all these people straight is to develop a Rolodex. Like a family Bible, your Rolodex should be protected and revered—it carries your career on its die-cut 3 x 5 cards.

What to put on each card: name, business, address, phone number, fax number, and e-mail address. Add: how you know this person (bowling, PTA, etc.), who intro-duced you, and two to three facts, such as mother of twins, Harvard grad, scratch golfer, name in news article on com-puter software. You should also categorize each name by how well you know the person: personal friend, friend of a friend, someone you'd like to know.

Everyone has a network, regardless of its power, its impact, its influence. If your circles are small, find ways to expand them. If your circles are large, then put them to use.

CHAPTER RECAP

- A network is a living, growing addition to business health.

- You already have a larger network than you realize.

- Developing a network requires continuing action.

- Networking skills are developed through practice.

Recommended Reading

Mackay, Harvey. *Dig Your Well Before You're Thirsty: The Only Networking Book You'll Ever Need.* New York: Doubleday, 1997.

Mackay, Harvey. *How to Build a Network of Power Relationships.* New York: Simon & Schuster, 1995.

Roane, Susan. *The Secrets of Savvy Networking: How to Make the Best Connections for Business and Personal Success.* New York: Warner Books, 1993.

Time Management

*S*uccessThink is not only a mental state, it's an active state as well. You have so much to do and only so much time in which to do it. Time—the one commodity that's never in surplus—must be actively controlled, used, squeezed, and respected. There can be no room for wasted time in anyone's day.

If you are a time-abuser, you most likely have a time-crusher in your department to use as a role model. Look for the young woman with two elementary school children. In her average day, she gets herself and her children up, dressed, fed, and out the door in record time. She gets her job done between 8:00 and 5:00, and during lunch hour meets with teachers, runs household errands and, occasionally, even eats lunch. Out the door at 5:00 on the dot, she then picks up the kids, stops at the supermarket, cooks and serves dinner, gets the youngest to bed, puts in a load of laundry, and takes the oldest to Brownies or Cub Scouts. A supermom makes more out of 24 hours than most of us can imagine. She even puts the army to shame.

Time—the one commodity that's never in surplus— must be actively controlled, used, squeezed, and respected. There is no room for wasted time in anyone's day.

The question is: How does she do it? It's simple. She has no choice. She doesn't have a wife to do these things for her, nor can she call home and say she'll be late because she didn't get around to finishing the Porterman project. Young mothers have learned to prioritize; they work smarter, condense time, and produce on a schedule.

If modeling yourself after this young woman seems like too much, perhaps a quick primer on time management would suit you better. Basically, all projects, tasks, chores, and jobs fall into one of five categories: Do It Now Or Else, Do It Soon, Just Do It Because I Say So, Busy Work, and Time Wasters.

- *Do It Now Or Else.* These are jobs that meet three criteria. They are critical, immediate, and necessary. An example: your company achieves most of its annual sales target at the Expo Grande, to be held three weeks from now. If your work is not ready on time, sales will plummet. So will your bonus, and, maybe, your job.

- *Do It Soon.* These jobs also meet three criteria: they are strategic and necessary, but they're not time-sensitive. An example: Human Resources wants every department to hold three employee motivational meetings a year. These meetings can be held at any time, even though they are important to the company and required of your department.

- *Just Do It.* These are chores that others think are important, so you do them right away. However, in the framework of what you are trying to accomplish, these tasks may be relatively unimportant. A good example: You normally have a weekly meeting to discuss ongoing projects. With the Expo Grande coming up, your boss decides to hold these meetings daily. You don't have anything new to say since yesterday, but you have to produce a report and attend the meeting anyway.

- *Busy Work.* Busy work is everything from signing invoices for payment to correspondence, monthly or quarterly reports, to a host of other jobs common to every department.

- *Time Wasters.* Wasting time results from gossiping, general malaise, daydreaming, or waiting for others. When a meeting is called for 9:00 and half the principals don't arrive until 9:15, you've wasted time.

Record Your Activities	EXERCISE

For one day, write down how you spend your time. Make a three-column chart. In the first column list the task, including time wasters. In the second column, put the time spent doing the task. In the third column, designate what category the project falls into: Now, Soon, Just Do It, Busy Work, Waste. Be honest. If you sit around waiting for a meeting to start and don't use that time, you've wasted it. Your entry should read:

TIME EXPENDITURE

Task	Time	Designation
waiting for meeting	8:55–9:15	waste
Internet chat group	9:15–11:45	just do it
chat with Frank	11:45–12:00	waste
return phone messages	12:00–12:30	busy

Don't be too surprised to discover you waste over an hour a day. It's impossible not to have some waste. Nobody can work full bore all the time without having a nervous breakdown. Says Edwin C. Bliss in *Getting Things Done,* "To work for long periods without taking a break is not an effective use of time. Energy decreases, boredom sets in, and physical stress and tension accumulate when a person stays with one thing too long."

Change the intensity of tasks you are doing on a regular basis. If you have been working at a task that requires exacting concentration for an hour or two, do fifteen minutes of busy work. Take a five-minute refresher. Make a phone call. Eat a granola bar. Give your mind and body a chance to recoup before starting the next exacting task.

BECOMING A SELF-STARTER

While he was painting the ceiling of the Sistine Chapel, Michelangelo seemed to be taking an inordinate amount of time to complete the task. Pope Julius, Michelangelo's boss in this case, was constantly hounding him to finish.

"When will you make an end?" Pope Julius shouted from the Chapel floor.

"When I am finished," Michelangelo shouted back from the scaffolding high above.

"And when will you be finished?" Pope Julius asked, hoping for a definite answer.

"When I make an end to it," stated the truculent Michelangelo.

The problem was a lack of communication. The Pope did not understand the complexities of painting a ceiling more than 80 feet above the floor. Michelangelo failed to tell the boss how long it would take and why. Communicating sub-tasks, time frames, and

> ### STAND UP!
>
> *The Declaration of Independence was written at Thomas Jefferson's stand-up desk. Thomas Wolfe, who was very tall, used the top of a refrigerator as a desk. Among noted executives who have helped popularize the stand-up desk in recent years are John Opel of IBM, C. Peter McColough and David T. Kearns of Xerox, and William LaMothe of Kellogg Company. People who work standing up are often passionate advocates of the practice. For some, their pulpit is their only desk, in which case a tall stool is usually kept nearby for occasional use.*
>
> —Edwin C. Bliss, Getting Things Done

obstacles to completion are part of managing time. Here are some additional pointers:

- *Break up every major task* into smaller sub-tasks. It's easier to approach a project that can be completed in a day or two than one to be completed in a month or two.

- *Give your supervisor a realistic time frame.* If she claims she wants it next week, explain how it can or cannot be done in that time.

- *Advise others* that you are involved in a time-sensitive project. If other projects will be delayed while you work on today's urgent demand, you need to let those involved know that prior commitments are on hold.

Why can't I get started? Why can't I make an end? Why do I lose focus, attention, productivity? You aren't the only one who has trouble with these problems. For some, the worst part of a project is getting started. It's like bearing bad tidings—there's nothing like tomorrow. Procrastination has no role in the life of a SuccessThinker unless you're a person who does his best work under pressure—even if the pressure is self-inflicted. For most of us there are several reasons we put off today what we'll most likely put off tomorrow:

- *Brain drain.* If you are tired, bored, or thoroughly disinterested in the project at hand, you will have trouble getting started. The solution: try to find one interesting or different element about the project that makes it worthwhile.

- *Lack of focus.* One problem getting started is not knowing where you're going. If you have an incomplete vision of the project, a vague goal, or insufficient data or input to begin, you won't know where to start. The solution: Briefly write down what the project is, what the goal is, what you need to complete the project satisfactorily. If you are missing elements required to get started, take the responsibility to fill in the gaps.

- *Fear of failure.* Nothing makes it harder to do a job than the impression that the project will be rejected, outdated, or valueless. Worse, it could be all three. The solution: Write a proposal outlining the aspects of the project, including time required, equipment and expenses, and anticipated results. Review the proposal with your supervisor. Get him to buy into the project. If he has a vested interest in the success of the venture, you are one step ahead of the game.

- *Low self-esteem.* Lack of internal or external motivation is a killer and usually related to a low sense of self-worth. You can't get yourself moving if you don't believe you are equal to the task. Without a sense of self-worth, you won't be a success at anything. The solution: Develop a sense of urgency. Nurture your self-esteem by convincing yourself you have the talent necessary to complete the task. Pump up your energy level.

CONTROLLING TIME

The key to controlling time is to recognize the demands on your time, prioritizing those demands, and becoming time-sensitive in all you do. It used to be that managing your time only meant writing a "to-do" list, which you then ignored for the rest of the day. Today's time management is a process of planning, ranking tasks, and fulfilling as many of these obligations as possible.

Don't let time become a source of frustration. Further, don't let time management control all your time. You can read a host of books, articles, and tips on time management. You can listen to time management tapes and take time management seminars, but here is a simple fact: *Time management is just common sense.*

Mail, Phone Calls, and Meetings

The following list of time management tips have been culled from numerous authorities on the subject. Don't try to incorporate everything into your routine at once. Choose those ideas that best suit you, and add them one at a time until each becomes second nature.

- *Get the largest wastebasket* you can bear to have in your space and keep it next to your desk. Sort your mail into two categories: read it and toss it. Junk mail should automatically go in the toss file unless it is for a seminar you might want to take. Don't waste your time on anything you didn't request or that isn't relevant to your work. This goes double for catalogs.

- *Answer memos, short notes, or information requests* by writing the answer directly on the original. Make a copy for your file, fold the correspondence and readdress it.

- *Don't ramble.* This is particularly important for internal memos and business letters. There is no need to reiterate every bit of information that has passed between you and the recipient. If she's been on the project, she knows what you're talking about.

- *Use the tools of mass production.* If you write many similar letters, try these short cuts. Create basic paragraphs, and a standard salutation and closure that you set up with your assistant or secretary. Number the paragraphs and keep the "paragraph" file on

"The more senior I became, the more precious became my time, the one commodity I could not stretch. I developed some simple rules: The staff was not to commit me to any meeting, speaking or social engagement, trip or ceremony without my approval. Not even for five minutes. And when I did schedule a meeting, it was to start on time. People who keep other people waiting are being inconsiderate. And my office was to return phone calls promptly."

—*Colin Powell,* My American Journey

your desk. When you need to respond to someone on a standard topic, write your letter this way:

> To: Sam Carlisle, Wellman Pumping
> Sal.
> ¶ 1,3,4,7
> Clo.

Your assistant will instantly know you are responding to Carlisle's request for a pricing catalog.

- *Handle your mail so you perform the fewest tasks.* For example: If you receive three memos scheduling meetings this week, sort them into a pile. Write the dates, times, locations, and topics in your planner all at the same time, then discard the memos unless they contain other needed information. Pack rats create endless files that they never look at again.

- *Learn how to read a magazine.* There is a table of contents in the front. Find it, select specific articles worth reading and paper clip them. Next time you are waiting for a meeting to start, open up the magazine and only read those articles. Don't read ads unless you are specifically looking for something.

- *Only do your mail once a day.* Just because another piece of paper is dropped in your in box doesn't mean you have to stop and read it.

Find similar ways of controlling your phone contacts:

- *Develop a script* or short list of topics before you call. That way you make sure you've covered the information you need and can keep the conversation brief.

- *Learn how to use voice mail.* Perry needs to get the latest figures on the Donaldson deal from Cassie.

He calls and leaves a voice mail asking her to call back. What a waste! A better message would be something like: "Cassie, this is Perry Smith. I need the Donaldson figures for the past quarter. Please call me back when you have them. My number is 555-1848."

- *Always leave your name and phone number,* even if the recipient is someone you talk to three times a week. Not everyone remembers numbers, and, if he picks up his messages away from the office, he might not have yours with him.

> **SUCCESSTHOUGHTS**
>
> There are times when you really should only be doing one thing at a time, and driving a car is one of them. Endless commuters watch their compatriots eat while driving, shave while driving, do business while driving, apply makeup while driving, and even get dressed while driving. Please note the number of nicks, dents, and scratches on their cars and the horrified looks of the people driven off the road by these part-time drivers. If you want to use your driving time wisely, rent or buy audiotapes and listen while you drive. You can learn a new language, read a bestseller, listen to a comedian, improve management or selling techniques, or discover ways to lessen stress in your life. Commuting is a necessary evil—except if you use the time to learn. Get off the phone! This tip can save your life.

- *Prioritize your phone messages* into immediate responses, respond within 24 hours, and trash basket. You can probably answer three quick calls in the ten minutes you wait for your lunch date to pick you up.

- *Keep phone calls short and to the point.* It's great to know that Wanda has a new grandchild. Congratulate her—then get back to the topic at hand.

- *Keep blank Rolodex cards by the phone.* When a new contact calls, write name and phone number on the card while you speak. Then, file while you're talking. This keeps your Rolodex updated without becoming one of those "to do" tasks that never gets done.

Finally, organize personal contacts to maximum advantage. At meetings, for example:

- *Start on time.* If a key player is late, call her office and ask when she will arrive—then start without her.

- *Never hold a meeting that doesn't have an agenda.* Make sure the agenda is complete and distributed to all attendees. Stick to it. Don't let others wander in their thinking or bring up extraneous, time-wasting items. Remind people of ideas that have already been rejected and won't be discussed at this meeting.

- *Take notes* on a flip chart for transposing later.

- *End on time.* Set a specific amount of time to meet and stick to it. One good way to do this is to set the meeting for an hour before lunch or an hour before quitting time. Tell all participants that you plan to be done in an hour or an hour and a half. Make sure when having meetings with outside suppliers or vendors that you set both start and end times for the meeting.

Generally Good Ideas

Figure out just how much you are really worth. You may be delighted to be a salaried employee, but just what is the value per minute for your time? If you earn $100,000 per year, you make about 67¢ per minute. Time wasting is an expensive proposition.

- *Find ways to organize your day.* Some people like day planners or organizers. Some like a write-on calendar on their desks. Some like to keep schedules on a computer. Ed keeps a spiral-bound notebook on his desk and writes down every significant task that has to be done. As he finishes, he puts a line through the item. If the item is delegated, he writes that down.

- *Learn how to say "no!"* This is easier said than done. When the pressure comes from the top, it's pretty hard to say, "I'm too busy." Instead, ask which of your current projects can be given to someone else.

- *Take time to recoup.* You can't perform every minute but don't let time dribble away. Find ways to make your storative time work for you. Try yoga or meditation or listen to music.

- *Accept the 90% rule:* If you perform each task to 90% of perfection, you are still ahead of 90% of everyone else.

- *Use a "to do" list,* marking off all completed items. For large, multi-action tasks, put separate actions on the list and check them off as they are completed. It enhances evaluating your productivity.

- *Be goal-oriented* if you want to manage your time better. If you don't know where you are going, how will you know when you get there?

Finally, if there is one element of SuccessThink that maximizes time use, it is setting up an effective follow up system. When you have set your priorities, delegated tasks, and put your plan into action, you don't want to fall down just before the finish line. Follow up with your people to make sure there are no unforeseen problems. Follow up on your own work to keep pace with your schedule. And, yes, you might even have to follow up on your boss. Be sure you do that with more than a dollop of diplomacy.

CHAPTER RECAP

- By controlling how you spend time, you will complete more tasks and feel more successful.

- Projects fall into five basic categories: Do It Now or Else, Do It Soon, Just Do It Because I Say So, Busy Work, and Time Wasters.

- Learn to manage your own time to avoid the pressure of looming deadlines.

- Time management is basically common sense.

- There are instances when you should do only one thing at a time, such as when you're driving.

- If you know how much you are worth per minute, you will be less likely to waste those minutes.

Recommended Reading

Axelrod, Alan, and Jim Holtje. *201 Ways to Manage Your Time Better.* New York: McGraw-Hill, 1997.

Bliss, Edwin C. *Getting Things Done.* New York: Charles Scribner's Sons, 1991.

Covey, Stephen R. *Seven Habits of Highly Effective People.* New York: Simon & Schuster, 1989.

Covey, Stephen R., A. Roger Merrill, and Rebecca R. Merrill. *First Things First.* New York: Simon & Schuster, 1994.

MacKenzie, R. Alec. *The Time Trap.* New York: AMACOM, 1997.

Keeping Perspective

Y ou're embroiled in a dozen projects, the printer calls with news of delays, your travel schedule puts you in Peoria the same day your supervisor has scheduled an essential meeting, and your dentist just called to say you need an expensive crown on your pesky bicuspid. And it's only 11:15 A.M. Quick—pass the antacid.

It's hard to stay with your personal game plan during the bustle of daily work and other people don't necessarily "keep your schedule." Relax, no one's conspiring against you, despite evidence to the contrary. It's simply a matter of agendas—you have yours, they have theirs. That's just part of life.

If you're going to succeed, it's important to develop patience, keep working on different aspects of your plan, and keep moving forward—despite minor setbacks, fluctuations, and interruptions. Go with the flow. Don't get your knickers in a knot. Avoid being up to your eyeballs in alligators. Choose any or all of the preceding clichés—just stay calm. A necessary ingredient in all these situations is keeping your perspective.

IN THIS CHAPTER:

• *Recognizing that stress is both a positive and negative motivator*

• *Identifying ways to deal with stress in the workplace*

• *Parlaying alternatives into positives*

• *Handling nepotism and favoritism*

Ted Frost in *The Second Coming of the Woolly Mammoth* claims, "Nothing is more likely to cause ruination in business than lack of perspective. Without a good sense of perspective, business management alternates between overreacting and under reacting. Lack of perspective causes people to respond to superficial stimuli rather than to underlying causes."

"It's a recession when your neighbor loses his job. It's a depression when you lose yours."

—*Harry S Truman*

START WITH STRESS MANAGEMENT

Yes, stress curls your hair from the roots out. You want to do your very best, but deadlines have a nasty way of creeping up despite all you've planned, plotted, scheduled, and prioritized, and even though you've agreed to pay your assistant double-time for working on the weekend. Learn how to get stress under control, how to make it work for you, not against you.

There are dozens of excellent books on stress management in your public library—if you only had time to drive there and take one out. And then, you'd have to schedule reading between rewriting the Valdese contract and developing the new ad campaign for Wally's Used Car World.

Let's first address lingering myths about stress:

- *You should eliminate all stress from your life.* Untrue. There is no way to completely eliminate stress, nor should you. Stress can be a positive factor, one that allows you to thoroughly enjoy your life. Here's an example: You like to jog and decide to enter a mini-marathon. This adds stress to your life, but the result can be positive. You may find that you can compete successfully on the local level, you achieve a personal goal, and you improve your health. The key is to recognize your stress levels and get them under control. It's only poorly managed stress that kills you, so get yours under control.

- *We all react to stress in the same way.* Not true. Some people thrive on chaos, others find the slightest disorder unbearable. People let off steam by yelling or being silent, crying or retreating, running away or attacking the problem head-on. The important thing is to know how you reduce stress and recognize stress release in others.

- *People who show no signs of stress probably don't have any.* Ever heard of ulcers, heart attacks, and nervous breakdowns? Plenty of people keep their stress under wraps until it's too late. Think of boilers. They have pressure valves and meters to mark when pressure becomes dangerous. Then, you either reduce the pressure or run for cover. In the workplace, it's better to walk away, let yourself calm down, and get that pressure valve back in the safety zone.

Job stress in the U.S. costs roughly $200 billion per year in worker's compensation, absenteeism, health insurance costs, and medical bills.

Stress is a serious factor in every business. According to the United Nations International Labor Organization, stress is a major cause of injury and lost productivity at work. Job stress in the U.S. costs roughly $200 billion per year in worker's compensation, absenteeism, health insurance costs, and medical bills.

Try one or a combination of these stress reducers, all of which can be done in your office, car, or during a commute:

- *Meditate.* No, meditation isn't just for seventies wannabes or fanatics. This is a proven method for getting your mind off the daily stress-makers that raise anxiety levels.

- *Relax to music.* There are dozens of relaxation programs available at every music or bookstore, including sounds of nature, quiet music, and relaxation readings. Look under the New Age section. Many music stores now have listening posts where you can listen before you buy. When you find one that makes you feel like you're lying in a recliner, buy it. Note: Don't get too relaxed while you're driving. You still need to get there alive.

- *Breathe deeply.* Remember when your mother told you to breathe deeply and slowly count to ten? She was giving you a quick stress reducer. Trust Mom to know the best way to get you to think before you say something you'll regret later.

- *Remember isometrics.* Tightening and relaxing specific muscle groups is a great way to relax. Find a book on isometrics at your public library. The combination of tensing and releasing muscles gives you an overall relaxed result.

- *Generate positive endorphins.* Those are chemical laugh drops running throughout your body. The more you do to content yourself, the more endorphins you'll make. Laugh, call a friend, think about something that delights you. Make a mental list of your favorite movies, books, sports heroes. Plan the perfect meal in your mind with so much detail you can taste how delicious it is.

- *Simplify—unclutter—toss.* There's nothing like a fresh start to reduce work-related tensions. Work methodically, sorting and organizing until your work space has a fresh, tidy look.

- *Exercise regularly.* You don't have to bench press 300 pounds or jog twelve miles a day to experience the energizing effect of exercise. Take a half-hour walk during lunch. Ride a stationary bike while you read through a week's worth of mail. Get your heart pumping to keep stress on the run.

- *Leave your desk or office and go visiting.* Don't make this a habit, or your boss will think you never do anything. However, when the tasks build up, a five-minute break with a friend will do wonders. If you can combine the visit with a walk around the building, all the better.

- *Eat real meals.* A can of cola and a package of cheese crackers are not a meal. Eat a healthy, balanced breakfast, lunch, and dinner. Food is the fuel that keeps your body and brain functioning. You can't drive a car without gas; you can't work your brain without food. Avoid snacks, especially high-fat snacks like chips and chocolate. Avoid empty calories like cola drinks and chocolate.

> ### MEDITATION AT WORK
>
> *Of all your environments, the workplace is where you probably spend the most time. Meditation in action at work can:*
> - *Lower your stress level.*
> - *Help you get that promotion.*
> - *Make a bad day not as bad.*
> - *Make a good day even better.*
> - *Help you connect with your colleagues.*
>
> —*Victor Davich,* The Best Guide to Meditation

- *Change, change, change.* If you normally read your mail, check your e-mail, and do all your correspondence first thing in the morning, you might find it's already 11:30 and you haven't "started" your day. You need a change. For some people, clocking the time spent on different tasks helps. For others, it's beginning at the top of a pile and working through to the bottom. Set small goals for managing a huge project. When you've ticked off each step along the way, you'll begin to see large projects in a more manageable way.

- *Don't think there is any job without stress.* A stress-free environment only exists in a graveyard, and then only if you're the one in the box, not the one digging the hole.

Has Stress Gotten to Me?

How can you tell if stress is getting ahead of you? Probably the most common signal is losing your temper. The less significant the cause for your explosion, the more likely it is stress-related.

Other signs of stress include headaches, indigestion, frequent bouts of bronchitis, sweaty palms, high blood pressure, anxiety attacks, confusion, nervousness, chest pains, gritting your teeth, rapid pulse.

Yes, headaches can also be brought on by changes in barometric pressure, chest pains could be gall bladder, and indigestion is probably the green pepper and anchovy pizza you had for lunch. However, if you have a combination of these stress symptoms or one that lingers despite attempts to relieve stress levels, you should see a doctor.

You need help controlling the physical and emotional effects of stress.

From Your Point of View

We usually associate peer pressure with teenagers, yet how many of us try to keep up with our friends in consumption of material goods? We buy into popular views of success: vacations in Aruba, a house in a specific area of town, a home entertainment center instead of a TV, a Volvo or BMW or Lexus in the garage, designer clothes, and so on.

Material goods add up on our personal scorecard, but what does it all mean? A brief translation: Money = Success.

However, this chapter is about keeping perspective. You know people who have bigger cars, take more exotic vacations, and wear custom-tailored clothes. On the scorecard they appear to be doing better than you. But that is not necessarily true. They may just have a bigger limit on their MasterCards. Keeping perspective requires you to put a fair valuation on more important things in life, the real signs of success.

Phil is a jeweler in a small Southern city. He owns two stores, a nice house, has a wife and grown children, a late model car. This is a person we might call a moderate success. If we look closer, we see that Phil is the kind of person most of us wish we could be. He participates in community affairs, including being active in his local Chamber of Commerce and regional Better Business Bureau. Phil's ethical approach to business continually brings in repeat customers. On a personal level, he is the man we'd like to call a friend; a man who is respected, valued, and admired by everyone.

True, Phil isn't a Getty or Vanderbilt. He doesn't wear thousand dollar suits or have a personal trainer at his beck and call. What he does have is balance, a keen perception of what is important in his life.

And that's what keeping perspective is about: creating a balanced life.

SETTING PRIORITIES

A principal ingredient in keeping perspective is realizing not everything you do is important. Does that hurt your feelings? Ah, well. . . . Make a mental list of tasks you perform during the average day. Are you saving the world or filling out yet another form for requisitioning diskettes?

Deciding What's Important   E X E R C I S E

Make a list of all the projects you're juggling at this moment. Add specific family and personal events, community commitments, social obligations, and business appointments. Determine whether each item is urgent or crucial (1), moderately important (2), or not essential (3). Is the item time-sensitive? Who does the project involve? Can you delegate the responsibility?

There are five priority items but only three have specific time constraints: lunch with the boss and two family events. Projects become urgent because a deadline is fast approaching. Those projects listed as long-range will become urgent—just as soon as your boss asks when he can see the report.

RESPONSIBILITIES

Items	Priority	Time Controlled	Involvement	Delegate?
Batten contract	1	deadline	JH, RK, me	yes
Matt's soccer game	1	6:00 Tuesday	me	no
lunch: boss	1	Thursday	FWM, me me, JH	no
training program	2	long-range	CM, LS, VP	yes
sales meeting	1	deadline	department	no
sales incentive program	2	long-range	me	no
interview new hires	3	as time allows	HR department sales department	yes
Linda's play	1	2:15 Friday	me	no
BBB meeting	3	12:00 Monday	RK or me	yes

You'll also notice Matt and Linda (your children, in case you didn't remember) are a top priority. Again, this is a matter of perspective. Long after you have moved to another job, your company loses the Batten account, and the sales forces turns over three times, your children will be your children. It becomes too easy to put off family when success dangles like a carrot in front of a donkey. However, keep your priorities in order: put family first.

If you don't think it makes a difference to your children if you're there or not; if you think because your spouse attends, you don't have to, guess again. Babs played the jar of mustard in *The Fairy Queen's Picnic* in first grade. Her Mom and Dad sat in the third row on the end. After the play, Dad took her out for a make-your-own sundae and told Babs she was the best jar of mustard he'd ever seen. That was over forty years ago. Your children will remember too.

PATIENCE AND OTHER ESSENTIAL VIRTUES

Everything can't happen at once. You have to be patient, and while it's difficult and contrary to your personality, you should consider that, like a good wine, success takes time. "My advice has always been to 'think positive' and find fuel in any failure," says basketball star Michael Jordan

> ### SUCCESSTHOUGHTS
>
> *Use a highlighter when entering items on your calendar to emphasize important deadlines, meetings, and appointments. Use one color for urgent items, another for follow ups. Hint: Your family is always highlighted with the urgent marker.*

in *I Can't Accept Not Trying*. "Sometimes failure actually just gets you closer to where you want to be. The greatest inventions in the world had hundreds of failures before the answers were found."

Develop patience, along with perseverance, determination, and stamina. These aren't the classic virtues of faith, hope, and charity, but they are the primary virtues of success. If you try, think, and work hard, you'll find success. You'll also have failures, mistakes, problems, and glitches. What makes the difference is how you handle those potholes, speed bumps, and flat tires. "There are ways to see our biggest problems as our greatest opportunities—if only we can step out of our trained patterns of perception," say Robbins and McClendon in *Unlimited Power, A Black Choice*.

Think about your biggest mistake or failure, a mammoth disaster you thought would never fade away. Now, let's look at the positive side—and don't say there was nothing positive about it.

- *Why was the result bad?* What did you do to achieve a poor result? Yes, you have to take some of the blame. This isn't easy, but it matters. Lack of responsibility = lack of sincere effort.

- *What went right?* No, the answer isn't nothing. Don't be a Chicken Little, running around in a panic because the sky is falling. Some things must have gone right. What are they?

- *What did you learn from the experience?* You'll never enter another trade show for the rest of your life? You'll never develop another software program, no matter how great the idea is? Again, be specific. There are small lessons learned in every major disaster.

If you don't believe that, think about the *Titanic.* Talk about disasters! However, you haven't heard of a ship since that has been billed as unsinkable or iceberg-proof, and all ships hold evacuation drills. Does that mean another ship won't ever hit an iceberg? Or sink? No, it just means there are lessons to be learned from even the most tragic events. And compared to the Titanic, really, how big was the mistake you made?

How did you grow, improve, develop, advance as a result of your disaster? If you did one thing better after the "event," you drew success from failure.

"That the circum-stances of my life pro-vide in such varied ways favorable condi-tions for my work, I accept as something of which I would prove myself worthy. How much of the work which I have planned and have in mind shall I be able to complete?"

—*Albert Schweitzer*

Accentuate the Positive

It's easy to dwell on negative aspects of life. David Mahoney, in his book *Confessions of a Street-Smart Manager,* describes this very human tendency: "Most of us fail—at least some-times—to view our problems in perspective. If your lives are 95% positive and 5% negative, it seems to be human nature to take the 95% for granted and focus on the 5%.

And no matter how small our biggest problem may be, we tend to balloon it up, worry about it, and let it encompass our thinking."

Like playing the piano or baking a soufflé, positive thinking requires practice, particularly if those around you always anticipate the worst. You have to form a positive thinking habit.

Developing Positive Thinking Habits	E X E R C I S E

Each morning next week, write down three things you will accomplish by the end of the day. These three things can be as simple as making a networking call, complimenting a colleague on a project well done, and cleaning out your "In" basket. At the end of the day, affirm your accomplishments. Now, you've begun developing positive-thinking habits.

Developing Peripheral Vision

Learn to look at every situation through the eyes of others. From where you sit, you see only part of the picture. Your subordinates have their viewpoints, your boss has hers, and the CEO has his. What do they see that you don't?

Taking a New Perspective	E X E R C I S E

You're in charge of a new sales campaign for the Everest, a four-wheel drive vehicle that climbs a 45% slope with no problem. You develop an ad blitz geared toward all those rugged young men who think of themselves as budding Edmund Hillarys. The cost, while slightly over budget, is well worth it. The Everest is going to be the vehicle to buy this year. For the next month, you'll be out of the office, traveling to regional sales meetings to introduce the Everest—your assistant will handle problems that arise in your absence. You've done a superb job—says you.

Now answer these questions:

- What is your boss' view of this scenario?

- What is your assistant's view?

- What does the CEO think?

- What do car buyers think?

"Choose a job you love, and you will never have to work a day in your life."

—Confucius

GAINING PERSPECTIVE

Most likely, your boss thinks you went over budget on a risky campaign, you failed to address all the soccer moms who buy four-wheel drive vehicles, and who gave you authority to have a novice run your department for a month?

Your assistant is offering thanks that you'll be out of her hair for a month and cursing her ill luck in having to deal with the day-to-day department hassles while you stay in posh hotels and eat at four-star restaurants.

The CEO doesn't much care who's in charge while you're gone, where you stay, what you eat, or that you're over budget. He knows if the Everest is a flop, the company will be sold to a Japanese conglomerate and all headquarters personnel will say "sayonara" to their jobs.

And the car buyers? Didn't your wife tell you women are the decision-makers when it comes to buying cars these days? You should have believed her. Suburbans are sold to plumbers, electricians, painters—and soccer moms.

Before you jump into a project, make a major request, or complain because your raise is only 3.5% this year, look at the whole picture. Consider all points of view. It's another way to balance out your perspective.

Basic Needs

We all have basic needs in our lives. We want to be loved, liked, appreciated. We want our egos in stable working condition. We'd like to be recognized for our accomplishments, admired for our efforts. We want people to think highly of our talents and abilities. We'd like a certain amount of freedom without impinging on the freedom of others. We want to control our destinies, feel safe in our careers and homes, and enjoy privacy in our personal lives.

We can achieve all of the above, within reason. That's where perspective comes into play. Take the time to adjust your vision and deal with the plusses and minuses of today from a balanced point of view.

CHAPTER RECAP

- The basic virtues of business life are patience, perseverance, determination, and stamina.

- Stress can be a positive factor, as long as you keep it under control. Not everything in life is important; most things don't even fall in the top 100.

- You can reduce stress with a few minutes of brain therapy.

- To maintain a balanced life, you must prioritize business, family, and friends.

- Human beings have fundamental needs. Among them are being loved, liked, and appreciated.

Recommended Reading

Davich, Victor. *The Best Guide to Meditation.* Los Angeles: Renaissance Books, 1998.

Mandino, Og. *Secrets for Success and Happiness.* New York: Fawcett Columbine, 1995.

Miller, Ph.D., Lyle H. *The Stress Solution.* New York: Pocket Books, 1994.

Peale, Norman Vincent. *The True Joy of Positive Living.* New York: William Morrow and Company, Inc., 1984.

Schweitzer, Albert. *Out of My Life and Thought.* New York: Holt Rinehart Winston, 1949.

Thomas, Dave. *Well Done!* Grand Rapids, MI: Zondervan Publishing House, 1994.

Success at Your Job

You were introduced to the basic ingredients of success in part 1. You have goals, and some general ideas about how to reach them. Now that you have a clear idea what success means for you, we can start talking about the finer points and how to get the most out of every job environment. In part 2, you will begin to think about your interpersonal relationships, and how these influence your life and your success dramatically. Your relationships with your boss, your subordinates, your peers—all of these are key in helping you achieve your goals. As you get familiar with the concepts in part 2, the power of these relationships will become clear and you will learn how to make the most of them.

Working with the Boss

*B*osses come in all shapes, sizes, personalities, and abilities. The one common thread linking all bosses together is that each has some control over you and your future. The perfect boss is rare and will likely be promoted, leaving you with a new boss to "learn." You'll have to get used to her habits, quirks and needs, just as you did with your last boss. Adjustment to each new boss is challenging—but you're up to it.

Less-than-great bosses—and who hasn't had her share of those—still have merits. After all, he must have done something right along the way to earn his position. Look for positive traits in your boss. Does he have superior industry knowledge, industry contacts, or street sales experience? Learn how to support whatever type of boss you have; it's well worth your effort—if your boss is happy, you're also likely to be happy.

Make an effort to determine what "type" boss you have, purely for the advantage you will have in dealing with her quirks and expectations. Knowing a person's character is key to dealing with them on a daily basis.

IN THIS CHAPTER:

- *Learning to view business from the boss' perspective*

- *Female v. male managers*

- *Manager stereotypes and how to deal with them*

- *Handling negative boss/employee relationships*

THE VIEW FROM THE BOSS' DESK

Take an objective look at your boss' job. He has a department with twenty-three employees. Of the four department secretaries, one is industrious, one is flighty, one is a terrific secretary but an ardent gossip, one tries hard but has minimal skills and even less talent. In the eleven entry-level positions, there isn't one employee with a full year's experience. Each one of these people has blown a basic tenet of customer service this week, and loyal customers are rebelling. One administrative assistant is on vacation, the office manager is in the midst of a divorce, and the regional manager with the largest territory had a coronary and will be out for about eight weeks. That's just personnel.

Are you starting to get the picture? Multiply your problems by a factor of ten, twenty, or thirty, and you might approach the critical factors your boss deals with daily.

Pressure from above (your boss' boss, the CEO, the board of directors, and shareholders) adds to the burden. And your boss, like you, has a family with all the complications arising from normal family life.

No, you don't have to love your boss. You don't even have to like her, but if you do, your life will be much easier. However, you should at least consider what your boss' burdens are and why she acts as she does. In short, try to think as your boss does. It will defuse many explosive situations.

TYPES OF BOSSES

"You've never met a boss like mine." Don't count on it! Anyone who's worked in corporate life has seen a fair share of supervisors. Can you recognize your boss from the following? Again, this is not so you can tell everyone you work for the School Yard Bully or The Power Monger, but so you can get a grip on working positively with this supervisor.

"In a bureaucracy it is always easier to beg forgiveness than to get permission."

—*Rear Admiral Grace Hooper*

The High School Quarterback

When Cal was in high school, he won the big game with a Hail Mary pass, dated the prom queen, and daily basks in the fading glory of it all. This boss lives in the past and relates everything to what happened "when I was." This is the sales manager who recalls that he won a green jacket for being a "master" salesman. So, this year, sales reps exceeding their targets will all get green jackets, whether they like them or not.

Handling Tips: Look for the basic elements that made this boss a success. If he won the master sales title four times, he knows something you can use. Utilize his ideas, blend them with yours, modernize the approach and help this boss learn a new play or two. Don't forget, this boss likes a cheering section, so rah, rah, rah!

Big Brother (or Sister)

Like George Orwell's Big Brother, this boss always watches you. Unlike the 1984 specter, she's actually looking out for your interests. She takes a parental approach. Listen carefully. This boss is a keeper. She'll teach you what she knows, give you credit for your efforts, and provide advice worth its weight in promotions, bonuses, and salary increases.

Handling Tips: To stay on the good side of this boss be open, honest, and above board. When you make a mistake, figure out how to correct it, tell her about the error and the solution, and she'll listen. Like your mom, this boss won't appreciate tattletales, back stabbers, or idlers. Do your job, keep her abreast of controversies and issues, and you'll get along just fine.

The Power Monger

"You will do it my way because I'm the boss." How many of us have heard this statement and winced. This boss might

"I think it is important for a boss to be frank about his temperament and work habits so that people working for him have a chance to understand and adjust. I warned the staff that when I am preoccupied, I can be short-tempered over interruptions or questions. I advised the staff not to overreact to these mood swings. Ride them out, and I would soon be back on an even keel."

—*Colin Powell,*
My American Journey

insist you do something against your moral or ethical code, and refusing carries significant repercussions. He'll take credit for your work and ideas, gleefully pocketing his bonus and running to the bank. This is not an easy person to work for—particularly if he has little or no knowledge in your area. You may wonder how he got to be in charge of merchandising when he's a purchasing person. Don't worry, the purchasing people who used to work for him wondered how he got into purchasing since he's really an accountant.

Handling Tips: Carefully educating this boss in a non-threatening way may be the key to success—particularly if you let him think the concept was initially his. If disaster strikes, don't look for this boss to take the brunt of the responsibility when the hurricane strikes. You'll be on your own when the going gets tough. The only way to deal with a Power Monger is to keep your nose to the grindstone, your back to a protective wall, and your profile low. Make your maximum leader look as good as you can—your only escape from the Power Monger may be his promotion to his next level of incompetence. After all, with all that accounting, purchasing, and merchandising experience he's so boastful about, he's bound to be a great CEO, right?

The Cheerleader

This boss contentedly sits on the sidelines and lets you enjoy the glory, then offers a few rousing cheers to keep you going. If you like to work independently, sink or swim on your own, this is your ideal boss. "Here's the project, let me know how it's going," she says at the beginning. "Do you need any help?" she asks toward the middle. And at the end, you get kudos galore. She's the manager whose people are fast-trackers because she stands behind you at all times, finds ways to expand your responsibilities (and thus your profile), and looks for opportunities to promote from within.

Handling tips: Don't worry about handling this boss, she's on your side all the way.

The Prom Queen

Prom queens are deadly. They combine the grace and charm of a Lizzie Borden or a Leona Helmsley. This is the manager who forgets that when the tiara comes off, she's just a normal human being. It's likely she started out on the bottom of the heap, although she doesn't have much compassion or interest in those current occupying her old position.

Handling tips: This manager is hard going, especially for men not used to working for women. Whatever you do, don't think flattering her hairstyle or new suit will earn points with this boss. Hard work and positive results are the key here. She'll expect you to do what she did: grind your way up on your own.

The Star Builder

Here's a boss who searches out talented people and trains them for the future. This boss will go far, and, hopefully, you'll get to ride along on his meteoric rise. He's another boss you don't have to worry about; he's too busy conjuring up strategies to get you a promotion to stand in your way.

The School Yard Bully

Despite the infinite number of seminars, courses, and self-help books available on progressive management techniques, there are some bosses who took the Ivan-the-Terrible Management Correspondence Course and never got over

"Managers who trust people improve their companies faster than those who try to control everything."

—*Jim Murphy*

it. This manager's primary technique is bluster and threats. "If you don't like the work load, get another job," he says smugly, knowing you have too much invested in the company right now to move. What this manager fails to understand is that he gets minimal effort from people because they spend their work time full of resentment and ill feeling.

On your bravest day, you might point out to the School Yard Bully that the U.S. Bureau of Labor Statistics ranks boss abuse as second in causes of workplace deaths in the U.S. In 1993, 1,063 people were murdered at work. Warning: Don't bring those homicidal thoughts to fruition or your next position will be in the prison license plate shop.

Handling tips: Seriously, hard work, proven results, and limited contact is worthwhile when working for a bully. It's also a good idea to keep along with keeping a low profile. But, after you've been through three or four agonizing reviews with this naysayer, you might question whether working in this company is worth the stress.

> ### EXCUSES YOU NEVER GIVE YOUR BOSS IF YOU INTEND TO ADVANCE
>
> - *It's not fair.*
> - *I'm not getting my share.*
> - *Why should I do his/her work?*
> - *I'm never included in anything important.*
> - *You're picking on me for no reason.*
> - *No matter what project I work on, someone else always messes up.*
> - *It's not my fault.*
> - *Is that in my job description?*
> - *Look, I'm doing as much as I can. Frank has plenty of free time—ask him.*

The Apple Polisher

Ingratiating to those above, always agreeable and always sucking up, this boss loves praise—especially when he's on the receiving end. He's what's classically called a "Yes man," doing whatever his supervisor asks without question. He's probably a pretty smooth talker. Yes, he'll eat it up when you praise his efforts or management style, but don't overdo it, or your colleagues will consider you just one more in a long line of sycophants. You may start your rise to the top by brown-nosing this manager, but your colleagues will undermine you every chance they get.

Handling tips: Don't be surprised if flattery gets you nowhere. The Apple Polisher only smiles at his own superiors—and you're not worth much in his list of priorities. He certainly won't buck the system to move you along. You'll have to produce major results to make headway with an Apple Polisher. It's best to find other outlets for your energy and attention.

Old Dog, No Tricks

A colleague once described our supervisor as being like an old dog: Blind to everything happening around him and peeing on everything in sight. Translated into working terminology: this manager puts his touch on every project, correction on every memo, comment in every conversation. This is the sort of boss who doesn't see the big picture, who doesn't make meaningful, far-reaching decisions. His actions are limited to monitoring employees and making minor changes to their work. He'll "volunteer" to sit in on meetings where you interview potential suppliers or employees, primarily because he doesn't trust you to do anything without his supervision.

Handling tips: Even hard work doesn't work here. The Old Dog is deeply entrenched in old management techniques and abuses. Luckily, he'll most likely be axed in the next big layoff, so bide your time.

Comparing Yourself to Your Boss	E X E R C I S E

Create a chart that compares your strengths and weaknesses with your boss' traits. In the example below, Jim is the head

EVALUATING TRAITS

The Boss	*Traits*	*Impact*	*Relationship to Me*
Strengths	1. delegates responsibility	1. allows others to show their ability	1. allows me to grow in my job
	2. organized	2. meets deadlines, stays on budget	2. makes me more efficient
	3. gives credit to others	3. subordinates shine in corporate view	3. gives me positive exposure to executives
Weaknesses	1. quick tempered	1. affects department morale	1. I have the most direct contact with Jim
	2. won't listen to reason	2. creates level of anxiety	2. puts me between boss and other department members
	3. little knowledge in customer service	3. occasionally rejects good ideas from ignorance	3. I have to oppose Jim to promote good ideas or they are lost

Me	*Traits*	*Impact*	*Relationship to Boss*
Strengths	1. experience in customer service	1. gives know-how to department	1. causes occasional tension
	2. easygoing	2. smoothes problems between Jim and others	2. can place me between the boss' view and others
	3. vision	3. gives department a long-range viewpoint	3. balances Jim's short-range viewpoint
Weaknesses	1. disorganized	1. poor time management	1. can learn this skill from Jim
	2. can't say "no"	2. overloads work schedule	2. Jim limits projects to those which better the department
	3. lack diplomacy	3. occasional conflicts arise	3. can learn this skill from Jim

of the customer service department, although his background is in sales.

It is important for you to understand the way you and your boss can balance each other in the workplace. It's your job to make his job easier; likewise it's his job to teach you by example and direct action, and to promote you within the company.

Comparing Philosophies	E X E R C I S E

Read the following list of characteristics. Mark in the first column those terms which best apply to your work and management philosophy. In the second column of boxes, mark your perception of what your supervisor's management philosophy is.

MANAGEMENT CHARACTERISTICS

Characteristics	*Me*	*Boss*	*Characteristics*	*Me*	*Boss*	*Characteristics*	*Me*	*Boss*
giant builder			dwarf mentality			easily intimidated		
controlling			leader			follower		
resists change			relaxed			delegates easily		
people person			do it my way			problem solver		
creative thinker			detail oriented			assertive		
knowledgeable			collector			process oriented		
innovator			policy follower			entrepreneur		
implementer			incompetent			over her head		
saboteur			reactionary			planner		
quality conscious			encourages opinions			hands-on management		

How closely does your style match your supervisor's? Do your styles complement each other? Do you fill in each other's gaps? Ideally, you should not match your supervisor item for item. If you do, you overlap skills and talents, and something will fall through the cracks.

Truly Abusive Bosses

It's one thing to work for an Apple Polisher or an Old Dog, it's another to endure serious abuse. It's also unnecessary.

Some bosses measure success in terms of might and territory. A tyrannical boss doesn't worry about casualties. You are replaceable—and he'll tell you so.

Some bosses worry constantly about their own competence, and they are usually justified. Inability fosters the need to belittle or backbite others to gain a sense of competence. You'll recognize this boss as a person who takes your information, presents it as his own, and rarely includes middle or lower management in upper-level conferences. Unless you appear inferior to him, you are a threat. This boss will never respect creativity because it is too frightening.

You may encounter chauvinists, bigots, and racists in management positions. This is particularly likely where the good old boy system is active. Don't try to change the mind-set of this type of boss—it's impossible. Besides, he doesn't see anything wrong with his thought processes because all his friends think the same way.

Sadists delight in having subordinates. They enjoy watching you work, knowing you're having a V-8 and stale peanut butter crackers from the canteen vending machines while they lunch at the local country club. Job perks sustain their personal image; your labor is one of those perks. For more information, see the books by Harvey Hornstein and Robert Hochheiser.

Handling Abusive Bosses

Enough is enough! You've doubtlessly found your boss in this cast of heroes and villains. If you have an abusive boss, your first step is to recognize you are not responsible for his negative attitudes or actions. "Abusive managers share a problem—and the problem is with themselves, not with us. We observe behavior in abusive managers which is obviously psychologically dysfunctional, in a category close to that of spouse abusers and child abusers and all the rest made famous by popular culture," says Bruce Tulgan in *Managing Generation X.*

You do not have to tolerate abusive behavior. Document abusive incidents in a professional manner. Use standard journalistic techniques: who was there, what happened, when it happened, where you were at the time, what was said.

If the incident is a one-shot event, don't be a nitpicker. There may be a logical reason for what happened.

> **SUCCESSTHOUGHTS**
>
> *Know your rights:*
> - *You do not have to submit to sexist, brutal, vulgar, demeaning, racist, or abusive language.*
> - *You do not have to allow your boss to humiliate you in public.*
> - *You do not have to tolerate physical abuse of any kind.*
> - *You do not have to endure retribution or revenge against you for seeking help from HR.*

However, if continuing incidents affront you, go to human resources management and discuss the problem. Be specific in explaining your side. Be fair. If your boss makes sexist or racial jokes but is helpful and supportive, say so. Give the positive with the negative.

It may prove a waste of time going to HR to complain about a chauvinist; they already know and are turning a blind eye. I once attended a planning session in which I was the only woman in a group of roughly 75 men. One of the senior vice-presidents told a vulgar, chauvinistic joke comparing dealing with certain suppliers to fondling a woman. Five male managers apologized to me for the remark, yet when I voiced a complaint to HR, I was told I had "misheard" the comment. The five male managers? They had the same hearing deficiency I do.

Hopefully, HR departments are taking a more positive, proactive approach to eliminating sexist, religious, and racist biases. The one thing in favor of filing a complaint: If you don't, nothing will ever be fixed.

While confidentiality would be delightful, you must realize HR can't investigate any issue without contacting your boss. He is entitled to tell his side of the story.

While the ideal situation would be for HR to act as mediator and help resolve all differences, don't expect it. You may be dealing with ingrained problems. With all the best intentions in the world, your boss may not be able to change or see change as an advantage. If no progress is made, investigate a lateral move to ease tensions.

MANAGING THE MANAGER

You don't want to be manipulated; neither does your boss. You can, however, take control of situations within your purview to make your boss/subordinate situation a win-win scenario. Keep in mind:

- *Your boss' success can also be your success.* Supporting your boss is part of your job description, whether it is in writing or not. Yes, this can be hard if your boss is difficult, but it is still part of your job.

- *Recognize your boss as a human being and an individual.* Bosses also have sick children, grumpy spouses, aging parents, bills to pay, and roofs that leak. If you expect your boss to understand what you are going through, return the favor and be considerate of his problems as well.

- *Be aware of your boss' limitations and weaknesses* and try to buoy him up when they arise. If your skills complement his, you will make a great team.

- *Discuss with your boss where you want your job to go.* He isn't a mind reader and can't guess your hopes and dreams. If he knows what you want, you can enlist his help to get there.

- *Make sure you get the stuff you need* (personnel, equipment, information) to succeed on a project.

- *Don't try to hide crises, dilemmas, or setbacks* from your boss. Consider the problem and solution—then go to your boss and tell her about what's happened. Give your boss a chance to support your efforts.

There is one exception to overcoming a negative boss—nepotism. Yes, the theory of relativity: If your boss was raised up on the shoulders of his gene pool, you can kiss any hope of change good-bye. Nepotism, like despotism, has nothing to do with ability and everything to do with power. In this case, relative power. Short of marrying the boss' child, you won't impress this boss.

Regardless of the type of boss you have, maintain an assertive posture. Work with the situation instead of having it overwhelm or defeat you. Keep a positive attitude, be forward thinking, and maneuver within your game plan. Bosses, like everything else in life, will pass.

"There are four kinds of homicide: felonious, excusable, justifiable and praiseworthy."

—*Ambrose Bierce*

CHAPTER RECAP

- Bosses have all the normal failings of human beings.

- You need to view your work from your boss' perspective as well as your own.

- You can get along better with your boss if you pinpoint his management style and learn to work with it.

- You have rights and need to know what they are. If your boss is abusive, you do not need to put up with it.

Recommended Reading

Drucker, Peter F. *Managing for the Future.* New York: Truman Talley Books, 1992.

Hochheiser, Robert. *How to Work for a Jerk.* New York: Vintage Books, 1987.

Hornstein, Harvey A. *Brutal Bosses and Their Prey.* New York: Riverhead Books, 1996.

Malburg, Chris. *How to Fire Your Boss.* New York: Berkeley, 1971.

Negotiating a Golden Egg

Negotiating is a skill many people believe is limited to sales and labor unions. Not true! When was the last time you went to a yard sale or a flea market? Did you pay the asking price? When you bought your last car or your house, did you write a check for whatever price the seller asked? Nonsense. You whittled and wangled the price until you were satisfied with the deal. Why should work be any different?

Negotiating is not a new concept. Travel abroad and shop at an open bazaar. There negotiating is an art, a science, a tradition, a necessity.

A good negotiator haggles for a larger bonus or a bigger pay raise, for better equipment for his/her group, or for added responsibility with a view to promotion. When asking for a raise, you're in the negotiating process, so it's a good idea to plan your tactics.

Basically, negotiating is a conversation between two parties, each with a goal in mind. The fact that the goals may differ dramatically is beside the point. This conversation can involve business, spousal relationships, friendships, services performed for your home or office, and even what time the kids go to bed on Saturday night. Apply normal conversational skills to every negotiation.

What is the first element of a good conversation? Showing interest in the person with whom you are speaking. Paying attention reaps great benefits. You learn about other considerations that are not on your list of priorities. The other person explains his position in a way you might not have considered before.

NEGOTIATE

The basis of the word negotiate *comes from the Latin* negotium, *meaning "not being at leisure." By the time Henry the Eighth was married to his third wife,* negotiate *had already evolved to mean "doing some form of business."*

Learn how to ask questions that gain more than a one-word answer. Become an investigator, an interviewer who pulls more information from the other side. Consider the five Ws of good interviewing: who, what, when, where, and why; then, ask how.

No negotiation can be all one-sided; that is a demand, not a compromise. You cannot always say "no" to every suggestion made by the opposite side. Be subtle in your negatives and vocal in your agreements. The other side will hear all negatives loud and clear, so control your voice levels. Sometimes there is greater advantage in a quiet, controlled voice than in shouting and tirades.

Listen. This can't be emphasized too much. Your turn to speak will come, but you need to listen at least half the time. Remember, this doesn't mean just hearing words, it means listening to what's said, how it is said, and what underlying meanings exist.

According to Herb Cohen in *You Can Negotiate Anything,* the basis of all negotiations are both the specific issues or demands openly stated during the negotiation process and the real needs of the other side—information which rarely comes out in the open.

Here's an example: You want to buy a painting for your hallway. You attend a gallery showing where there are dozens of potential buyers and a wide variety of artworks available. Business at the gallery is brisk, competitive, and intense. You say you want a painting and plan to spend less than $1,000. Your initial selection is The Birches at Holly Farm, priced at $1,250. Those are the specific facts surrounding your negotiation. The gallery does not "need" your business—they have plenty of prospects for this picture. Your ability to negotiate is limited, and someone else walks away with your picture.

However, you get the artist's name and address. You visit the artist in his studio, where he has a half dozen pictures. You tell him you like his work and are interested in a painting, if it came at the right price. The artist has no other prospects in the studio and has a greater "need" to sell to you. Your bargaining position has increased. You purchase a landscape similar to your original choice for a bargain $800.00.

THREE CRUCIAL VARIABLES

There are three crucial variables in any negotiating process: power, time, and information. It doesn't matter whether you deal over a used car or the perks attached to a new COO position.

Power, says top negotiator Herb Cohen, is the capacity or ability to get things done by controlling other people, events, or yourself. When you negotiate, the other side always seems to have more power than you do. Power should be a vehicle from one destination to another, not a goal in itself. Your personal power depends on your perception of power: If you believe you have power, you do. If you believe yourself powerless, you are. In the negotiating process, your understanding of the process, your experience, and your emotional control comprise elements of power.

Time is one variable that can seriously work against you—particularly if the other side knows you are in a crunch. When the other side seems to have no specific deadlines, no pressures to reach a deal, or no restrictive time frames, they may have an advantage over you.

Consider your time frame in a different light. Is the deadline the absolute, drop-dead deadline or is it the first, possibly flexible, deadline? What happens if you don't meet the deadline? Most likely, very little. Imagine this situation: While you are negotiating the purchase of a major piece of equipment you honestly tell your boss you'll likely miss the January 15 deadline but may be able to save the company $13,500 by extending the negotiation process. You won't hear too much about the missed date. To put time on your side, be flexible and never let the opposition know you are sweating.

Gathering information prior to meetings or discussions

provides you with a real edge at the negotiating table. This is the typical Boy Scout situation—prepare for any eventuality, know your opponent and determine her pressure points, so you can negotiate to your advantage.

THE BATTLE OF THE SEXES

Yes, there are strategies for negotiations between men and women. No, sex is *not* one of them.

For women who want men to listen to them, try these strategies. Remember that men are raised differently from women. This is not a sexist stereotype, it's just plain truth. Men are taught that crying is a sign of weakness, while women consider crying an excellent way to release their anger or frustration. Women have a different hormonal structure that also affects emotions. To get along at the negotiating table with a man, keep calm, cool, and collected. Be as businesslike as possible, and keep your emotions in check. Be honest, open, and forthright.

For men who want women to listen to them, try these strategies. Many men get their own way by using emotion. No, they don't break down and sob on the blotter. They yell, scream, curse, threaten, and bully. This is just as bad as the emotional weeping of women. Control your temper and talk to women in a businesslike manner. You wouldn't call a man "stud muffin"; don't call women "honey," "dear," or "sweetheart." You wouldn't pat a man on his hand; don't touch a woman, either. A natural, open approach will win points from the women you work with.

SETTING PRIORITIES

"Negotiating is a game. Some writers on the topic of negotiating refer to win-win situations, claiming the proper aim of the negotiating process is to reach an agreement that is just fair and benefit-maximizing to all by identifying common ground and mutual interests," says Geraldine Henze in *Winning Career Moves*.

A win-win scenario is always crucial for a successful negotiation:

- If you walk away from the table dissatisfied with the deal, you'll feel less likely to work with the other party again.

- If the other side walks away unhappy, they won't want to work with you.

- Long-term relationships ease negotiation tensions and establish common ground. In the long run, a solid rapport between both parties creates a better business environment.

Develop a list of priorities. Know what's important to you and your company before sitting down at the table. Logical criteria are price, delivery conditions, quality, supply, service, variety, and dependability.

Do not assume price is the primary consideration in every negotiation. Kristen was in the job market. In her mid-forties she had very specific job needs. First, she wanted to relocate in Denver or Colorado Springs. Second, she didn't want a job that required constant travel. And third, she wanted to reduce stress and spend more time away from work. You'll note salary was not a key consideration for Kristen. It's not that it didn't matter; but her priorities had shifted.

Thus, when she negotiated with her new employer, location, travel (or lack of it), and reduced job stress were priorities. Other negotiation points included relocation expenses, a company car, a two-week vacation during the first year (although this was contrary to company policy) and, of course, salary. Because Kristen's new employer assumed salary was a critical bargaining factor, the negotiations proceeded in an interesting fashion. The employer gave in on

"Have regard for your name, since it will remain for you longer than a great store of gold."

—*Ecclesiastes 41:12*

all three of Kristen's top priorities, paid relocation expenses, gave her a vacation, and settled on a salary level comfortable for them both. The only thing Kristen gave up was a company car, which she didn't need anyway. Oddly enough, six months after starting her new job, Kristen received a raise in pay, increasing her salary by 50%.

ASKING FOR—AND GETTING— WHAT YOU WANT

Larry was offered a great job with a major publishing firm. It was a job he really wanted, but couldn't afford to take. Why? Because moving would devastate his finances. There was only one way for Larry to handle the situation: tell the company he really wanted the job, but needed more money for relocation expenses.

This was a minor detail; one the firm agreed to immediately. What company would willingly lose a potential star over $2,500? The point here is not that Larry had an unusual request, but that he voiced his concerns and asked for the money.

Most sales fail, most relationships fail, and most negotiations fail because of a lack of clear communication. People don't ask for commitments or openly express their needs. You have spe-

> ### NEGOTIATING
>
> *Negotiating ideally is a win-win process, be it global diplomacy or in closing a sale on industrial equipment. When the buyer makes a firm demand, you cannot blandly stick to your cards.*
>
> *The secret: give a little, get a little, continue to work toward the long-term relationship. You may think of negotiation as billion-dollar deals in boardrooms or hostages on hold involving the government and terrorists. It's high time we applied the word to day-to-day life.*
>
> *—Charles B. Roth and Roy Alexander,* Secrets of Closing Sales

cific priorities, but only one item fills the number one slot. Don't let any deal, regardless of its size or content, fall apart by getting hung up over a minor point. Surrender the battle, win the war.

Look for the hidden agenda. If it's not price, then what is the sticking point? For example: is it credit terms? service standards? failed or unreasonable expectations? lack of trust? Listen to what's being said around the table. Can you pinpoint the obstacles to agreement? If not, ask the participants to voice their objections and listen for any "between the lines" concerns.

You get nothing if you don't ask for it. You've heard this all through your life. Make reasonable demands, and you will find rejections few and acceptances increasing.

Hardly anyone in business today hasn't heard the saying "You can have it fast, cheap, or good. Pick any two." This is the basis of negotiation: prioritizing and compromising. Know where you stand in a bargaining scenario. If time is critical, then is price flexible? If quality is essential, is time still fixed?

When the item you negotiate is your career, decide in advance what elements you must have and what you can live without. Once you've eliminated an element from the discussion, don't go back to it. It's over. You'll weaken your position and cast doubts on your integrity.

> **RAISES**
>
> *One of the cleverest ways of asking the boss for a raise was the approach used by John Kieran when he was the sports columnist of the* New York Times. *Feeling the need for an increase, but wanting to be tactful about it, Kieran went to his employer, Adolph Ochs, and said respectfully, "Mr. Ochs, working for the* Times *is a luxury I can no longer afford." He got the raise.*
> —Lance Davidson, The Ultimate Reference Book: The Wit's Thesaurus

Being Reviewed

The one time you can guarantee you and your performance will be the central topic is at your annual review. Okay, it's your show, so what do you want to say? Robert

Hochheiser offers some suggestions on how to get the most from a meaningful review in *How to Work for a Jerk:*

- *Have a plan.* Know in advance what you want, what your strategy is to get it, and what contingency tactics you'll adopt if what you try first doesn't work.

- *Make sure you get a face-to-face review.* You can't negotiate with a piece of paper. Don't let management get away with simply sending you a memo about your raise or your review. Insist on a one-on-one meeting with your boss.

- *Send him an accomplishment list.* Do this in writing before the review. Use the list to remind him of what you've done, how well you've done it, and how indispensable you are.

- *Make up a "wish list."* What do you want? More money? How much? A different title? Which one? Decide how much of what you want you intend to ask for, and also how little of it you would settle for.

Contract Negotiation	EXERCISE

You have been assigned the task of negotiating a new contract with your company's maintenance staff. What are five possible issues the maintenance staff might bring up? What are five possible issues on your side of the table? Prioritize the issues for both sides.

Plan your negotiation strategy. Where will you hold the meetings? Who will you want to attend on your side? On the other side? What points are you willing to compromise on? What points are non-negotiable? Why?

Who has the power? What information do you need? What is the time frame or deadline? Who has the advantage in each of these crucial issues? What is the ideal result?

CONTRACT ISSUES

Management	Maintenance Staff
Your issues: 1. pay rate 2. hours 3. drug testing 4. vacation time 5. working conditions	Their issues: 1. pay rate 2. safety concerns 3. hours 4. safety training and protective equipment 5. profit sharing
Issues in priority order: 1. pay rate 2. working conditions 3. drug testing 4. hours 5. vacation time	Issues in priority order: 1. safety concerns 2. safety training and protective equipment 3. pay rate 4. profit sharing 5. hours
Meeting location: off-site at local hotel conference room	
Attending: you, secretary, HR benefits manager, COO	Attending: three staff representatives
Source of power: 1. layoff of personnel 2. authority to make deals	Source of power: 1. work stoppage 2. critical to production schedule
Information: 1. What are their demands? How rigid are they? Areas of potential compromise?	Information: 1. What will management do to avert a strike? What concessions will maintenance make?
Areas for compromise: 1. pay rate 2. safety training and equipment, creating a safer environment	Areas for compromise: 1. drug testing program 2. work hours 3. pay rate
Areas of no compromise: 1. vacation days per year 2. work hours 3. drug testing program	Areas of no compromise: 1. safety concerns, training and equipment

Management and labor agree that safety is a concern and money/efforts will be put toward that end. Labor then agrees that drug testing is a safety issue and agrees to the program as offered by the company. The hourly pay rate goes back and forth, with both sides compromising on an acceptable rate; $1.50 less than labor asked for, $1.00 more than management wanted to give. The difference covered the increased expenditures in safety by the company. Labor agreed that the 12-hour on, 12-hour off, 36-hour week will remain intact, as it parallels the production crew. Both sides agreed to disagree about vacation and sick time, with that issue tabled until next year. The company already has plans for a 401K with profit-sharing built in. This program will be implemented in two years; those changes satisfied the maintenance group.

Can't Take It Back, Jack

Be positive, be confident, and be careful. Don't make threats you can't or don't intend to carry out. Sometimes, in the heat of the moment, you might say something you really don't mean. Some people believe threatening to quit will land them a better raise. More often, the boss wishes you well in your new position and offers to help clean out your cubicle. On the other side, managers who threaten dismissal may find themselves involved in lawsuits or with significant turnover rates. Are you willing to take either risk? Before you put yourself in a bind, take three deep breaths and say to yourself, "Think, think, think."

You also need to be levelheaded and strategic in what you ask for. There are times when requests will meet with approval and others when it's best to keep quiet. When do you keep quiet?

- When your company has just posted negative sales results.

- When your company recently downsized.

- When your most recent projects were less than successful.

- When your company loses its largest client, a major contract, or any other significant business.

When should you ask for a raise?

- When sales figures are high—particularly if your contribution was significant.

- When you have taken on added responsibility and proven yourself capable of handling it.

- When you have a history of successes that impact the company favorably.

- When you have a solid alternative waiting in the wings. An example: Brenda worked for a major textile company. As a single parent, salary was definitely Brenda's number one priority. A competitor offered Brenda a $7,000 raise to come work for them—she couldn't easily turn this down. Brenda liked her job and the people she worked with. She went to her boss and candidly explained her position. She wanted to stay, but couldn't afford to. Her boss valued Brenda highly and arranged a $5,000 raise. No, it wasn't as much money as the competitor offered, but considering the continuation of health benefits, Brenda came out on top.

- Be prepared with a list of trade-offs when negotiating job specs, salary, vacation time, moving expenses, promotion. Note several things you want and several things you are willing to give up. Don't get stuck on the first rung of the ladder. If you are given a boost in another way, accept it, and continue to work your list. Give yourself plenty of time to make your desires known and have them come to fruition. You can't—and won't—be a winner on every point.

When to Back Away

There are times when no amount of negotiation is going to achieve a positive result. That's the time that no deal is the best deal.

It's hard to give up, but when no progress is possible, the best strategy is retreat. You only waste time and effort by continuing once you've reached an impasse.

Keep in mind that today's "no," may be the start of your next deal with someone else, between you and some other company, or for a different opportunity.

Your Word, Your Bond

Once you have reached an agreement, you are honor bound to keep it to the best of your ability. Make your word count for something. It doesn't matter if everyone else you meet reneges on his agreements—so long as your word is your bond.

CHAPTER RECAP

- Negotiation is not an "I win" situation, but a win-win situation.

- You must make concessions on minor issues for a negotiation to be successful.

- Prepare for every negotiation by determining what your priorities are before you sit down at the table.

- Ask questions. Information is power.

- Step away from any negotiation where you are not given the opportunity to feel some success. There is always another deal.

Recommended Reading

Donaldson, Michael C., and Mimi Donaldson. *Negotiating for Dummies*. Foster City, CA: IDG Books Worldwide, 1996.

McCormack, Mark H. *On Negotiating*. Beverly Hills, CA: Dove Books, 1995.

Roth, Charles B., and Roy Alexander. *Secrets of Closing Sales*. Englewood Cliffs, NJ: Prentice Hall, 1993.

Selling Your Most Valuable Product—You

Like negotiating, fundamental sales techniques are essential if you are on the way up. What are you selling? Your greatest asset: You.

Consider yourself like a product. What are your features? benefits? What are you worth? Are you on the market strictly for price? If so, you are selling yourself at a discount and will be valued accordingly.

We sell ourselves on a daily basis in meetings, reviews, presentations, and even in casual business conversation. How you present yourself—*sell* yourself—can mean the difference between advancing and getting stuck in a rut.

WHY AND WHEN TO SELL YOURSELF

Essentially, you sell yourself on a daily basis, through your work, your ideas, the way you interact with others, the presentations you make, and your appreciation of others. In this chapter, you are the product. Who will buy your product? What do they get for their money? What criteria will encourage a sale?

IN THIS CHAPTER:

- *Learning how and why to sell yourself*
- *Assessing your features and benefits*
- *Tips on controlling your behavior*
- *Exercises on setting yourself up for a "big sale"*

Tom Reilly, in *Value-Added Selling Techniques,* says, 'Buyers go through many stages in their decision process. First, they agree to a need. Next, they agree to a product, supplier, and so on. Be sure that your buyer agrees first to needing something before discussing your product. This is conceptual selling: convincing your prospect of a need."

Here's an example: Mitchell is an architect with a large regional firm. Together with being an adequate architect, he excelled at overseeing a project from concept to construction. However, his firm did not have designated project managers. Mitchell's first job was to convince his firm's decision makers that a new position—project manager—was necessary. Once they saw the need, he sold himself in the role.

Why do you need to sell yourself? So that you are not passed by at promotion time. The phrase "It pays to advertise" applies to selling yourself. Make your boss aware of your qualities and desire to advance. While you don't want to nag, regular repetitions of your "ad" are valuable.

When do you sell yourself? Keep in mind the following scenarios: meetings, presentations, reviews, conferences, and training sessions. Anytime you are in the spotlight (or can move into the spotlight) is the time to sell yourself.

QUALITY, FEATURES, AND BENEFITS

Are you a Nash Rambler or a Cadillac Eldorado? A used VW bus or a Lexus? You choose a car, a house, a major appliance, a computer, and a vacation package on the quality, features, and benefits. Your boss or potential employer shops the same way. She wants to get the best buy for her company's money.

Knowing this, you should evaluate what features make you the best buy. What qualities do top performers display? In their book, *The Selling Edge,* Michael and Celeste Levokove include the following characteristics of top performers:

- They understand success depends on one's ability to efficiently manage one's position.

- They develop and utilize several tools and techniques to enhance their success.

- They are always open and receptive to new ideas that might improve performance.

- They tend to be driven.

Some features that will increase your future potential include long-range planning, leadership, and strategic thinking. If you do not possess these skills now, you need to establish a program of skill building to add to your "saleability."

"We are all salespeople every day of our lives, selling our ideas, plans, and enthusiasm to everyone we meet."
—*Charles M. Schwab*

Selling Yourself

EXERCISE

Write a features-and-benefits ad to sell yourself. First, determine what your major features are, then the benefit of each feature. Next write an ad to promote yourself. Review this sample before you start.

Features:

- Excellent written and oral communicator.

- Visionary approach to management.

- Highly productive manager.

- Varied experience in several connected fields.

Benefits:

- Communication skills translate into better manager/employee relations, customer/company relations, improved media relations.

- A visionary approach addresses new markets and new products and turns potential into profits.

- High productivity means meeting and exceeding targets on all levels.

- Varied experience uncovers parallel solutions to problems.

The Ad:

Gregory Johnson—experienced, energetic, effective. In sales and marketing, there are few who equal Greg's ability to motivate others, generate enthusiasm, and achieve results. Among Greg's assets are a knack for communicating via all media, to all levels. You'll find improved relationships with employees, customers, and industry representatives turn into long-term business partnerships. Greg approaches each opportunity with a unique, yet practical, vision. He draws solutions from his experience in the automotive industry, while applying valuable lessons learned in aerospace and large-scale construction. Gregory Johnson—the solution you're looking for.

Give that man the job!

WHAT MAKES A GOOD SALESPERSON?

The art of selling is simple: You find out what the buyer wants and sell it to him. This applies to work situations, personal relationships, and social situations.

How do you know what to sell? Ask! As a freelance writer, Babs contacts people from a variety of fields when she is looking for work. She sends sample copies of her writing to potential clients, along with a resumé, and project list. Since Babs writes

> ### SUCCESSTHOUGHTS
>
> *Never ask questions that can be answered with a simple "yes" or "no." You won't get worthwhile information unless you can elicit a full, detailed answer.*

for education, business, healthcare, fiction, and scripts, one resumé would never do. Instead, Babs has developed a different resumé for each market she works in. She sells her writing talents with a directed "benefit" of experience in the field she's pursuing. In short, she sells what customers want.

Learning to ask the right questions is a talent. Even greater is developing the listening skills to absorb the answers. Let's say you are considering a new job with BBB Nuts & Bolts. Here are a few questions to ask the interviewer:

- *Can you tell me how the company began?* How it has grown in the past five years?

- *What is the company's mission statement?* How do employees work to fulfill this mission statement?

- *May I have some printed materials* about the company and its benefits?

- *What duties will my job entail?* What training will I receive? Who will I report to? What is his experience in the industry? Who else will I be working with? In what capacity?

- *Where will I get my leads?* Which customers will I be calling on?

- *When are your slow times?*

- *May I go on a sales call* with a sales representative?

- *What gives you an edge in your market?*

- *What can I learn working for this company?* What opportunities will be open to me in the future?

- *May I have a tour* of this facility?

At this point, you should know quite a bit about BBB Nuts & Bolts. If you still feel you don't know enough, ask more questions until you're satisfied.

A good salesperson takes the initiative when faced with opportunity. "Initiative is the element essential to getting things started and 'off and running.' You can never have enough initiative in your tool kit," says Darrell Simms, author of *Black Experience Strategies & Tactics in the Business World.*

Finally, perseverance is a basic sales techniques. Regardless of the field or position, if you work with a determined, constant pace, you will be a winner. Remember the tortoise and the hare? Aesop knew that slow and steady really does win the race.

You can't just ask for the sale, promotion, raise, job—you must also follow up and ensure you get what you ask for. Ask for the sale; ask again; ask a third time.

"Our self-feeling in this world depends entirely on what we back ourselves to be and do."

—*Henry James,* The Principles of Psychology

What Makes a Good Product

I know, you're a person, not a product. However, you will still need skills and talents—the "features and benefits" of your person-product.

EXERCISE	*Comparing Yourself to a New Car*

Let's compare you, the "product," to those criteria people most want when buying a new car. After you've done that let's see how you stack up against what your customers will want from you, the "salesperson."

Review your answers. If you said "yes" to 17 out of 20, go ask for a raise, you are a Lexus in your industry. If you said "yes" to 12 out of 16, consider ways to improve. Fewer than 12 "yes" answers? Rethink your approach to your job.

Remember: Price is not the only variable in any deal. When selling yourself, avoid price as an issue. If you fulfill most of the above criteria, price won't be a problem.

There is no such thing as job security anymore. Even the boss' son can get the ax when a conglomerate

DESIRED CRITERIA

Most Wanted Criteria	*Do You Have It?*	*Yes/No*
quality	Is your work always top-notch?	
responsibility	Can others depend on you?	
consistency	Is your work consistently superior?	
price	Do you earn your salary and bonus?	
stamina	Do you hop from job to job?	
brand identity	Do you do the "right things"?	
appearance	Do you present yourself in a positive light?	
diversity	Are you multi-faceted or multi-talented?	
availability	Can you be counted on to take on new projects despite a busy work load?	
usefulness	Do your skills and talents work for the company?	

What Customers want from Salespeople	*Do You Have It?*	*Yes/No*
follow-through	Do you follow up on requests?	
dependability	Can others depend on you?	
communication skills	Do you communicate clearly and openly?	
availability	Can others reach you if they need to?	
knowledge	Do you know your stuff?	
perseverance	Do you persist?	
organization	Are you methodical?	
internal selling skills	Do you sell ideas and customer requests with enthusiasm?	
honesty	Are you honest with the people you work with?	
service mentality	Do you know what your customers want and provide that service level?	

acquires Dad's company and ousts current management. However, you can develop skill security: Make your skills your "product," and you'll find yourself valued by your company.

Pre-sell Preparation

Where are the Boy Scouts when you need them? Before you can sell yourself well, you have to prepare. Here's how:

- Know your strengths and tout them regularly. This doesn't mean bragging or bluster, but a humble offering of your skills at crucial moments.

- Know what your company needs in terms of skills and acquire them.

- Know what activities will help your boss and do them.

- Know your value to yourself, your family, and your company and insure it through continued success.

We have talked at great length about skills and talents—features and benefits—you can use to sell yourself. But what reduces your value? Here are a few negatives, which detract from you, the "product," as pointed out by Burton Kaplan in *Winning People Over:*

- Creating an obstacle course that thwarts success.

- General anarchy in your work style. No method, no persistence, no results.

- Overly volatile, temperamental, difficult to work with.

- Worrying to the point you can't, or don't, function.

Body Language Speaks for You

Not surprisingly, success is not only what you say, but also how you say it. There can be many reasons your body language doesn't equal your conversation. You may be tired, preoccupied, or have trouble communicating. Regardless of the reason, be careful that your body gives positive cues.

> **THREE STEPS TO CONTROLLING YOUR BEHAVIOR**
>
> 1. See your goal. *Fix the image in your mind. Focus tightly. Release the power of your unconscious mind. Hold tight to the dream.*
> 2. Sell yourself. *No one is more persuasive than you. Remind yourself that you're about to make a fresh start.*
> 3. Act as if. *Want to be confident? Even if you do not feel particularly confident, act as if you are.*
>
> (Source: Walter Anderson, The Confidence Course)

- *Send positive vibes.* You can do this by smiling, leaning toward the other party, or maintaining eye contact.

- *Leave an adequate amount of space* between yourself and the other party, particularly when standing. You don't want to be too close, as this closeness can be taken as intimidation.

- *Think about how you sit.* Relax in the chair without appearing stiff or uncomfortable. Keep your arms open or use your hands to gesture. Crossing your arms implies closing out the other person.

One Last Thing

You control your success or failure. Darrell Simms suggests, "You will never make it in the business world if self-control is not a part of your tool kit. In fact, you will fail miserably without this element."

This is true regardless of your education, your vocation, or your situation. You can avoid failure or allow it to rule your actions. Much depends on how you behave toward others.

CHAPTER RECAP

- You sell yourself with every project you do, every meeting you attend, every time you work with others.

- We all have features and benefits that are valuable to employers. Knowing your features and benefits and how to sell them are key elements toward promotion.

- You must control your emotions when dealing with others.

- Preparation is the primary step in selling anything—including yourself.

Recommended Reading

Mandino, Og. *The Return of the Ragpicker.* New York: Bantam, 1992.

_____. *Secrets for Success and Happiness.* New York: Fawcett Columbine, 1995.

Munro, Barry Graham. *Smart Salespeople Sometimes Wear Plaid.* Rocklin, CA: Prima Publishing, 1994.

Reilly, Tom. *Value-Added Selling Techniques.* Chicago: Congdon & Weed, 1989.

Roth, Charles B., and Roy Alexander. *Secrets of Closing Sales.* Englewood Cliffs, NJ: Prentice Hall, 1993.

Coaches, Mentors, and the Mentored

P erhaps the best thing that ever happens to anyone in business life is finding a great mentor. An active, interested mentor is the fast track to the fast track. If you are lucky enough to have a mentor, appreciate it. If you don't have one, get busy and find one. According to Nancy W. Collins in *Professional Women and Their Mentors,* "In a professional sense, powerful mentor figures can make a critical difference in one's career. They are important not only at the beginning and the mid-levels, but to provide a final push into senior positions."

The titles from the past—boss, supervisor, manager, director—are on the wane. Today businesses look for facilitators, coordinators, sponsors, coaches—and, yes, mentors. Mentoring has come back into fashion. Unfortunately, too many people claim to be mentors or have mentors without understanding the significance and responsibilities inherent in the mentor-mentoree relationship.

The mentor mentality is a pass-it-along favor. He mentored me, I'll mentor you. If getting ahead is your goal, a mentor can make advancement easier. Later on,

IN THIS CHAPTER:

- *Learning the dialogue of mentoring*

- *Identifying the difference between a mentor and a coach*

- *Locating a mentor*

- *The give-and-take of mentoring*

you can repay the debt—and this is one area in which pay-back is wonderful and fulfilling.

THE ROLE OF MENTOR

Perhaps the best thing that ever happens to anyone in business life is finding a great mentor.

What do you remember from your ancient Greek myths and legends? In *The Odyssey* Mentor is an elderly advisor to Odysseus. When Odysseus leaves his home to fight in the Trojan Wars, he entrusts his son Telemachus to the care of Mentor. Mentor guides Telemachus from infancy to maturity through his wisdom, experience, and nurturing. Mentor is wise, loving, responsible, and sensitive, just the thing for a child who will one day rule his land.

Today's business mentors are like business parents—guides from "infancy" through "maturity" in the business environment. It is a caring, responsible role, and one that should not be taken lightly. Like parenting, mentoring is a long-term commitment.

It all sounds so delightful, pleasant, simple. But . . . there's always a "but." "There are countless traps along the path . . . ," says mentoring guru Chip Bell. "Mentoring can be a power trip for those seeking an admirer, a manifestation of greed for those who must have slaves."

While mentoring is not a guaranteed avenue to success, there are paths along which mentors and their protégés should definitely trek.

One such path is a mutual dialogue. Mentoring is not lecturing, it's discussing, planning, questioning, and answering. It requires a dialogue in which both parties listen to each other. Occasionally, there is disagreement, although there should always be a goal of learning in every discussion. There is no set pattern for these discussions, but a good mentor should never expect the protégé to mimic her answers or follow her dictates.

Another path of mentoring is guidance. There is the difference between rescuing a subordinate and supporting him. When you support, you allow the subordinate to stay in control. When you rescue, you take control. Too often mentors act like firemen, standing by with large hoses ready to douse the fires inadvertently lit by naive protégés. How can a protégé learn personal responsibility if he is always bailed out of his problems?

Listen, listen, listen is the advice most experts recommend to prospective mentors. Learn to listen between the lines. What is your protégé really saying? What else might be involved?

A problem arises between your protégé and Gretchen, the head of InfoSystems. Sure, you know Gretchen really well, and you could quickly smooth out the problem. Don't do it! Discuss possible ways to correct the problem, then let your protégé fix his own mistakes. If you are the protégé, ask for advice, recommendations, insights on handling a problem. Thank your mentor for the advice and go to it.

Why consider being a mentor? It is imperative to prepare a group of successors to follow in your footsteps, not just one. If you have any hope of moving ahead, you will need strong people to come behind you. Unless you make the effort to prepare them, you will find your department falls on its face the minute you leave. The legacy you leave behind should be a department in which people can step into your shoes and productivity never suffers.

Climb high
Climb far
Your goal the sky
Your aim the star.

—*Inscription,*
Williams College

Mentor v. Coach

There is a subtle distinction between being a mentor and being a coach. Basically, mentors seek out potential stars and guide them to success. A coach leads a team, creates camaraderie amongst team members, encourages the best performance from every team member, and trains the team to succeed.

Becoming a good coach requires knowing when and how to criticize an employee. Consider the result. Criticize the result. Build up the person. Here are a few tips on offering criticism:

- *Can the problem or behavior be changed?* The problem is a specific result, error, behavior—not a person. Identify the problem as such and address it.

- *Choose a proper time and place.* Never criticize a subordinate in front of others or when you are angry. Get yourself under control, then address the issue.

- *Criticism should be positive, not threatening.* Don't threaten a person's livelihood because he made a mistake. You make mistakes too.

- *Be specific.* If you can't define what is wrong and what you want done to correct it, how do you expect the employee to fix the problem?

- *Help with the fix.* Develop a plan for correcting the problem. If there is a time frame under which the correction needs to be made, say so. Don't compound one problem with another by failing to let the person be successful in correcting the problem.

- *Offer praise.* Be there tomorrow to remind the person that you are confident of success or that you already see progress. Praise, unlike punishment, is always a good public event.

A good coach has a number of attributes, which should become part of her management style. In *Coaching, Mentoring & Managing* William Hendricks says, "No coach has ever had the 'perfect team.' The best teams you've even seen—the ones you may have wished you had—all have their share of personality types that could drive anyone crazy. The difference between the success and failure of any team is how well the coach understands its members and motivates them."

"Everyman's work, whether it be literature or music or pictures or architecture or anything else, is always a portrait of himself."

—Samuel Butler

Every day you have the opportunity to encourage someone on your team. Failure to do so will lower self-esteem, reduce productivity, and adversely affect everyone on the team. There are plenty of chances for praise if you look for them. Let people know you appreciate long hours, missed lunches, helping others, and offering positive ideas. Be sure to offer honest praise whenever you have the chance—for ideas, for work, for pitching in when deadlines are looming. And, never miss an opportunity to let your superiors know who contributed to the success of the project.

> **SUCCESSTHOUGHTS**
>
> *If you decide to be a mentor, avoid certain traps:*
> - *Let the learner struggle to succeed in the same way a child falls a dozen times before learning to take a step on his own. No one ever learned to take giant steps by being carried everywhere.*
> - *Ego can get in the way of solid mentoring. Don't let praise, earned or not, become the focus of your relationship with the "mentoree."*
> - *Don't make promises you can't keep. Big raises, big bonuses, promotions, and key appointments are not easily attained.*
> - *Just like a drug addict or an alcoholic needs a facilitator to break his addiction, a protégé may cling to his mentor as essential to his business success. This is as damaging for the protégé as it is for the mentor.*
> - *Don't spread yourself too thin or allow your protégé to consume your time. You each have a job to do. Be helpful, be active, be determined to encourage the protégé to stand on his own two feet.*

Finally, if you are going to be a coach, you have to show up for the practices as well as the games, accept responsibility for defeats, and keep your team moving forward. Absentee or negligent management undermines the structure of a successful team.

The Responsibility of Being Mentored

Learning is the business mode of the future. Without continued learning, people's skills, abilities, and value to the company will dwindle, and they will no longer be employable. When you sign on as a protégé, you make a serious commitment. This is not a one-sided relationship where everything is done for you and you do nothing in return.

At the outset, you and your mentor should identify and establish realistic, firm goals for your future. Where do you want to go? Why? How will you get there? How can your mentor help? What is your role in achieving these goals? A strategic plan is essential for both of you.

You have to trust your mentor to look out for your best interests. She has to trust you, too. Much of what you do reflects on her leadership and advice. If you go from one blunder to the next without considering how your actions reflect on your mentor, you are not living up to your responsibility.

A good mentor will push you, challenge you, encourage you to step beyond the familiar to another level of performance. Sometimes this can be frightening, intimidating, and even overwhelming. You may feel that your mentor's expectations are too high. If so, it's time to sit down and discuss your feelings. Don't be afraid to admit your concerns.

Finally, a mentor relationship is like gaining a new best friend. It takes time to develop a friendship that is both long-term and mutually beneficial. It also takes a lot of work. Show appreciation for all the extra help and attention your mentor offers. It may be that the best way of repaying your mentor is to mentor someone else.

"If you pick up a starving dog and make him prosperous, he will not bite you. This is the principal difference between a dog and a man."

—Mark Twain

Finding a Mentor

According to Nancy Collins, a mentor should not be your boss but should hold a higher position than you, must show interest in you and your growth, and must be able to commit time to being your mentor.

Because of the abundance of men at higher levels in business, it is very likely that your mentor will be a man. In an ideal world, it would not matter if your mentor were male or female. Realistically, male/female chemistry, social mores, and family pressures can overburden today's mixed-gender mentor/mentoree relationships. While it sounds politically incorrect, it may be easier for men to mentor men and women to mentor women. Unfortunately, there is a serious lack of women at the top who can or are willing to mentor women on the rise. Women might have to investigate professional women's organizations to find potential mentors.

A mentor does not need to work in your company. You should be looking for a mentor from any avenue of your life. Where do you look? Try the Better Business Bureau or the Chamber of Commerce. Get involved in your local business community—there are plenty of eligible mentors there. Join a service organization like the Elks, Rotary, or Lions. Join a professional organization in your field. Be aggressive in finding the right person—don't wait to be noticed.

Finding a Mentor	E X E R C I S E

Make a chart with five columns and as many rows as you need. Title the columns: Contact Source, Person, Position, Assets as Mentor, Debits as Mentor. Consider as few as three and as many as a dozen potential mentors. Key in on those with the best

POTENTIAL MENTORS

Contact Source	Person	Position	Assets as Mentor	Debits as Mentor
Women's Business Network	Susan Abbott	VP, Marketing	• position • influence • well-known	• time factor • interest?
Lion's Club	Jerry Sarner	small business owner	• knowledge • contacts • interest in me	• influence

XYZ Corporation	John Towart	Director, HR	• influence
			• position
			• interest in me
			• location
			  (same company)
			• previous success
			  as mentor
				• time
				• experience in
				  my field

opportunity to mentor you. This will pare down your list of potentials and move you closer to finding the mentor you need.

In a way, mentoring is an easier concept for men. From their earliest days in competitive sports, boys learned that a coach could guide them. So it is easy for men to envision the coach/athlete relationship. Now that girls participate in sports more actively than in past decades, they too will begin to benefit from the coach/athlete model. In addition, growing numbers of women aspire to high positions in their professions. Many will find the mentor/protégé relationship an ideal first step on the ladder.

> **SUCCESSTHOUGHTS**
>
> *How a mentor is helpful:*
>   1. *Guides a neophyte first starting out in a company through the maze of corporate politics.*
>   2. *Facilitates recognition, recommendation for larger responsibility, bigger salary, new position, key appointments within the corporate structure.*
>   3. *Assists in long-range planning toward career goals.*

Payback Is Great

As a thirty-something divorced mother, Priscilla began working in a well-known carpet and rug company. Her supervisor, Ed, also became her mentor, even though the boss/mentor combination is not usually a good one. He told Priscilla how his supervisor in his previous job "took him on." He was given opportunities for success, advanced quickly in responsibility and job level, and was paid accordingly. Ed arranged for Priscilla to have increasing responsibility for projects and both the praise and pay that went with it. He said, "The only way I can pay back my mentor is to do for you what he did for me."

If you don't have a person to help, try Big Brothers/Big Sisters, the Jaycees, scouting, the Guardian Ad Litem program in your area, or sponsoring an intern from a nearby high school or college. Become someone else's best chance for success. You will discover that the luster of her success shines right back on you.

CHAPTER RECAP

- Mentoring is a give/take relationship.

- A mentor can be found outside your company.

- Mentors should cultivate independence in those mentored.

- A mentor serves as a business parent, showing the road to success to a younger, less experienced person.

Recommended Reading

Bell, Chip R. *Managers as Mentors.* San Francisco: Berrett-Koehler, 1996.

Bick, Julie. *All I Really Need to Know in Business I Learned at Microsoft.* New York: Pocket Books, 1997.

Collins, Nancy W. *Professional Women and Their Mentors.* Englewood Cliffs, NJ: Prentice Hall, 1983.

Hendricks, William, ed. *Coaching, Mentoring and Managing.* Franklin Lakes, NJ: Career Press, 1996.

Ogilvy, David. *Confessions of an Advertising Man.* New York: Atheneum, 1988.

Woodring, Susan Fowler. *Mentoring: How to Foster Your Career's Most Crucial Relationships* (audiotape). Boulder, CO: Career Track, Inc., 1992.

So, You're the Boss

Congratulations! You got the promotion. You're the boss. Big deal? Yes, it is—but don't let it go to your head.

Being new to "bossdom" is a power trip, a financial boost, and a serious commitment. You have plenty to learn and had better listen to your subordinates. Your secretary, who has survived your four predecessors, has plenty of inside information to make your job easier and your department more successful.

There is a world of difference between being managed and managing others. One place to start is by realizing that while you manage others, someone also manages you—there's no escape. Even the Pope has a manager.

DIFFERENCES BETWEEN MANAGER AND THE MANAGED

Today, you move into the corner office with a window and plush carpeting. You're hyped; this is the position you've worked toward for six years. You unpack the pictures of the kids and the Rolodex. You sort your books into the bookcase alphabetically. And it's only 7:15 A.M.

Now what? Go make a pot of coffee—it will impress your department to know you not only can make coffee, you actually did make coffee.

As manager, you are responsible for your own work and that of everyone in your department. Jack's low sales figures or Alice's error-filled reports reflect negatively on your management abilities. Similarly, a 22% increase in sales and professional presentations reflect positively on your talents. Ideally, you should put aside your personal interests in favor of the group. While it is unrealistic to expect such benevolence on a continuous basis, the premise is sound: If the group prospers, so do you.

First Day in the Hot Seat

It's your first day as "the boss": sweaty palms and a grin plastered across your face. There are no numbers to reflect your skills—yet. Instead, you are being evaluated by the people whose efforts impact your future: the people in the department.

If you are totally new to the company or department, begin by reviewing the personnel profiles of the people who will report to you. Get an idea of their backgrounds, their past history with the company, and what talents or skills they bring to your department.

Call a quick meeting to introduce yourself. Hopefully, your supervisor will introduce you, but if not, then introduce yourself. Explain who you are, why you were hired, your goals for the department, and a bit about you the "person." You don't have to tell everyone about winning the state wrestling championship in high school or the Pillsbury bake-off eight years ago, but give them an idea of who you are. Then go around the room and ask each person to tell you about himself.

Take notes—particularly if the department is large. Dedicate a piece of paper to each person, and note her job, interests, projects she mentions. Ask at least one question of each person, calling that person by name. This fixes names and faces in your mind.

At that meeting, schedule short individual meetings with each person. Fifteen minutes should be more than enough; you can always have longer meetings as required. You will likely have other items on your calendar, so just fit in a few people each day without creating a traffic jam outside your door.

Your initial challenge is getting your department to trust you, cooperate with you, and work both with and for you. This can be a formidable task, especially when you realize you can't do the jobs of 75% of your department. Don't worry, you were not promoted to do their jobs, but to facilitate the success of their jobs.

> **SUCCESSTHOUGHTS**
>
> *Four rules of delegation:*
>   1. *Don't keep all the plums to yourself. Everyone likes to do fun projects, interesting projects, be challenged. Spreading around key opportunities will solidify your relationships.*
>   2. *Don't dump the dirty work on the same person every time.*
>   3. *Don't be afraid to roll up your sleeves and pitch in—regardless of how menial the task.*
>   4. *Don't ask anyone to undertake a task that is contrary to the law, their moral code, their religion, or their emotional well-being.*

If you feel at a loss, just realize that several of these people could have been selected for the job, but your superior chose you. If you don't know why, ask her. Be sure to let your department know why you were chosen—it will smooth your road considerably.

While you learn about your people and position, relax. No one expects perfection; you are once again at the bottom of a learning curve.

Remember: As the boss, you don't have to do all the work. You can keep tasks that suit your talents and personality and delegate those that do not. It is important to spend time in areas where you are capable, effective, efficient, and happy. That's also true of your employees.

Matching an employee's abilities to the tasks at hand is an admirable skill. Before you have a grasp of who does what well, ask. Employees will quickly own up to their talents.

MEETINGS, PRESENTATIONS, CREDIT

"The makeup of a good executive is 40% perception, 40% implementation, and 20% all other."

—*David Mahoney*

From now on you will attend and run more meetings, give endless presentations, and offer ideas given to you by others.

Meeting management prevents endless hours of wasted time. For meetings you control:

1. Set meeting times in the morning when people are fresh and not yet involved in their project list. Ninety minutes before lunch will keep a meeting on track.

2. Set an agenda with definite time limits.

3. Set a goal for what the meeting will accomplish. This can be only one of three things: dissemination of information, assignment of tasks, and decision-making. If the purpose of the meeting doesn't meet one of these criteria, don't hold it.

4. Send a copy of the agenda and meeting goals to all attendees.

5. Start on time.

6. Have someone take notes and convert them into memo form after the meeting.

7. Keep people on task. Don't allow attendees to go off on tangents, spend half an hour talking about Saturday's big game, or compare pictures of their new grandchildren. Do this politely, but firmly.

If you are an attendee, you have similar obligations:

1. Arrive on time for the meeting, prepared to work.

2. Bring any information for which you are responsible. If you need to distribute copies, make sure you have an adequate number.

3. Ask for an agenda before the meeting.

4. Don't go off on tangents.

5. Fulfill any commitments you make at the meeting.

6. Afterward, communicate to your department all commitments, information, or decisions that affect them.

Keep meetings as short as practical. Long-winded meetings make the attendees comatose. In *The Second Coming of the Woolly Mammoth*, Ted Frost recommends the following: "Use the sound bite principle. The average person's attention span is pitifully short. It starts to fade after only 20 minutes, even if the person is intensely interested in the subject matter. Utilize this in your dealings with people. Here are some useful tips from successful people, namely, trial attorneys:

• Listeners are most receptive to facts, ideas, and conclusions during the opening statements.

• Eighty percent of listeners form their final opinions after hearing opening arguments.

• People tend to remember the first and last things they hear and forget what was said in the middle.

• Eighty-five percent of what we learn comes through our sense of sight. Thus, visual presentations are more effective than verbal ones."

This may be the only free legal advice you ever get. It translates well from the courtroom to the boardroom.

Finally, when you attend meetings in which you present someone else's brainstorm, give her credit up front, then remind everyone again who came up with the idea. If possible, have the person make her own presentation, but in any event, make sure she receives credit.

RESPONSIBILITIES OF MANAGERS TO SUBORDINATES

Managers bear certain responsibilities for their employees. These include: expanding skills, offering opportunities, teaching others, and assuring the success of those employees.

A good manager is a good teacher. Teach your subordinates better and more effective means to complete their work. Expand job profiles by giving away larger chunks of projects, challenging your people with new ideas and asking them to solve new problems. Then, empower your people to complete their projects successfully. That's good management. "It all boils down to motivation with a focus. When you're working with people, focus means giving people you rely on trust and real responsibility," says Dave Thomas, founder of Wendy's.

Says Bruce Tulgan in *Managing Generation X,* "We need managers who can keep pace with our voracious appetites for information by constantly refueling the work environment with endless supplies of challenging experience, new projects, new skill areas, new technology, new interpretations, and new meaning."

Employee Surveys, Standards of Performance, Employee Reviews

One of the most onerous and difficult tasks managers face is evaluating employees. You can make this job easier by regular attention to employee situations.

- *Keep an up-to-date file* on each person under your supervision. At least once a month add information about projects completed and other successes. If an "atta-boy" arrives on your desk about Cassie, congratulate her personally, then add the memo to her file. By the end of the year, you'll have plenty of ammo to shoot for Cassie's big raise.

- *Deal with problem areas one at a time.* Too many managers collect a sack full of grievances and use an annual review to correct behaviors the employee doesn't even remember. If a confrontation arises, handle it immediately, then move on.

- *In a review, always begin and end with positives.* If there are areas that need work, explain what they are and what changes you expect. Ask each employee to give you a list of topics he would like to discuss during the review.

- *Never tell someone you are "giving" him a raise.* Instead, tell him he "earned" a raise.

- *Set a time to discuss next year's standards of performance, goals and opportunities,* and means of measuring success. This can be part of the review process or separate from it. You will find most people appreciate the chance to control their own performance ratings, which happens when future standards of performance are agreed upon in advance.

> *"Start with good people, lay out the rules, communicate with your employees, motivate them, and reward them. If you do all those things effectively, you can't miss."*
>
> —*Lee Iacocca*

Listen, Listen, Listen—Building Listening Skills at All Levels

I'll bet you thought when you became the boss you could do all the talking, and everyone else would have to listen. That is definitely one approach—but the boss who really listens is valued far more by everyone.

Consider this scenario: Wendy, Mark, and Phil are assigned joint responsibility for the Keppler account. In addition to her regular job, Wendy recently assumed the Membership Chairman's slot for a professional organization. The Keppler contract requires entirely too much of the time Wendy planned to spend on her membership drive, so she doesn't pull her weight. Mark and Phil want to strangle her, but grit their teeth through the initial phases, until Wendy's slackness threatens contract negotiations. Wendy, a smart cookie, beats the men to the boss' door and lays down a tissue of half-truths about Mark and Phil's participation. What happens when Mark and Phil go to the boss? They sound like a pair of whiners, and the boss is suspicious because of Wendy's insinuations.

There are some managers who believe the "first in is telling the truth." How does this happen? It's simple. The manager listens to the story the first employee tells explaining why the project didn't produce the needed results. He believes that person is "fessing up" to the problem. Don't fall into this trap.

Take a tip from your mom. Mothers never do this. They always look at the tattling child with a jaundiced eye. It's not that the first one never tells the truth. It's just that you need the complete story, the whole picture, to determine what is really happening.

When a "Wendy" comes into your office, thank her for the information and tell her you'll look into it. Then, ask Mark and Phil individually to give you their version. Keep in mind that every employee has a personal agenda. Don't expect other agendas to match yours.

Become receptive—but reserve your opinion until you have all the facts. How do you improve your listening skills?

Face-to-Face Contact

A face-to-face conversation requires eye contact. Try to hold it 60–70% of the time. That seems like a lot, but you'll find that keeping eye contact also allows you to pay closer attention to what others are saying.

If you are in your office or a conference room, don't fidget, pick lint from your socks, or play with rubber bands or paper clips. Don't answer the phone; don't clean your desk; don't thumb through magazines; don't stare out the window.

Avoid asking too many questions by putting more effort into listening than trying to figure out ways to argue with what the other person is saying. Make sure the questions you ask are pertinent, informative, and show your interest.

On the Phone

It is easier to get distracted when you are on the phone. There is no one to look at, no one to notice you aren't really paying attention. First, set out a pad and take notes, including the name and company of the caller. Say "Yes" or "I agree" to let the speaker know you are listening. Make a pertinent comment about the topic, like "The Whitehead deadline isn't for three weeks. Do you really want us to stop everything else at this point?"

Listening to Complaints

When listening to a complaint about someone, be polite and attentive. At the end of the complaint, ask the person what she would like to happen next. If she says she wants a decision immediately, explain that you will get back to her as soon as you have all the facts. Then, see each other person involved in the situation and make your decision based on all possible information.

Adjusting to the Change in Status

The change from manager or subordinate to boss is drastic. You have more people to worry about, more problems to deal with, more things to go wrong, more work than you can do in a lifetime, more money and less time to enjoy it.

You also have a social change; you're no longer one of the guys. Don't be surprised if the people who now depend on you for their raises and promotions don't want to socialize with you during the lunch hour. If they did, when would they have time to talk about you?

Here are some settling-in tips for a new boss:

- *Don't flaunt cash.* Yes, you're making more money now, but you don't have to buy a Beemer the first week you're the boss.

- *Keep your door and mind open* to suggestions, but maintain a level of privacy.

- *Remember your status,* even outside the office. Keep a sense of dignity and self-respect at all times.

- *Always say "please" and "thank you."*

- *Don't forget to practice praise.* Praise is a funny thing. We can always find a fault, but we're uncomfortable giving or accepting compliments. Offer praise regularly, promptly, in both oral and written form, and consistently. Spread praise around like soft butter on toast, smoothly, and evenly to all corners.

- *Don't show favoritism.* Once you start, you'll be stuck in that rut until you move into a new job. Favorites soon take advantage of the situation and you'll regret having initiated it.

Keeping on an Even Keel

Despite frustrations, disasters, and a falling sky, there is no room for a boss who explodes like a bomb, erupts like Vesuvius, or leaves a path of destruction like a Class-5 tornado. Yes, you are only human. Yes, you have a temper that occasionally gets the better of you. But do you want people to cringe when they see you coming?

Recognize that during periods of stress or extreme pressure, you change your approach to work. On a regular basis, you are easygoing, creative, and patient. When the pillars start to crumble, you want to shore them up single handedly. While this is natural, it is counterproductive. Ask yourself these questions:

- Do your people understand the crisis?

- Did you trust Mary or Lou to complete their work successfully before?

- Don't your people usually rise to challenges? Will your micro-management help or hinder the completion of the project?

If your people are loyal, productive, and hard working, why don't you trust them to do their jobs? Do you intend to flog everyone just because the CEO stepped on your toes?

When the urge to interfere strikes, however desperately you want to do so, close your office door, sit on your hands and count to 2,100 by sevens. Once you are calm again, ask if there is anything you can do to help. When the answer is "no," accept it. And wait.

All's Fair...or Is It?

In addition to all your other obligations, you are now in a position to hire, promote, and advance the people who work for you. As you consider hiring or moving people up, make sure you do so based on sound reasoning and not because Steve is your golfing buddy or Helen is fun to be around.

Job offers and promotions should be based on merit—an unusual occurrence. Know where you stand in regard to employee rights, both legal and moral.

- Equal opportunity employment laws prohibit discrimination in employment based on color, race, religion, national origin, gender, age, or disability. This is not just a law, it is your moral obligation. Tuck your prejudices in a pocket and leave them there.

- Job specs should be determined by what's necessary for success on the job, not by stereotypical views. Just because you've always had white male vice presidents, doesn't mean the trend should continue. Diversity based on talent and experience will add more to a company's future than maintaining the status quo. Andy McKenna, President of Schwarz Paper Company, says, "Success comes from blending people from different corners of society. That kind of success does not come easily, but it forms a lasting foundation."

- Don't ask either men or women applicants questions relating to their marital status or family. In the same way, don't promote Al because he has a big family and needs the money, or Martha because she's a struggling single mother. The law is very particular about failing to promote women because they are pregnant. Know what the law requires of you as a manager. Also, be aware that family emergencies do exist and are valid reasons to miss work or leave early.

- You can't refuse to hire or force to retire anyone over the age of 40 just because of age. Nor can you pass someone up for promotion because, in your view, she is too old. With age comes wisdom; tap it, don't ignore it.

- Focus on people's abilities, not their disabilities. In return, people will focus on your abilities and forgive your failings.

Dr. Jekyll or Ms. Hyde

Remember all those bosses you hated— which one have you become? It is easy to let promotion or advancement go to your head. When reality sets in you'll feel like a twit.

Choose a role model, that boss you admire, and emulate him. If it helps, make a short list of the qualities you want to acquire, tape it to your blotter, daily calendar, or computer and read it several times daily.

If that doesn't keep your ego under control, create a "humility list." This is a list of people who have talents you don't have, people who have overcome obstacles you've never faced, people whom you admire for whatever reason. Your list might include Mother Teresa, Helen Keller, Admiral Grace Hooper, Leonardo da Vinci, Oprah Winfrey, Ken Follett, and Colin Powell. When you're feeling a bit ego-bloated, think about what these people have done with their lives. It is a definite leveler.

A promotion creates vast opportunities. Choose your path carefully, mindful of those who follow in your footsteps. Enjoy the trip—you've earned it.

CHAPTER RECAP

- Becoming a boss changes your perspective; be prepared for the change.

- You have a responsibility to your people to praise them, elevate them, teach them, and help them succeed.

- The law requires you to hire and fire based on valid criteria. Personality differences are not considered valid.

- You cannot and should not discriminate against anyone because of marital status, sexual orientation, age, sex, or disability.

Recommended Reading

Bick, Julie. *All I Really Need to Know in Business I Learned at Microsoft.* New York: Pocket Books, 1997.

Covey, Stephen R. *Seven Habits of Highly Effective People.* New York: Simon & Schuster, 1989.

Gibbons, Barry. *This Indecision Is Final.* Burr Ridge, IL: Irwin Professional Publishing, 1996.

James, Jennifer. *Thinking in the Future Tense: Leadership Skills for a New Age.* New York: Simon & Schuster, 1996.

Kaplan, Burton. *Winning People Over.* Englewood Cliffs, NJ: Prentice Hall, 1996.

McCormack, John, with David R. Legge. *Self-Made in America.* Reading, MA: Addison-Wesley, 1990.

Managing on the Cutting Edge

There is a world of difference between being managed and managing others. Management styles abound, and it is up to you, the manager, to carefully select the techniques that work for you. It's also important to realize that managing people is not the same as knowing the business. Becoming a manager is not a *carte blanche* to do whatever you please—it is a responsibility, a commitment, and an obligation to lead, develop, and promote.

One favorite management theory comes from David Ogilvy of Ogilvy & Mather. Paraphrased, Ogilvy's theory is that creative giants tend to hire current or potential giants and develop a network of creative, talented people. The corollary is that mental dwarves hire lesser dwarves and develop a company populated by Lilliputians. If you are a giant among the dwarves, get out fast. You will forever be head and shoulders above your boss, and he will be so intimidated that he'll forever seek ways to lop off your head. Become a giant builder and fear not. The worst your giants will do is make you look good. After all, you had the sense to hire them, didn't you?

IN THIS CHAPTER:

- *Identifying future trends: leadership, empowerment, delegation, diversification*

- *Six past trends worth another look*

- *Four current trends*

- *Six best management practices*

LEADERSHIP, EMPOWERMENT, DELEGATION, DIVERSIFICATION

Gary entered his subordinate's office and looked around. The desk was covered with piles of papers. Photos and layouts clung to every imaginable surface. Keylines were spread out on the art desk. He shook his head and said, "A cluttered desk is a cluttered mind."

Caroline looked at him from amid the clutter and smiled, "An empty desk is an empty mind." The point? Personal work styles differ. So do management styles. You can't easily shift your style to accommodate someone else, and you can't expect anyone else to change to suit you.

In today's business world management buzzwords abound. Everyone speaks the same management babble—without ever applying the techniques that accompany the jargon. How many middle- and lower-level managers have sat through meetings in which the CEO declared the company was going to build participative management teams, gave his list of reasons why, then ended the meeting without ever letting anyone else voice an opinion? It is still the "do as I say, not as I do" concept of management.

Why do upper managers talk change without ever making adjustments to their own style? There is no simple answer, but you can bet control is close to the top of the list—in capital letters. Today's management practices are all about releasing information and power to employees, but many upper management people were trained that another way to spell "boss" is "c-o-n-t-r-o-l." They simply can't let go.

However, you want to be a success as a manager, and you're not going to make those same mistakes, are you? You will embrace the current modes of management: *leadership, empowerment, delegation,* and *diversification.*

It is idealistic to think that teams, clusters, or departments can work efficiently without leadership. Says Bob

"If you've done your best, then you will have had some accomplishments along the way. Not everyone is going to get the entire picture. Not everyone is going to be the greatest salesman or the greatest basketball player. But you can still be considered one of the best, and you can still be considered a success."

—*Michael Jordan,*
I Can't Accept
Not Trying

Geller in *How to Survive in the Nonprofit World,* "When it comes to management, democracy is a great concept—but it just doesn't work. No decisions are ever made by committees without leadership."

Leadership, however, is not based on Attila the Hun leading hordes of frenzied warriors into battle. Today's leader is a facilitator, a greaser of wheels. Real leadership means granting freedom to subordinates and creating room for people to use their strength, inventiveness, and knowledge. Leaders, by nature, are planners, instructors, guides, and agents.

> ### SUCCESSTHOUGHTS
>
> *Leading others to success puts them in the limelight; you can bask in the reflection of that light. Don't let your ego get in the way of this uniquely wonderful event.*

"Managers will be people who are comfortable facilitating, greasing, finding ways to make it all seamless, not controllers and directors, we've got to take out the boss element," says GE's Jack Welch in *Fortune,* March 1991.

When you lead others, you must let them work in their own way. You must also give them credit for their work—a method that can cause a major hit to your ego. The leader gains his success vicariously—through the success of his subordinates.

Empowerment—the "in" management concept of the '90s creates an unusual work environment. Employees now have access to information that was once monopolized by management. "As knowledge is redistributed, so too, is the power based on it. Power is shifting not because of fuzzy-minded do-goodism, but because it is essential for survival. Employees aren't made to feel important, they are important," says Alvin Toffler in *Powershift: Knowledge, Wealth, and Violence at the Edge of the 21st Century.*

Empowered employees influence organizations, people, and events. They plan and act based on their commitment to the company. Empowerment allows employees to take risks, to step beyond the safety net of "business as usual." Managers who empower their employees must be risk takers as well. They must be willing to trust their employees to act in a way that benefits the company and the department. They must release the bonds that hold the employees and allow them to work independently. Explains Harvey A. Hornstein in *Brutal Bosses and Their Prey*, "A modern management credo has redefined the requirements of being an effective boss to include the empowerment of subordinates." In short: To be viewed as a success you must also empower those around you to succeed.

SUCCESSTHOUGHTS

Delegating:
- *Choose employees with appropriate skills and desire to take on responsibility.*
- *Delegate projects that are guaranteed success for the subordinate.*
- *Set out the parameters of the project, goals, and deadlines on paper.*
- *Give as much positive feedback, support, and encouragement as possible.*

(Source: Gail Gabriel, "Delegating Do's and Don'ts," Executive Female, May 1998)

Part of that success will come from two prominent management techniques: delegation and participative management, which are basically the two sides of the empowerment coin. Delegation is when a manager develops employees by giving them added responsibility, increasingly important projects, and the freedom to both find solutions and achieve results. Participative management allows employees to participate in major decision making, planning and innovating processes and products. Both are ways to empower employees.

Consider this definition of management: *"Management is getting things done through others.* By that definition, the ultimate measure of management is results—the staff"s output resulting from the manager's input. Other things being equal, the greater the ratio of output-to-input, the more effective the manager is," says Kenneth Blanchard in *The One Minute Manager Meets the Monkey.*

Once you give the task away, sit on your hands until the circulation stops. Don't interfere, no matter how much the desire grows. You'll never develop skills in others if you give away a task, then take it back again. You'll defeat not only the purpose of delegating the task but also your employees.

Participative management is the most practical management technique because it utilizes the experience, savvy, skills, and creative thinking of everyone. Participation in decision making is not a luxury for today's corporation, but a necessity. Look at it this way: The company has problems. You need solutions. You can hire an outside consultant to identify the problems and solutions, or you can rely on your own people to find better ways to work. Guess which one is cheaper? Guess which one is most successful? The answer to both questions is participative management.

In *Productive Workplaces* Marvin Weisbord says, "The action needed to create (the change) is so simple that people often cannot, will not, believe it works. It requires that those with the biggest stake in the change sit down together and figure out, from all angles, the right thing to do. Given some minimal guidance, most work groups produce designs 85-90% congruent with what the best outside pros can do—with vastly more commitment to implement."

One problem frequently overlooked in project planning and implementation is resistance from the very employees the project is designed to help. You must create situations in which your employees take ownership of problem solving, or you will undermine change, regardless of how miraculous the solutions appear to be.

Business writer John Greenwald explains in the article "Is Mr. Nice Guy Back?" from *Time,* "To help bring good ideas to life, GE holds 'work-out' sessions in which groups of workers and managers spend three days in shirt-sleeve meetings on anything from gripes to pitches for new products. In a session at an aircraft-engine plant, one team pitched a plan that cut the time needed to produce a

Participation in decision making is not a luxury for today's corporation, but a necessity.

jet-combustion part nearly 90%. And an electrician proposed a design for an aluminum reflector that has cut the plant's light bill in half."

Worth Another Look

Just because a management theory is considered passé doesn't mean it isn't worthwhile. Theories are like hemlines—they go in and out, up and down, changing with the seasons. This section is a brief primer on some theories that are well worth another look:

- *One-Minute Managing*—The one-minute managing concept was introduced by Kenneth Blanchard and his cohorts in the '80s. There are several "One-Minute" books, and all are quick reads. They are practical business guides for managers wanting to get the most from their employees. The strategies offered are designed to promote employee morale; the manager is taught to look for opportunities to "find someone doing the right thing."

- *Corporate Culture*—The corporate culture concept is simple: Whatever management techniques your company espouses creates a culture or style. Microsoft is loaded with mentors and has a relatively casual dress policy. For years IBM required its management to wear white shirts. Some companies prefer employees to use voice mail and e-mail; some encourage management to have secretaries screen calls, others tell employees to answer their own phones. You can create your own mini-culture in your department by setting an example and encouraging people to follow it.

- *Entrepreneuring*—If ever there was a movement to subvert the American corporation, it's entrepreneuring. The brainchild of Gifford Pinchot III, entrepreneuring encourages creative thinkers to find ways around the bureaucracy of modern corporate life and pursue their visions. Entrepreneurs take risks happily, circumvent counter-creative orders, do any job that needs doing, follows intuitive lines of thought, and work underground because publicity automatically triggers the corporate immune system that thwarts creativity.

- *MBWA*—Whether you call this theory Management By Wandering Around or Management By Walking Around, the credit for this concept goes to Excellence guru Tom Peters. This technique mandates exactly what the title implies: you wander around the department, office, other parts of the company, clients' businesses, and competitors' businesses to see how they do things, why they do things, and what they're doing. Then, you choose what might work for you and incorporate it into your office culture.

- *Restructuring*—When times get tough, the tough restructure. Restructuring should mean reconfiguring the company to work more effectively. In most cases, we just shuffle deadwood around, create reams of paperwork, layoff the boat rockers, and settle into business as usual.

- *Excellence*—Who can say anything against excellence? Again, this is a concept that Tom Peters has amplified and all success-minded people will want to read at least one of his "Excellence" books.

> *"The price of greatness is responsibility."*
> —*Winston Churchill*

TQM and Assorted Other Buzzwords

There is managing people, and there is managing stuff. Many management techniques are all about stuff and ignore that people are needed to think up the stuff, make it, sell it, and buy it. Stuff management has its ardent detractors and followers. For example, here's one point of view from John A. Byrne: "What's dead as a pet rock? It's total quality management. TQM, the approach of eliminating errors that increase costs and reduce customer satisfaction, promised more than it could deliver and spawned mini-bureaucracies charged with putting it into action."

On the other hand, David Luthy wrote, "TQM is the cornerstone of success in today's competitive environment. Businesses, large and small, have discovered that attention to quality can have a significant impact on the bottom line. TQM doesn't cost; it pays! The goal of TQM is to meet the long-term demands of the marketplace and, thereby, make money. Quality is defined in terms of 'fitness for use of goods or services as perceived by the customer.' Attention to customers, products, processes, and related business operations results in total quality management."

The debate rages on. TQM, like many other management concepts, is limited by the implementation process. Some companies jump into TQM with both feet, then jump with equal zeal into the next management fad. If you are going to adopt a technique, don't do it recklessly. Evaluate the process first, then cull out the aspects that won't work for your department or company. While you're at it, check out other management concepts that might offer excellent advantages.

- *Value Chain Management*—This is the process of maximizing the flow of services and information from raw materials to end use through a value-added network of suppliers. In a survey of 225 large manufacturers, value chain systems were considered more flexible in meeting customer demands. Value Chain Management deals with inventory, fill levels, processing costs, distribution, and profitability.

- *Experience Curve*—The experience curve predicts a percent decrease in unit costs with each doubling of production volume. What is that in English? Here's an example: It costs $100 per unit to produce a widget. Production is expected to grow by 20%, and the experience curve will be roughly 85%. If you make 1,000 widgets, production costs per unit = $100. When are making 2000 widgets, production costs per unit = $85. Think computers. How much did the 1950s IBM full-room/small-brain computer cost? What does a PC cost today?

- *Quality Circles*—Toyota employs Quality Circles in its manufacturing plants. A Circle consists of small groups of team members (2-10 people) plus a Circle leader. The Circle meets weekly to identify problems, investigate causes, implement solutions, and report results. This is simply another form of participative management.

COMMON SENSE AND COMPASSION

Yvette has a serious problem. Her son was in a car crash and needs surgery. He'll be in the hospital for three days and at home recuperating for three weeks. The company policy says that Yvette cannot take time off to care for her son without loss of pay. As a manager, what are you supposed to do?

Managers must use common sense and compassion. If you look for it, there is a way around just about every problem. Can Yvette do some work from home? Can she work through lunch and have flex hours? Can she make up time when she gets back? Can you devise a plan by which Yvette meets both family and job obligations?

It is not a bad thing to question the decision-making process. Who is making all the decisions? What are decisions based on? Who is giving input? How are creative ideas, suggestions handled? Is the final decision communicated to the employees? In what way? What misapprehensions do the employees have? Does everyone understand the goals of management? Do they buy into those goals?

Flexibility, common sense, and compassion go a long way toward creating loyal staff. You won't find these covered in management books because they don't make measurable contributions to the bottom line. However, every successful manager remembers that he works with people, and people have problems that need to be dealt with. You can be compassionate and still get the job done. Live by the Golden Rule; manage by the Golden Rule.

BEST PRACTICES

As a manager you need to follow what are considered "best practices"—the best, most profitable, most effective methods for achieving results. Regardless of your position, you will need to follow a path toward success.

- *Be a Leader.* "When a company is meandering, its management staff is demoralized. When the management staff is demoralized, nothing works: Every employee feels paralyzed. This is exactly when you need to have a strong leader setting a direction. And it doesn't even have to be the best direction— just a strong, clear one," says Andrew S. Grove in *Only the Paranoid Survive.* Taking a leadership position is a key component of "best practices."

- *Serve Your Customers.* Excellent customer service is crucial. Your customers are the reason you are in business. Management should visit customers to maintain a close relationship and iron out any difficulties. Usually purchasing and sales are the only people who have direct contact with customers. There is no reason people in any other departments shouldn't accompany sales reps, attend vendor or supplier meetings, or visit customers. How can employees connect with customer needs if they never see a customer?

- *Manage Information Flow.* Make sure all your people have the know-how to do their jobs.

- *Benchmarking.* It can give you the data to see what has been achieved and help identify methods by which your company can achieve similar results. Benchmarking is a measure of best practice performance. This is MBWA by visiting the best places. You can benchmark against another company, another department, another division of your corporation.

- *Teamwork Really Works.* According to John Greenwald, "This apparent New Age emphasis on teamwork and trust is really a homecoming to theories that U.S. companies cold-shouldered—and Japanese managers embraced—when American social scientists first proposed them in the 1950s and '60s as a key to creating high-quality products."

- *Teams Create Success.* Here are a couple of examples: Conrail's problem-solving team found ways to reduce the error rate on one customer's bills from 14% to 3%. Their ultimate goal is total accuracy on billing. Oil giant Mobil follows the team concept in the oil fields, where upper management allows field crews to make decisions on when and where to drill. Risky? Perhaps, but field crews are at the heart of the business and know their stuff.

- *Praise Your People.* Writer and businessman Elbert Hubbard said, "One machine can do the work of fifty ordinary men. No machine can do the work of one extraordinary man." If you have extraordinary employees working with you, let them know how much you appreciate their work. The worst thing a manager can ever do is forget to say, "You did a good job! Thank you."

TAKING CHARGE

Sooner or later you will have to put your foot down about something. It can be minor, major, or middling. Empower, delegate, encourage all you can, but always remember you are ultimately responsible for yourself, your department, and the development of your people. Take that responsibility seriously. On it rests the growth and opportunity of everyone who ever works with you.

Without your sponsorship and tutelage, your subordinates will be stuck in your department forever—and so will you. Give them a chance to prove themselves, then, like a doting parent, send them off into the big world to fend for themselves.

ENCOURAGING SUBORDINATES

Everyone shares certain aspects of life. We all have fears, hopes, pride, and uncertainties. As manager, you hold the future of your subordinates in your hands. If they do not succeed, this is as much a reflection on your leadership as on their talents.

We all have basic fears. We want to be liked and appreciated. We are afraid of being inferior, unable to measure up. We feel defenseless against criticism. We fear having our weaknesses and failings revealed to others.

Do you add to these fears or create an environment in which your employees become fearless? Albert arranges a mailing list for a mass mailing. By accident, he omits all

Florida addresses—the primary target market for the mailing. What do you do when Albert comes to your office, head down in shame, ready to take the whipping for his mistake? Today's manager should (and *you will*) listen to the problem, ask what the solution is, then encourage Albert to act quickly.

Here are a few ways to develop your employees:

- *Bring subordinates to meetings* or send them in your place. They'll see the decision making process in action, feel important and trusted, and you'll save some time.

- *Report back to your department* on any meetings you attend. There is nothing worse than finding out that you will be involved in a time-consuming, urgent project that you learn about three days too late to get the work done.

- *Involve everyone in planning* and making presentations. If you have a major presentation to make, break it up into smaller parts and let your subordinates have a chance to gain valuable experience.

- *Give credit to all participants* and idea originators. Do this both in front of them and when they are absent. There is nothing quite so delightful as finding out that your supervisor said something positive about your work to others.

Part of administration is setting standards of performance for subordinates and doing annual reviews. When setting performance criteria, be realistic and fair. Set attainable goals—let your subordinates know that you will help them reach those goals. Don't hoard up grievances for a year and spring them on the unwary subordinate when it's time for the annual review. Correction should be made when the problem arises; reviews are a time for rewards.

CHAPTER RECAP

- If you hire and cultivate stars in your department or company, productivity, creativity, and contentment will be high.

- Participative management shares input, output, and decision making.

- Do not discard previous management ideas because they aren't fashionable. Choose a style that suits your personality.

- Common sense is worth any three management concepts.

Recommended Reading

Allen, Robert. *The Challenge.* New York: Simon & Schuster, 1987.

Anderson, Walter. *The Confidence Course.* New York: HarperCollins, 1997.

Covey, Stephen R. *Seven Habits of Highly Effective People.* New York: Simon & Schuster, 1989.

Drucker, Peter F. *Managing for the Future.* New York: Truman Talley Books, 1992.

Mahoney, David, with Richard Conarroe. *Confessions of a Street-Smart Manager.* New York: Simon & Schuster, 1988.

Peters, Tom, and Nancy Austin. *A Passion for Excellence.* New York: Random House, 1985. Or any other Tom Peters *Excellence* book.

Hill, Napoleon. *Keys to Success.* New York: Dutton, 1994.

Rancourt, Karen. *The Empowered Professional: How to Succeed in the 90s.* Harvard, MA, 1996.

Simms, Darrell. *Black Experience Strategies and Tactics in the Business World.* Beaverton, OR: Management Aspects Inc., 1991.

Leadership — The Basic Element of Team Building

*I*f you don't have leadership skills in your bag of tricks, you'll need to consider developing those techniques posthaste. While it is true that leaders are generally born and not made, you can build on your current leadership abilities through seminars, mentoring, and practice, practice, practice.

Leadership is vision-based—it is not management. The difference between the two is significant. Leadership is a "must have" for the next generation of business chiefs; it is the long-range view of where a business is going and why. Management is the "how" whereby a business reaches the goals of a visionary plan.

"What is needed is enlightened leadership—leaders who not only have the vision but who have the ability to get the members of the organization to accept ownership for that vision as their own, thus developing the commitment to carry it through to completion," say Ed Oakley and Doug Krug in *Enlightened Leadership*.

It is important to recognize the difference between a leader and a manager, primarily because true leaders are a

IN THIS CHAPTER:

• *Leadership is vision-based*

• *Learning to develop leadership skills*

• *Understanding how to lead yourself to success*

• *Leading groups*

rare commodity. Here's an example: Fuzzy Toy Company struggles to make ends meet. A new line of super hero figures or something equally spectacular is needed to pull Fuzzy out of the fire. At the annual long-range planning meeting, Sam suggests there are few super hero lines directed toward girls, and a new line—complete with a book series, videos, costume changes, puzzles, a board game, audio tapes, and figures based on fictional women adventurers—could be just the concept to dig Fuzzy Toy out of the red. More than two-thirds of the managers sitting around the board room think the idea is stupid, but don't have a better one. So various people take on the necesssary roles in the project. Max, head of marketing, commits to studying the super hero figure market, girls' book series, and the feasibility of this concept. Joanne, head of design, commits to creating six introductory prototypes as the foundation of the line. Alan commits to working the numbers—he's in finance.

In this group, Sam shows vision, creativity, and leadership. Max and Alan, influential vice-presidents in the company, are managers; they implement someone else's ideas. Joanne shows both leadership and managerial skills. It will be her creative vision that develops the new line, and her managerial input that brings the concepts to fruition.

Becoming a creative thinker, an innovator, requires tossing away the old and embracing the new. Without a good "spring cleaning," mindsets tend to be reactive rather than proactive.

It is a simple fact that you can't be a true leader, a true visionary, if you spend all day putting out fires. Consider

---

CLASSICAL LEADERSHIP

While Alexander the Great was leading his thirsty army across the desert, a soldier came up to him, knelt down, and offered him a helmet full of water.

"Is there enough for 10,000 men?" asked Alexander.

When the soldier shook his head, Alexander poured the water out on the ground.

(Source: Lance Davidson, The Ultimate Reference Book: The Wit's Thesaurus*)*

MINDSETS

Looking forward	*Remembering the past*
lights fires under self and others	douses every creative fire
change is valuable	the old way is better
"I can" philosophy	"I can't (or won't)" philosophy
success is a cornerstone for the future	problems, problems, problems
creates the plan	follows the plan
"Let's do it."	"I'll get back to you on that."
leads his people	defeats his people

what creates obstacles for you and your department. Determine possible solutions and implement them. When today's business runs hassle-free, you make time to address the business of tomorrow.

VISION AND ACTIVE THINKING

Proactive thinking demands creative communication. Remember the three learning modes: auditory, visual, and kinesthetic. Those learning modes enable a leader to communicate his vision. A leader explains his vision in simple terms, calling on a number of images to create a picture in the listener's mind. Stories, analogies, comparisons, even jokes all help "sell" a visionary concept.

What difference does it make? It's the message, not the method—or is it? Here are two descriptions of the same back-to-school community service program:

A. Every year low-income children return to school without the tools necessary for success. This year our company will collect cash contributions toward supplies for disadvantaged children. A representative in your department will collect next Thursday. Checks are acceptable.

B. As summer draws to a close, children in our community gear up for another school year. But what about low-income children, whose parents must choose between bread on the table or a backpack, between meat for supper or a new pair of shoes? Next Thursday, join us for "School Lunch Day." For $4.00, you get a complete "school lunch" (sandwich, chips, apple, cookie, and milk). The profits will buy pencils, notebooks, backpacks, and new school clothes for 24 disadvantaged children in our community. Let's send them to school with a smile! See you there!

Which one of these programs would you support? It's the same program—but "B" has so much more appeal. You can imagine having to choose between food and school supplies. Knowing how the money will be spent adds to the incentive.

When you communicate your vision, give graphic examples, tell stories, draw pictures—and generate excitement in your goals.

GROUP DYNAMICS

Before you can lead a group, you must understand how it works—or doesn't work. From the days of cavedwellers, humans have lived in families, clans, tribes—groups. And the dynamics of those families, clans, and tribes were much like the dynamics of today's groups: a mixture of workers and slackers, leaders and followers, optimists, and pessimists, stars and plodders.

The only difference between Neanderthal groups and today's work teams is when Og refused to hunt mastodons, Urg whacked him over the head with a club, thereby ridding the group of an unwanted slug. Today's team is slightly more complex; a good swat with a club will land you out of work and into court.

What are the advantages of working in a group? Groups or teams provide a blend of talents, skills, and knowledge. Members of the group have different jobs, they act and interact from different viewpoints. The financial analyst sees future profits in the results of a group project; his focus is to enhance bottom line numbers for the next three years. The sales manager sees opportunity for her regional representatives to grow their customer base. The administrative assistant sees the workload involved in creating a new product or service; he views the project in terms of the number of support personnel needed to accomplish the tasks on time. Each contribution has value—and a good leader draws out each contributor to maximize the effectiveness of the group.

Ideally, the group becomes self-regenerating, drawing on mutual ideas, cooperating on all levels, and coordinating efforts to achieve a superior end. Talk about idealistic! Maybe this happens at Pie-in-the-Sky Corp., but your company doesn't seem to have the same experience with teams. As a leader, your role is to communicate, motivate, facilitate, and mediate. Do not expect the team to always work together smoothly. There will be normal jockeying for position, necessary development of a work style with new people, and moderate bickering as the group shifts into gear. Leading a team is work, and don't forget it.

TODAY, YOU'RE THE LEADER

As leader of the group, you allow the natural evolutionary dynamics to occur. You can't stop the flow, but you can erect an occasional dam to redirect efforts. It is your job as leader to . . .

- *Use the skills and talents of each team member* to the maximum. That means assigning tasks to the lazy one, the quiet one, and the one who pretends to be too busy. There is a reason each person is in the group; make sure all members pull their weight.

*"Everybody is saying
that we need to stop
putting leaders on
pedestals. I'm not so
sure. The real problem
is finding leaders who
truly deserve to keep
their pedestals. In
fact, I think we ought
to be putting a lot
more 'little people'—
people who have
really achieved some-
thing—on pedestals
so that ordinary folks
have a better, clearer
idea of who's doing
the job and who's
setting the pace."*

—*Dave Thomas,*
Well Done!

- *Communicate, communicate, communicate.* This is perhaps the greatest obstacle to overcome in group leadership. You must let group members know where you are going, what is expected of them, why you are working on this project, what their roles are, who they are working with, when each aspect of the project must be completed and whether elements of the project are on schedule. If you have late-breaking developments, send out e-mail or voice mail to the group. Don't tell some and not others—you'll divide the very group you are trying to pull together.

- *Develop a schedule* that all members sign off on. This makes sure everyone knows who is doing what and when it is due. Once he signs off on a schedule, each person becomes responsible for meeting deadlines.

- *Motivate people* to fulfill their obligations. One good way is to check the progress each member is making on assigned tasks. Offer your help; offer to listen; offer suggestions on how to overcome obstacles—do not offer to do the work.

- *Become a cheerleader.* Offer public (group) praise for a task well done, regardless of who did it.

- *Offer criticism or negative comments behind closed doors.* I know this has been said before, but this is a must! Never berate members of the group in front of each other.

- *Start every meeting with an agenda* and stick to it. Have someone take minutes at the meeting and distribute copies within a day.

- *Allow key group members to present their own work* when presenting the project to others. Introduce

the project and its participants, then step back
and let others take credit.

- *Let group members know in advance* if there is a need
for confidentiality. Don't tell someone after the fact
that project information was need-to-know only.

- *After the project is finished, hold a final group meeting*
to rehash the pros and cons of the project's completion, work methods, and scheduling. This brings
closure to the project and eliminates start-up problems on your next group effort.

- *Send a memo congratulating each member* on their
participation in the group effort. Be specific. If
someone kept track of large amounts of data, say so
and explain why this contribution was valuable. Be
sure to copy the individual's direct supervisor. Don't
send a generic memo that suits everyone from the
CFO to the junior mail clerk. Even Publisher's
Clearinghouse Sweepstakes addresses each individual as a person—it's their secret to success.

Manage Things, Lead People

Just as you need to acquire a balance between work and
recreation, between business and family, you must also
acquire a balance between managing and leading. In most
management positions, assets are listed as follows: furniture, computer hardware and software, inventory, people,
wastebaskets, etc. People are not things—don't treat them
that way; don't manage them at all. Lead your people.

Distinguishing Leadership from Management	E X E R C I S E

Which items are leadership-oriented; which are management-
oriented? Review the following chart. (Answers on page 212.)

LEADERSHIP V. MANAGEMENT

Administrative Tasks	Leadership	Management
1. developing an annual operating plan		
2. evaluating a department member		
3. mentoring an employee		
4. embracing cultural differences		
5. originating a customer service program		
6. developing a strategic plan		
7. generating new goals		
8. complying with company policies		
9. following company procedures		
10. setting standards of performance		
11. motivating others		
12. originating a training program		
13. developing new skills or knowledge in others		
14. letting employees develop a successful work style		
15. following principles instead of pursuing the bottom line		

Leadership roles require flexibility in looking at yourself and others to teach others to view their work styles in a different way, "creating a major shift in their people's mindsets from one that keeps them stuck in boxes to one that naturally searches for new and innovative solutions," state Ed Oakley and Doug Krug in *Enlightened Leadership.*

There can be nothing less motivating than feeling like just another cog in the wheel, each cog the same as every other one. By making each subordinate feel unique, by giving each person an opportunity to grow and develop, you lead your company toward a solid future. Why? Because employees who are challenged, respected, valued, and motivated by supervisors who believe in them perform like stars.

Canadian leadership guru, Jim Clemmer, in *Pathways to Performance: A Guide to Transforming Yourself, Your Team and Your Organization,* describes leadership as "an action, not a position.

"A leader doesn't just react and respond, but rather takes the initiative and generates action. Leaders help people believe the impossible is possible, which makes it highly probable."

In your role as leader, consider ways to make the impossible possible. Generate the same enthusiasm you have for a project in those who work with you. Share in the triumphs but bear the brunt of defeat on your own shoulders. Don't worry, they're plenty broad enough.

Keep in mind Walter Lippmann's words from *Roosevelt Has Gone:* "The final test of a leader is that he leaves behind him in other men the conviction and the will to carry on. The genius of a good leader is to leave behind him a situation which common sense, without the grace of genius, can deal with successfully."

> *"It is time for a new generation of leadership, to cope with new problems and new opportunities. For there is a new world to be won."*
>
> —*John F. Kennedy*

CHAPTER RECAP

- There is a major difference between leaders and managers. Leadership envisions the future; management handles today.

- Businesses with no leadership stagnate.

- To become a leader you must develop skills and envision a plan for the future.

- Leaders bring out the best in workers by assessing strengths and using them.

- Manage things; lead people.

Recommended Reading

Kotter, John P. *Leading Change.* Boston: Harvard Business School Press, 1996.

Oakley, Ed, and Doug Krug. *Enlightened Leadership.* New York: Simon & Schuster, 1991.

Rancourt, Karen. *The Empowered Professional: How to Succeed in the 90s.* Harvard, MA, 1996.

Thomas, Dave. *Well Done!* Grand Rapids, MI: Zondervan Publishing House, 1994.

Tulgan, Bruce. *Managing Generation X.* Santa Monica: Merritt Publishing, 1995.

Answers from chart on page 210. Leadership-oriented items are #3, 4, 6, 7, 11, 12, 13, 14, 15. Management-oriented items are #1, 2, 5, 8, 9, 10.

Becoming a Motivator

*H*ow do you, as a manager, reward your people for a job well done? All too frequently, you don't. After all, they get paid, don't they?

Perhaps, but there is more to life than money. If you hope to motivate your subordinates, get their best possible work on a regular basis, or even reach departmental sales or marketing targets, you have to energize them to perform their best. If you don't, you'll find employee turnover leaps out of proportion and dissatisfaction rages rampant through your cubicle jungle.

Somewhere along the line, feeling lucky to have productive, innovative employees turned around 180 degrees. Now, managers tell subordinates they're lucky to have jobs. Ouch! Is that what you want to hear when you meet with your supervisor?

"People are motivated by different things and on two basic levels: their needs and their values. All people have some very basic needs like food, water, and shelter. These basic needs provide motivation for most of us to get up each morning and go to work. Earning a living allows us to care for our families by putting a roof over their heads and food on the table.

"For motivation to be truly effective, it must involve more complex issues, dealing with quality of life—status, salary, family—and self-actualization—knowledge, independence, and creativity. These complex issues are known as values. Values generally are better motivators because they are long-term and they tend to remain constant over time." (Source: *Motivation and Goal-Setting*, Second Edition)

So, how do you keep employees happy? "By creating an atmosphere in which workers feel they are not mere factors of production, but organic elements of an enterprise that respects them and will bend itself to make their lives richer in ways that go beyond money," says Kerry A. Dolan in a *Forbes* article entitled "When Money Isn't Enough."

In *A Passion for Excellence*, Tom Peters and Nancy Austin discuss the way Bill and Vieve Gore treat people who work for them. They don't have employees, they have associates whom they treat according to "four principles: fairness, which controls destructive dissension; freedom, which allows associates to experience failure; commitment, the power behind the desire to succeed; and discretion, which reduces the chances for behavior that could damage the company's reputation and profitability."

Winning teams are careful constructions requiring expert architectural design, talented builders, and a daily maintenance crew to keep everything in tiptop shape. Most often, you'll find a winning team consists of goal-oriented, self-motivated people. Directing a winning team means recognizing the dynamics of team structures.

The team should be made up of equals. This means that no single person is the star, no one a drudge. Every role played is an important one. This will require redirecting the focus of people who usually fill starring roles and getting them to see the value of teamwork. It also means the team is recognized as a unit, not individually.

"I can live for two months on a good compliment."

—*Mark Twain*

WHAT COST HAPPINESS?

Until last month, you thought you had a contented department. After the Blankenship project reaches a successful completion, the team took on the Klengson/Trammell merger, followed by the tough Parker product recall. Who knows how much overtime the team put in or what sacrifices they made in their family lives? Sure, you appreciate the effort, but, it's all part of the job, so you didn't bother ladling on the praise, offering compensatory time, or putting Dave and Sandra up for promotion to the branch office directorship.

Within a few short weeks, Dave took a job with your competition, Sandra decided to start her own small CPA shop, and Kevin told you—well, that's just not printable here. Whoa! Three unnecessary—and costly—departures.

NEW EMPLOYEE COSTS

Employee Hiring	*Accountant, gr. 1*	*Accountant, gr. 2*	*Accounts Payable gr. 1*
newspaper ads	$75.00	$75.00	$75.00
administrative screening of applicants @ $25/hr.	150.00	150.00	200.00
your time for interviews @ $50/hr.	600.00	600.00	400.00
drug screening	25.00	25.00	25.00
training classes	1,500.00	1,500.00	0
months before employee works productively	3 months	3 months	1 month
% annual salary	11,000.00	12,500.00	2,500.00
% annual benefits	4,500.00	5,000.00	1,000.00
start up cost	17,850.00	19,850.00	4,200.00

You now have three slots in your department that need to be filled as quickly as possible. Those three were stars, and all the temps in the world can't make up for their loss. The salary range is not overly impressive, $30,000–$35,000, and you'll probably be interviewing about two dozen applicants to fill the positions.

Let's do some calculations on replacement cost per slot, not counting the loss of productivity your department suffers by not having the positions currently filled.

SUCCESSTHOUGHTS

What works:
- *Recognizing talent as a corporate asset is essential.*
- *Giving recognition when it is due and making it tangible requires initiative, creativity, and understanding.*
- *Motivating employees to perform at peak levels is essential in today's business world.*

Replacing an employee costs a lot more than you probably imagine. Remember these costs are only "start up" costs: locating and hiring, training, and time before an employee pulls his full weight. If you have to move one of these employees, you can add $5,000–$10,000 to the bill. Turnovers are an expensive business, so keeping employees happy and content makes sense—or should that be "cents"?

No one would deny that this is true. But it's easier said than done. People seem to find it easier to criticize than praise, break down rather than build up, denigrate rather than motivate. If you incline toward the negative, adjust your thinking. Remember promote, progress, and produce all begin with "pro," the suffix that means "for." Be "pro" the people who work with you and your team will be proactive.

"There are four ingredients to lighting a fire under your company, team, or organization. They are Urgency, Inspiration, Ownership, and Rewards," explains Arnie Rincover in an article on motivation. (Source: Arnie Rincover, "Motivation.")

Urgency

A sense of urgency comes from understanding the long and short views of how a vision can come to fruition. Communicate the big picture to your people. When people don't know the destination, they're in no hurry to reach it. Let your people know the direction, the timeliness, and the importance of a goal, and they'll be more inclined to reach for it. Here's a typical scenario:

Holiday Sweaters, Ltd. is introducing a new product line that must be in the stores by October 1 for the

> **SUCCESSTHOUGHTS**
>
> *Urgency must be real. You can't tell people the situation is urgent, expect them to work overtime, and offer no rewards (either financial or otherwise) unless there really is a crisis. When rare crises do occur, tell everyone up front what the problem is, ask for help finding solutions, implement as many solutions as time allows, and provide the necessary resources (equipment, people, supplies, outside sources). If you do this only on rare, true-crisis occasions, you can ask a great deal from your people. If you do it every week, when a real crisis occurs, no one will care. And if you do have real crises every week, you should reevaluate your management style.*

Christmas season. Failure to meet Christmas orders represents a loss of $285,000 to the company and all Christmas bonuses to the employees. The $285,000 makes the situation urgent to upper management; the loss of Christmas bonuses brings the urgency to everyone.

If you work in teams, look to team leaders to create a sense of urgency among their players. This means finding the leader whom team members admire and will follow; giving that leader the authority and resources to meet whatever deadlines are set; and making the team responsible for the completion of its tasks in a timely and profitable manner. To find this team leader, look for people others already follow, not necessarily your "favorite" among the team members.

Inspiration

Arnie Rincover offers five ways people get inspired in the workplace:

- if they are involved in a project they think is great
- if they get to do something new they've never done before
- if they get to do something they didn't think they could do
- if they work to improve their community
- if they learn something new and vital

To inspire someone, give her a goal she will value. You'll never inspire anyone by telling her meeting projected targets will fulfill departmental objectives. That's what inspires you.

Instead, find a motivating factor your subordinates can buy into: beating the competition, creating a project that betters the community or educates young people, promoting learning for you and your team, or establishing a mentoring relationship which will put someone on the "fast track."

Ownership

"If I work on it, I want it to have my stamp, my thumbprint, my name, my identity." That's not an unusual request, but one employees often hesitate to make. Why? Because in antiquated management situations, the "I" was suppressed for the greater good of the company. Memos that focus on the "I" in them were laughed at. People who thought about themselves before considering the company weren't considered "team players."

Employees provided ideas to their superiors, who in turn fed them to upper management, who likewise discussed the brilliant idea originated by Ellen Goodwin, administrative assistant. The idea was great; upper management patted its joint self on the back for coming up with another winner. There may have been some trickle down, but the next Ellen knew about her idea was when she saw it on the shelves at Piggly Wiggly.

In that old-fashioned environment, people did not ask for the credit due them. However, times have changed.

Your employees want to be acknowledged for their ideas. They want you to know who came up with the idea, and they want you to promote it with their name tag still attached.

If you allow people to "own" their projects and give them credit for what they do, you will motivate them. However, do not give credit without giving two other things: responsibility and accountability.

When they buy into a project, people must also be responsible for its outcome and accountable for successes and failures. You don't get praise without the possibility of censure.

> *"Far and away the best prize that life offers is the chance to work hard at work worth doing."*
>
> —*Theodore Roosevelt*

Rewards

Rewards fall into two categories: tangible and intangible. Tangible rewards are raises, bonuses, trips, cars, wall plaques, and paperweights bearing the company logo. Intangibles are a bit trickier: praise, credit for one's ideas, respect, freedom to act, choices, flexibility in hours or workplace.

Your first step in offering appropriate rewards is knowing what your employees want, need, and appreciate. Unfortunately, this differs for everyone. Yolanda would rather have compensatory time off to spend with her children; Simon prefers cash; and José would rather be named Employee of the Month than have a week off with pay. Progressive-thinking companies are revamping reward programs to meet individual needs and expectations.

How do you find out what they want? Ask! Be a good "asker" and a good "listener." Tailor your questions like a magazine interview. Encourage people to think, express their opinions, offer personal solutions, analyze problems, and explain personal preferences. Don't ask anything that can be answered with a simple yes or no. This is all personal opinion—there are no right or wrong answers.

$$$$$$

While money still motivates many, its effectiveness doesn't last. As soon as an employee gets accustomed to her current take-home pay, the motivation from a salary increase is gone.

In addition, look realistically at the increase. For example: This year your employees receive a maximum 5% pay increase. It sounds very generous, especially considering the average increase in your industry is only 3.5% this year. Steve is in his third year with you and is making $31,200 per year, or $1,200 per pay period. Five percent of his annual salary is $1,560, or $60 per pay period. Steve is single and claims one withholding allowance.

What happens to Steve's $60? He pays roughly $16.00 additional federal withholding, about $4.70 in Social Security and Medicare taxes, $4.00 in state withholding, and $4.80 towards his 401K. Steve's $60 is now $30.50, or the equivalent of one night at the movies with his girlfriend and a large pepperoni pizza after the show.

The fact is, considering inflation, Steve's generous 5% raise doesn't look so great on his paycheck. It's no wonder money fails as a perpetual incentive—unless you find a way to extend the life of monetary rewards.

Hubbard Hall, a chemical manufacturer headquartered in Waterbury, Connecticut, has a solid grip on how to use money as an incentive. For one thing, bonuses, given monthly, are distributed company-wide based on position and tenure with the company. A production-line employee, the receptionist, and the mail clerk get bonuses, just like the CEO and corporate vice presidents. Other rewards include company-paid lunches for teams exceeding monthly production or sales targets and company-paid dinners for employees and spouses for exceeding targets. Hubbard Hall's plan is methodical and continuously active. While the rewards are tangible, the monthly or quarterly nature keeps the reward factor predominant in the minds of Hubbard Hall employees. At the company's Inman, South Carolina, plant, bonus lunches have become a common event—a regular reminder of long-range production goals and a reward for short-term successes.

Other companies provide unique reward programs based on employee concerns. Kerry Dolan in *Forbes* reports that Illinois Trade Association pays for chiropractic care, herbal therapy, and other forms of alternative medical care, including a once-monthly free massage for any employee who wants one. Medical costs are high, and more people are turning to alternative forms of medical care to maintain wellness—forms not commonly covered by standard health insurance policies.

Benefits Are in the Eye of the Beholder

What motivates your people? Is it having supplemented, on-site daycare so parents can spend lunch hours with their children? Is it bringing one's pet to work? Don't laugh, there are work environments allowing dogs at the desk.

Do your employees have trouble seeing to their household chores during lunch hours? Consider arranging dry cleaning or laundry pick up. Or perhaps, you could have automatic teller machines from a local bank at your work site.

According to Kerry Dolan, "a concierge service at Chicago-based Andersen Consulting will arrange for someone to be at an employee's home when the cable guy comes, or send someone to pick up a car from the repair shop."

The opportunity to buy postage stamps, mail packages UPS or FedEx from work, cash a check on-site, or purchase subway tokens makes life easier for employees, and, because these are recurring events, rather than a once yearly review-and-raise scenario, these benefits are much appreciated.

WHEN EMPLOYEES LACK MOTIVATION

What makes people lazy? Why isn't everyone a firebrand like you? It could be that while you have an inbuilt, gung-ho generator, those around you need a hefty shove to get going. What leads a department or team into complacency?

Partially, apathy derived from satisfaction. Don't forget, those in the number two slot try harder because they're still hungry. Satisfaction, resting on one's laurels, kills incentive.

Frequently, management plays a subversive role in creating apathy. First, management informs employees everything is great, profits are up, no worries, no problems. If people continue to get that message and no other, there is no impetus to get moving. Further, lack of communication from management keeps people in blinders: no destination = no motivation to reach a goal.

Finally, a negative, destructive grapevine, nepotism or favoritism in promotions, and elitism in distribution of rewards contribute significantly to malaise in the general workforce.

EXERCISE   *Understanding Motivation*

Ask yourself the questions on the next page about your company, your department, and yourself.

How many checks have you put in the "yes" columns? You may not be able to realign your company's rewards program, but you can influence matters within your department, and you definitely control your own motivations and personal reward system.

MOTIVATING FACTORS

Question	Company		Department		Self	
	Yes	No	Yes	No	Yes	No
Are people your company's greatest assets?						
Do employees feel valued?						
Are all employees aware of company-wide goals?						
Are rewards perceived as fair by all levels?						
Do promotions come from within?						
Is credit given for good ideas or work?						
Are subordinates praised openly for their work?						
Is criticism a private affair?						
Does a sense of urgency exist?						
Are natural leaders in leadership positions?						
Do employees complain about their supervisors?						
Is the workload too heavy?						
Are pay and incentive policies sufficient?						
Are rewards tangible?						
Are employees motivated to achieve?						
Does your company reward achievement at all levels, including hourly employees?						

Lighting the Proverbial Fire

Once a company or group wallows in apathy, generating enough interest to regain momentum becomes essential for survival and about as easy as crossing Antarctica on a tricycle.

Dr. Rick Brinkman and Dr. Rick Kirschner, authors of *Dealing With People You Can't Stand,* recommend two essential skills for energizing stagnant team members: blending and redirecting. "Blending is any behavior by which you reduce the differences between you and another in order to meet them where they are and move to common ground. The result of blending is an increase in rapport. Redirecting is any behavior by which you use that rapport to change the trajectory of that interaction."

In simple terms, meet your people halfway and bring them along with you on the path to success. The key is to develop positive interaction. You will find sincerity and candor to be excellent tools for one-on-one conversations. Tell the person what the problem is and why you want it fixed. Explain the direction you're moving and her role in reaching the destination. Build up her skills and spirits rather than destroy her ego.

Learn to accept differences in the people around you. "Everybody responds to different situations with different levels of assertiveness. During times of challenge, difficulty, or stress, people tend to move out of their comfort zone, and become either more passive or more aggressive than their normal mode of operation," say Drs. Brinkman and Kirschner.

Things to Work On

There are techniques you can use to develop active motivational skills:

- *Have open, honest discussions* with your people on an individual basis. Learn what matters to your people; and let them voice their personal concerns.

- *Be open to unusual suggestions,* special situations that differ from the norm.

- *Do not use fear, coercion, greed, or humiliation* as motivators. They are destructive.

- *Make criticisms timely,* short, and behavior-, rather than person-oriented.

- *Look for one thing each day to praise* in every employee in your group. This could be appreciation for a thoughtful task, a job well done, an idea that helps the company or department.

- *Make praise sincere, public, and personal.* Too many managers use praise to bolster their own reputations, "Boy, I'm a great guy, I just told Amy how much I appreciate her." Amy is the focus here, not you.

- *Encourage people to participate* in decision making. That doesn't mean giving up authority, it means explaining the situation and asking for suggestions. You don't have to follow them, just listen.

- *Encourage your people to work smarter, not harder.* Sam was a manager who valued staying late at work more than efficiency. Sounds absurd, doesn't it? Think about it. He saw several people regularly staying late, still working diligently at 7:00 P.M., while others left daily at five. Clearly, the late-leavers were working harder. But were they working smarter? If you have a person who completes assigned tasks within an eight-hour day and does so at a superior level, she should be rewarded. On the other hand, you should certainly provide time management classes for the late-leavers. They need it.

Give your employees and yourself a reason to show up every day. Be a motivator, an energizer, and a star maker.

CHAPTER RECAP

- Help team members adjust to group rather than individual rewards.

- Only your employees can identify what rewards mean most to them.

- Praise in public, criticize in private.

- Money is a short-lived motivator.

- Laziness is a contagion that is usually rooted in the company structure.

Recommended Reading

Clemmer, Jim. *Pathways to Performance: A Guide to Transforming Yourself, Your Team and Your Organization.* Toronto: Macmillan Canada, 1996.

Covey, Stephen R. *Seven Habits of Highly Effective People.* New York: Simon & Schuster, 1989.

Peters, Tom, and Nancy Austin. *A Passion for Excellence.* New York: Random House, 1985.

_____. *Motivation and Goal-Setting, Second Edition.* Hawthorne, NJ: Career Press, 1993.

Teamwork—
A Reincarnation

*T*he dominant trend for the new millennium will be—drum roll, please—teamwork. Sound familiar? It is. Quality teams, R&D teams, marketing teams, and softball teams have been significant management factors for the past two decades. And really, most of us are more familiar with teamwork than we perhaps realize. We grow up in family teams, develop civic pride through community teams, and play on sports teams. Corporations are, ideally, teams of people working toward a common goal.

"You might liken the farm family to a small corporation. Fundamentally, it was a team of people working toward the common and critical goal: survival. Each family member was assigned tasks based on his or her age, capability, physical strength, and stamina. With the years came 'promotion'—and more demanding tasks," says Janet Hauter in *The Smart Woman's Guide to Career Success.*

Survival is still the goal, and teamwork the means to survival, as competition from global giants threatens the foundations of American business. Most companies report a 20–40% gain in productivity after eighteen months of working through self-directed teams. In the late 1980s General Electric anticipated a 40–50% improvement in productivity by reconfiguring its work force into teams. It's a matter of logistics and practicality. As corporations pare down middle management to keep a competitive edge, there are simply too few GIs left to do the work. The Generals have to get in the trenches or the company's productivity will suffer. In the new millennium, teamwork and team management will take on new dimensions and become even more valuable. Your success will depend on being a team player in all aspects of your job.

TEAMWORK CONCEPTS AND TRENDS

Be prepared for teamwork to take on new titles, new faces, new parameters, but don't be surprised if everything you learned in Little League comes into play in your future teams. Remember:

- Four singles are as good as one homerun with the bases empty.

- Not everyone can be pitcher.

- Everyone gets a turn at bat.

- RBIs can win the game, even if they come from a pinch hitter.

- The pitcher can't play every position.

- Batting .400 is better than most major leaguers ever dream of.

- You can't always win.

- Sometimes the game gets called on account of rain.

- Pizza with the team is ten times better than pizza alone.

According to John Kotter in *Leading Change,* "In a fast moving world, teamwork is helpful almost all the time. In an environment of constant change, individuals, even if supremely talented, won't have enough time or expertise to absorb rapidly shifting competitor, customer, and technological information."

It is just not practical to expect every person to be talented in every performance aspect of a project. Creative thinkers don't make good bean counters, and vice versa. Going back to Little League: Every team member has a different job according to each member's different talent. On a well-balanced team you need divergent talents.

> ### SUCCESSTHOUGHTS
>
> *When planning a team, choose people from different departments, areas of expertise, and levels of employment. The best ideas can—and often do—come from secretaries, assembly-line workers, and other hourly employees. Teams should have a balance of talents and types of experience.*

It is difficult to evaluate the potential of a team, particularly from the inside. If your team does not perform up to expectations, ask someone from outside to observe the team at work. Give them criteria on which to base their assessment. Here are some questions to ask when evaluating team dynamics:

- *How well does the team communicate?* Does all input come from one source? Are there team members who don't communicate with others? Do some members consider the team a social event? Is there a reason for this?

- *How does the team make decisions?* Is there one leader who sways the opinions of everyone else? Does the team fail to make important or timely decisions?

- *Has the team established a work routine?* Do meetings go on and on with no action taken? Do team

"Teamwork is the
essence of life."

—*Pat Riley,*
The Winner Within

members listen and act on suggestions presented by everyone, regardless of status in the company?

- *Do team members pull their weight?* Does each person come to meetings prepared? Are tasks doled out equitably? Do you have grandstanders, prima donnas, or attention hogs on your team?

- *Who is the leader in the group?* If there are two or more people who are normally leaders, is there conflict? Is the conflict productive or destructive? Is there a power struggle within the team?

- *Are goals and roles set for the good of the team or the good of individuals?* Are rewards equitably distributed? Do all members of the team get recognition for their participation? Do they all contribute to problem solving? Is everyone on the team given a role to play and a chance to succeed?

Once you have a good appraisal of your team's dynamics, you can find ways to progress. Take steps to remove obstacles one at a time. For example, if you have a non-participant, find a task that person can do well, assign it, then praise the results as a way to encourage further participation.

Don't be too upset by friction within the team. Confrontation, criticism, and a certain amount of rejection (of ideas, not people) are vital elements of a productive team. You will have to decide if the conflict is productive or destructive. If it is the latter, take action immediately to halt the negative slide. Remind members what the team goals are and how they can work to achieve them.

When a team works too smoothly, it may be cause to worry. "Conflict is inevitable and necessary in reaching effective and creative solutions for problems. How is conflict handled in the group—avoidance, compromise, competition, collaboration, etc.?" says Kenneth Blanchard in *The One-Minute Manager Builds High Performing Teams.*

| **Building a Team** | E X E R C I S E |

Imagine that you are given the opportunity to build a team from the ground up. Your project is to investigate shipping costs, identify problems, and develop and implement solutions. First, you need to choose team members. You can have no more than eight people on your team. Whom do you choose? Why? What do you think each will contribute to the team? Assess your team for balance, experience, and talent.

Team Trends

Along with teams comes a new terminology. There are no plain vanilla teams any more and there is a new name for every new team. We have Empowered Teams, High Performance Teams, Superior Work Teams, Self-Directed Teams, Self-Managed Teams, and Clusters. You can hardly see the forest for the trees!

An Empowered Team is a group of people who can investigate a project fully, develop processes and products, and implement their results. They have support from upper management and the power to act as needed.

High Performance Teams and Superior Work Teams are groups of effective people who have a clear direction, communicate effectively, make decisions, and produce results in a timely manner.

Self-Directed and Self-Managed Teams are groups of 5 to 15 employees responsible for a whole product or process. The team develops an idea from creation to fruition, plans and performs tasks, and, frequently, undertakes many roles formerly assigned to management.

A Cluster is a group of people from various fields who work together more or less permanently. There can be as many as fifty people in a cluster, with it broken down into smaller work units. Clusters work well in engineering, architecture, or similar fields in which projects require expertise from a number of areas.

Some of us have difficulty visualizing the organization of a group without a chart. Most organization charts are like trees or pyramids with the CEO on top and hourly employees some place off the bottom of the page. Cluster organizations and team corporations don't work that way. If you can't "see" the way a team or cluster concept works, visualize a spider web in contrast to a pyramid. There is greater teamwork in the web con-

cept, as each thread bears an equal portion of the weight. That is not to say that these companies don't have a central figure—the spider web still has the spider, doesn't it?

Perhaps the most interesting trend in team concepts is diversity. What makes a diverse work environment? Is it a mixture of ideas, provocative thinking that is respected, and innovative planning? How many companies can honestly say they have a diverse workforce?

A division of a major U.S. corporation, buying into the concept of diversity, decided to make a recruitment video proclaiming its diverse nature. There was only one African American man in corporate headquarters and three African American women, all in subordinate positions. There were no Native Americans, Hispanics, or Asians. All the offices with doors and windows were occupied by white men, cubicles by a mix of men and women. Teams had white male leaders with little or no training in teamwork concepts. Thus, teams were run under the premise, "Do as I say, or you're fired." What could this company possible show as "diversity" in their video? You can imagine the opening scene: Fade up to Tonto peering over a cactus and telling the Lone Ranger, "Too many white men, Kemo Sabe!"

Regardless of what your team is called, it will only perform as well as its members. Everyone on the team needs positive reinforcement, so make sure team members feel included and committed. By rewarding team members, you will develop a sense of accomplishment and pride. It all goes back to those sports teams you played on as a kid. Didn't you just love the banquet when you got your trophy or sports letter?

Yeah, Team!

It should come as no surprise that sports inspires teamwork. That's why business conferences hire speakers like football's Lou Holtz and basketball's Pat Riley to give speeches on motivating teams and improving performance.

Let's dissect sports teams down to their foundations, then say farewell to sweaty locker rooms, athlete's foot, and "Win one for the Gipper." Just how do sports teams work?

Every good sports team starts with a coach and management staff that scouts for potential players. They look for players to fill the gaps in the current team. If the team needs muscle on the defensive line, managers don't draft quarterbacks and tight ends. In corporations, replace the scout with a headhunter or recruiter. How does your company recruit management-level

> SUCCESSTHOUGHTS
>
> *Before you establish a team, understand the parameters under which you can aid the team's success and how you can undermine its productivity. Train, support, prepare, set goals—then step back to the sidelines and cheer.*

employees? Most likely, a position comes open, and the company hires someone who can perform the tasks. Where do these people come from? Are they recruited from outside or promoted from within?

Every year the most seasoned professional baseball player is expected to show up for spring training. In business, it is called a "learning curve." When you take on new responsibilities, a new position, or a new company, you don't begin at peak performance level. You need to work into the job.

During the regular season teams still have practice. Why? They won last Saturday, so who needs to practice? This is one area in which business really needs to pay attention. New projects bring new challenges and opportunities that require honing old skills and developing new techniques. All personnel need refresher courses that will energize them and improve their performance. They also need training that allows them to learn and apply new techniques. Considering how much a professional sports team spends on training—and how often big business reverts to sports for inspiration—it is astounding how the one budget item that suffers in every corporate cutback is training and education.

SUCCESSTHOUGHTS

Cling to that training budget like a lifeline—it is!

Last year's World Series champions will have a hard time being this year's World Series champions. Pat Riley in The Winner Within *explains, "Complacency is the last hurdle any winner, any team must overcome before attaining potential greatness. Complacency is the Success Disease: It takes root when you're feeling good about who you are and not what you've achieved." Just remember that a successful career is not based on one event, but on a series of repeat victories.*

One final sports analogy: A group of individuals, regardless of their talent or potential, will not be a team until they are trained by their coach to work together. Once the training element is in place, the coach has to let the team go out and play its game. In Self-Directed Work Teams: The New American Challenge, *Jack Orsburn and colleagues claim, "When you stop training self-directed teams, they starve to death." Team building is a continuous training process, not a buzzword for success. As vital as the team concept is to the success of a company, it may still fail if the coach—or boss, CEO, COO, and so on—cannot or will not let go of her control over the team.*

How Teams Work

You've got the team in place. You've got a project to do. Now, what? To be a good coach, you'll need to understand how a team works.

1. Prepare the team with information about the project, the work involved, the goal, why it is important, what their roles will be. Create an agenda.

2. Bring the team together for an initial meeting. Have each person introduce himself, telling a bit about his job in the company. Your job here is to let everyone on the team know why Sam or Fred has been chosen for this team. It might go something like this:

Sam: I'm Sam Gray and I work on the loading dock. I've been with XYZ for eight years.

Coach: Sam has valuable hands-on experience that will help the team understand our shipping problems and whether our proposed solutions will work.

3. Present the important material and get feedback from the team members. During the meeting, assign tasks, making sure that everyone has something to do. Set a schedule so everyone knows when each task must be done. Set a date for the next meeting.

4. Supervise performance from a distance. Get regular updates, see problems before they happen and smooth the path to success.

5. Add additional team members, both temporary and permanent, if you find a talent or manpower personnel gap in your team. Take suggestions from the team about whom to add, but make the final choice yourself, based on the needs of the team.

6. Follow up with the team to let them know how far along other players are on their parts of the project, how the schedule is going, whether it fits the required time frame. Keep track of what changes need to be made.

To have a real team you have to have goals, rules, and a mission. Everyone on the team must buy into the mission, or the goals will not be reached. Likewise, everyone on the team should reap the rewards of reaching the goal. It's always a good idea to remind people of the primary goals at the beginning of every meeting and as part of every memo. Coach Pat Riley calls this agreemeent the Constructive Covenant. He says, "A covenant is an agreement that binds people together. The Constructive Covenant:

- binds people together

- creates an equal footing

- helps people shoulder their own responsibilities

- prescribes terms for the help and support of others

- and creates a foundation for team work."

Team Goal Setting

Setting goals is critical for team success. Be sure to incorporate company, team, and personal goals into your planning. Be very specific in defining goals. One of the greatest frustrations employees face is trying to achieve nebulous goals with no measurable standards.

- *Make sure the goals you set are clear, specific, attainable.* People need to understand their roles in reaching the goal. Make sure goals are measurable against written criteria. Do not assume that team members will automatically agree with the goals you have set or use the same standard of evaluation. Remember: Clear, specific, attainable.

- *Set three small, attainable goals,* then add three more once the first goals have been reached. It is more important to give team members a sense of accomplishment than it is to establish an endless list of goals that have people shooting off in all directions. Set priorities within the team. Make sure everyone knows which tasks must be completed first, when the results are due, and why.

- *Plan the work—work the plan.* But be flexible. Not everyone works the same way you do and trying to make someone work in a style alien to them is counterproductive. Tell team members that the goal is to get from point A to point B— how they get there is their business—as long as the group reaches point B by the set deadline.

- *Don't leave schedules to chance.* Go over the initial schedule in the first meeting. Ask about conflicts, other projects, other commitments. Be flexible in making adjustments.

- *Set budgets that will provide the funds necessary* to accomplish a job in the specified time frame. If temps are needed to do tasks, hire them. If specific equipment can be rented to speed up the process, rent it. Don't expect a miracle on a shoestring— it won't happen.

- *Arrange in advance for the equipment,* computer time, personnel, and materials you need for a project. Support staff is vital to every project—make sure support is available to do the tasks and on the schedule required.

- *Keep on top of any problems that arise.* As coach, your job is to smooth the path for team success. Handle problems efficiently, effectively, and without repercussions. Better yet, discuss possible solutions with a team member and delegate the problem solving to her. Remember: Train, train, train.

> *"If you really believe in quality, when you cut through everything, it's empowering your people, and it's empowering your people that leads to teams."*
>
> —Jamie Houghton, CEO, Corning

TEAM-BUILDING, THE KEY TO SUCCESS

"A management team—or any group of people working under you—is like an investment portfolio," says David Mahoney in *Confessions of a Street Smart Manager*. You don't start out with the perfect portfolio—you don't start out with a perfect team, either. You will have to build your team from the ground up, recognizing in team members not only what they do, but how they do it.

Performance is a variable that you must control if you are a team leader. If you are a team member, your obligation is to support the team and its goals by performing assigned tasks, enabling others, and being the "value-added" component to the team.

Team members usually fall into one of five categories: the cooperator, the visionary, the facilitator, the challenger, and the slug.

- *Cooperators* provide technical information, use accessible resources, and organize tasks and functions for the team. This is your accounting manager, computer programmer, or administrative assistant.

- *Visionaries* see goals and creative ways to reach those goals. They are your thinkers, your big-picture people.

- *Facilitators* communicate among members; they are "people" people and are usually considered easy to work with and for.

- *Challengers* question everything: the composition of the team, its goals, its methods, its success. Challengers are outspoken, candid, and assertive.

- *Slugs* are self-defining.

Despite all your planning, you many well wind up with the odd slug. The only recourse is to remove all slugs from the team. You don't have time to adjust stodgy thinking, nor can you afford non-performing members on the team. The other four you need for balance.

You may face resistance when dealing with team members who are set in their ways. But don't believe you can't teach an old dog new tricks. If the rewards are sufficient and the motivation is high enough, anyone can learn just about anything. If team members need specific skill building to reach team goals, make sure those skills are in place before they are needed.

"The worst mistake a boss can make is not to say 'well done.'"

—John Ashcroft, former chairman, Coloroll

Benefits of Teamwork

Teamwork is not a benefit, it is a process to achieve an end. However, there must be benefits for both the company and the participants. Company benefits will include some, or all, of the following:

- Improved productivity, problem solving, utilization of personnel.

- Increased employee commitment, loyalty, personal growth.

- A satisfied, effective work environment.

- Improved communications throughout the company.

- Maximum utilization of ideas, creativity, training.

- Increased profitability.

Team members will also see benefits, such as:

- Increased training, skill building, problem solving, and decision making opportunities.

- Increased involvement in company policies and programs.

- Opportunities to participate in company planning.

- Personal pride, ownership, commitment.

- Variety, challenge, opportunity.

- Financial and personal rewards.

Tomorrow's team can be the path to your success. Go into team programs with the right attitude. Your benefits will be much greater than the effort you put in.

CHAPTER RECAP

- As companies reduce their personnel, every employee will have more responsibility. Work will be accomplished through teams.

- Diversity in team formation leads to greater success.

- All teams have some conflict. It is the team leader's role to smooth out conflicts and resolve problems.

- Teams develop a work style very similar to individual work styles.

- Setting goals is a primary element for team success.

- Teamwork is a process toward achieving an end.

Recommended Reading

Blanchard, Kenneth, Donald Carew, and Eunice Parisi-Carew. *The One-Minute Manager Builds High Performing Teams.* New York: William Morrow and Company, 1990.

McNally, David. *Even Eagles Need a Push.* New York: DTP, 1994.

Parker, Glenn. Team Players and Teamwork: *The New Competitive Business Strategy.* San Francisco: Jossey Bass, 1996.

Riley, Pat. *The Winner Within.* New York: GP Putnam's Sons, 1993.

Roberts, Wess. *Leadership Secrets of Attila the Hun.* New York: Warner, 1991.

Success in Your
Future

*I*n parts 1 and 2 you got to know the elements of success and how to apply them on a personal and interpersonal level—you're on your way to a successful career and life. In part 3 you will learn what to do when things change—the job market, your interests, or your needs. These chapters will tell you how to survive a layoff and how to keep yourself prepared in an ever-changing job market. You'll also begin to consider what to do in the event of a dramatic life change. Do you want to work from your home? Do you want to be your own boss? As you grow, you may find your career goals and expectations changing. Part 3 will prepare you for these changes.

Your Next Career

*O*nly eight more months until my next vacation!"
People who live from vacation to vacation, or on a lesser scale, from weekend to weekend, are in the wrong job. It may be the company or corporation. It may be a difficult boss. It may be that the current job no longer meets the current mind-set. It may be that the employee has outgrown the job.

Regardless of the reason, experts agree that this is not the right job to be in. "There is only one success—to be able to spend your life in your own way," says Christopher Morley. Work, to be successful, should have elements of fun. Are you having fun yet? Treading water in a stagnant pond is no way to reach future goals. Assertive people investigate positive changes to correct inertia.

LATERAL MOVES

One way to get out of a bad situation and into a better one is through a lateral move, taking a job on the same pay or status level in a different department or area of the company.

"Right," you're saying to yourself, "I really want to stay in this deadbeat hole."

Before you discount the value of a lateral move, let's investigate the rationale behind such a move:

- You get a new boss, new responsibilities, and new people to work with.

- You don't lose touch with the positive people you built relationships with over the past few years.

- You may be able to last until your retirement is vested. Vesting occurs after five full years with a corporation. If you have only eighteen months to go, take a lateral move so you can keep the investment you've made. That's right, you've invested your time and effort, so don't throw away the money the corporation owes you.

- You'll broaden your skill and experience base. Combination skills are a valuable resumé builder and help find that next job.

- The grass is not necessarily greener on the other side of the fence. Your next corporation may be worse to work for than the one you work for today.

- Lateral moves keep needed health and other benefits in place. If anyone in your family has a pre-existing condition, you'll want to take this into consideration.

- Lateral moves often do not entail moving to a new location. If you have school-aged children and a spouse with a good job, a lateral move can give you the change you need without disrupting the family.

- Occasionally, a lateral move gives you a chance to move to an exotic or preferred location: closer to or farther away from your in-laws, to a foreign country, or to an area where you've always dreamed of living.

So, now that a lateral move improves in appeal, how do you get one? You can volunteer to work on committees or programs in conjunction with your target department. You can let colleagues know how much you've always wanted to live in Jersey City. Or, you can take the quick and easy route—tell the people in Human Resources you are interested in lateral moves that will let you (a) work in a related field, (b) work in a particular location, or (c) expand your value to the corporation. Be careful not to point out that you want to move because (a) your boss is an imbecile, (b) you hate the corporate culture and would do anything to get away from it, or (c) you're only hanging on until your retirement is vested.

Considering Lateral Moves | EXERCISE

Make a list of all the possible lateral moves available within your company. For example: Today, you are secretary to the director of purchasing. Obviously, you could be a secretary to any other director, vice-president, or company officer. However, you do have some purchasing knowledge. Could you also be a purchasing trainee? Could you be a customer service rep? Once you have your list compiled, list the pros and cons for each move. Some things to consider are location, potential for advancement, people you'll work with, experiences you'll have, salary range of the new position, and the opportunity to do something you've wanted to do for a long time. If you have an understanding, supportive supervisor, you might ask her whether she thinks you would make a good _____. A positive response means you have an ally for taking a new direction. Note: Even though you may not see an increase in your current salary, the move to a position with a slightly higher salary range gives you added earning potential.

LOOKING FOR OTHER PROJECTS

One of the problems in departmentalized work is that you frequently lose sight of other opportunities within the corporation. If you have a central headquarters with multiple branches, you may not realize how much more interesting it would be to work in one of the other locations. One way to find out if you would like a different setting is by volunteering for short term assignments at branches or the central headquarters.

Even if you don't plan to leave your current location, you should try to expand your experience by reaching out to different areas. Here's an example: Your company sells cleaning supplies to healthcare facilities. You are a sales rep with a varied customer base. At the next sales meeting, you learn that the company wants to expand into the hotel/motel segment of cleaning supplies, and a task force is being formed to look into that market. Volunteer! You have street sales experience and product knowledge that can help this team. Headquarters types will also see you as a team player, a knowledgeable resource, and a savvy sales rep. This could be your leg up the corporate ladder.

If nothing else, finding new and exciting projects outside your normal job can motivate you, energize you, and give ho-hum daily drudgery that element of fun all jobs need. Never pass up a chance to do something different. Who knows where it may lead?

Expanding the Scope of Your Job

Judy had a background in home economics—fabrics, textiles, and associated crafts. When an opportunity opened to teach an extension course at her local university, she recognized her "in." Once she had her foot in the door, she created new courses and new opportunities for herself. Within three years, Judy created her own job. And you can, too.

When your job is no longer challenging, find ways to give it a boost. Get involved in transforming the job you have into the job you want. You may meet a fair bit of resistance, but you will eventually expand the scope of your job into a position you'll enjoy.

Seeking Consulting or Freelance Opportunities

Consulting and freelancing can be excellent ways of expanding your profile, increasing your value, and filling your bank account. One caveat: Make doubly certain your company does not see a conflict of interest in your moonlighting. A major advertising firm that isn't interested in small business projects might willingly let you freelance ads for local restaurants or gift shops. An industrial architecture firm might not frown on your doing landscape architecture for homeowners. The rule of thumb is that you never take potential clients or money from the company that pays your regular salary.

If you are going to get into part-time consulting, you'll need to set yourself up in business. Here are a few tips to gain that professional look a consultant must have:

- *Get professional business cards,* stationery, and brochures if you need them.

- *Get an outside phone line,* if needed, along with the equipment you'll need to work.

- *Establish a separate business bank account.* You can't run your business through your personal bank account.

- *Build a portfolio* of work to show clients. Also, build a reference list of satisfied clients.

- *Set up accounting procedures* for billing, statements, payables, and receivables.

"It is difficulties that show what stuff men are made of."

—Epictetus

- *Get a business license* and pay your taxes as required by city, state, and federal governments. Don't try to circumvent the law—if they catch you, you'll be sorry.

- *Get the word out* that you are interested in small projects along specific lines.

SKILL-BUILDING

One of the biggest problems in the business world today is the gap between worker skills and job demands. A 1997 survey by the Society for Human Resource Management (SHRM) and Aon Consulting shows that 43% of survey participants (HR managers) believe that current employees do not have skill levels to match job demands. These skill shortages include both attitude and aptitude. According to the survey, the weakest competency among non-management personnel was creativity and innovation followed by dealing with change, problem solving and reasoning, and communications.

There are basic skills that can help you, regardless of the field you pursue: interpersonal, listening, presentation, computer, and team building.

Interpersonal Skills

Interpersonal skills are two-fold: verbal skills (speaking and writing) and nonverbal skills (body language, voice, timing, eye contact, and so on). Good interpersonal skills are based on recognizing the primary needs of other human beings, like security, recognition, self-esteem, belonging, trust, and understanding. While it is true that you can't learn compassion in a classroom, you can take lessons on body language, voice, speaking, and business writing. There are classes at your local community college that cover these areas, or you can hire a "personal trainer"—a consultant that specializes in improved communications skills.

Listening Skills

What could be more frustrating that sitting opposite your boss while he reconfigures half a dozen paper clips, answers phone calls while you're speaking, reads his mail, or picks the lint from his suit? Worse, you could have a boss that does all these things during one brief discussion. You can adapt yourself to becoming a better listener by using these techniques:

- *Remove or ignore distractions.* If you are mid-project, leave your desk and sit by the person meeting with you. Close up the folders, put mail aside, switch your phone to voice mail, and turn your attention to the speaker.

- *Learn to make eye contact.* Too many people these days can't look someone else in the eye. Don't let that be you.

- *Smile.* Sounds simple, but a smile can put people at ease and change a stilted conversation into a comfortable one. Smiling at appropriate times shows the speaker you are listening to what she's saying.

- *Don't relax too much.* If your mind tends to wander the more comfortable you get, you'll need to sit up straight or move to the edge of your seat.

- *Take notes on key points.* Write down key words or phrases from the conversation, particularly if they are points you need to act upon. They should serve as reminders of what the speaker is promoting, selling, or advancing.

- *Listen with your ears, your body, and your heart.* Sit close enough so you can hear everything that's being said. Show by body language that you are listening. Be compassionate, particularly if the speaker is discussing a personal issue. Put yourself in the speaker's position and make it easier for her to talk to you.

Presentation Skills

With today's modern technology, producing readable slides, overheads, graphs, and other visual aids is a snap. However, there is a major difference between quality presentation materials and a quality presentation. Pursuing better speaking and presentation styles is valuable in every position you will ever hold. A speech course can help here, in addition to these tips:

- *Organize your thoughts by making an outline.* This sounds like elementary school, but is essential to keeping your presentation on target.

- *Limit your material to no more than 8–12 minutes.* Any longer and you have people snoozing in the rear. More than 20 minutes, and they'll openly snore in the front row.

- *Use effective graphics.* Anything flashed on a screen should have no more than 8–10 words and be readable from the last row. How many times have you sat through a presentation in which endless tables, spreadsheets, or full pages of text are projected on the screen and can only be read by the presenter? Then you turn around and do the exact same thing. Have someone project each piece while you sit as far away as you can. If you can't read it, don't show it.

- *Don't hand out printed material* before you are ready to speak about it. This is a classic taught in Education 101. The reason? People will be reading page 14 while you are talking about the material on page 6.

- *Practice, practice, practice.* You have to practice every presentation, even if you are doing it in the taxi on the way to the meeting. Make your family your audience. If you can't keep the people who love you listening, how can you keep the people who don't?

- *Take questions only after you have completed a presentation.* Let the audience know that you'll answer questions when you are finished.

- *Move around.* Walk around the room, keeping eye contact with a variety of people. Use a cordless mike if speaking to a large room. Speakers who stand like statues are ignored like statues, except by roosting pigeons, and we know what they do, don't we?

- *Don't try to be humorous* unless it's your natural style. We're not all Jay Lenos. Jokes, unless they are well told, are a speaking disaster.

- *Use a flip chart.* Have an assistant write down key issues as they are discussed, or prepare the chart in advance. Remember: Print big so that everyone can read it. Also: write in upper and lower case letters. Don't use all upper case letters or script. Mixed case print is much easier to read.

- *Use an easy-to-read, large, bold type* font on all presentation materials. Again: Use upper and lower case type. Print should be black. Reversed type is hard to read. Yellow, orange, red, or other pale colors do not make for good reading either. If they did, this book would be printed in one of those colors, wouldn't it?

- *Do a wrap-up of key points* at the end of your presentation. Don't say, "in conclusion," because you'll lose everyone before the last syllable is out of your mouth. End with "Thank you."

Computer and team-building skills have already been discussed thoroughly, so we'll leave it at this: Learn to use a computer. Become a team player. That's all, folks!

DEVELOPING A JOB OUTLOOK FOCUSED ON YOU

"Do you feel you're at a crisis point in your life? When written in Chinese, the word *crisis* is composed of two characters. One represents danger, the other opportunity. Recognize that you can choose to succumb to the danger by letting circumstances control you, and end up feeling hurt, depressed, angry, or powerless. Or, you can embrace the opportunity and use this time to seek a more dynamic future," says Donna MacDougall Ferris in "Don't Let a Job Loss Knock You Off Your Feet."

A company or corporation will not take responsibility for your success, your future, or your retirement. Only you can look out for yourself. While loyalty is admirable, loyalty to yourself and your family is more so. Don't sacrifice the ultimate good of yourself and your family for the promise of a fancy title, corner office, and a silver BMW.

Evaluating What a Job Offers

You've been offered a new position. It's sounds wonderful, and you're seriously thinking of accepting. Stop! Before you take a job, consider both the positives and negatives of the offer. What does it pay—and what will it cost? Costs include family time, personal time, pressure and stress, travel, and so on. What will you gain—and sacrifice? What can you learn—and is it worth it? Is the title real or a fabrication? Will this job help you reach your goal?

Here are a few more things to think about before you take the job:

- *How do the people dress?* Is the dress casual or business attire? Are you going to have to go into debt in order to dress for work?

- *Who's in which office?* Are the enclosed offices only for men, while the cubicles house women?

- *What is the general age makeup?* Is there a potential for you to make personal friends among the other employees? Is friendship in the workplace a concern for you?

- *What is the normal pace of work?* Do people seem relaxed or harried? Ask people about their workload. If several say that Tuesday is slow, but Thursday is hectic, ask to come back and visit on Thursday.

- *What is the attitude of employees?* If you don't have a chance to talk to people in private, ask about employee turnover. In mid- to high-paying positions, high turnover rates could indicate unhappy personnel.

- *What is the company's take on teamwork,* recognition, its mission?

- *What do customers say about the company?* This is particularly important if you deal with the public.

- *What benefits are you entitled to?* Are they equal to the benefits available to someone else who is doing a comparable job? Will you get a bonus? If you need childcare, what provisions are available?

Many jobs sound like a great deal before and turn out to be nothing more than spun sugar after. Titles can be misleading. In an effort to make a corporation look diverse or equal opportunity, everyone, including a janitor, will have

CAREER UPGRADE MAGAZINES

Business Week

Forbes

Fortune

Money

Working Woman

"Things may come to those who wait, but only the things left by those who hustle."

—*Abraham Lincoln*

"manager" attached to her position. Look at the meat of the job—what you'll do, who you'll do it with, the level of responsibility, the intrinsic opportunity (learning, growth, experience), and the pay. Notice that pay comes last. No amount of money will make a job you hate worthwhile.

The job, whatever it is, meets the criteria you have set for yourself. It moves you up a rung on your personal success ladder. Take it. The job, whatever it is, falls far short of your needs. Pass it by. Just evaluate carefully before you do either. Success can only come to those who strive for it, not to those who settle for second best.

CHAPTER RECAP

- Lateral moves offer variety without endangering partially-vested retirement funds.

- Work on projects outside of your department.

- You can expand the scope of your work by using what you know to create new jobs, like teaching a course or adding new responsibilities to what you do now.

- Consulting and freelancing open new doors and add money to the family coffers. Just be sure you don't have a conflict of interest that will cause you to lose your regular job.

Recommended Reading

Anderson, Walter. *The Confidence Course.* New York:HarperCollins, 1997.

Bick, Julie. *All I Really Need to Know in Business I Learned at Microsoft.* New York: Pocket Books, 1997.

Celente, Gerald. *Trends 2000: How to Prepare for and Profit from the Changes of the 21st Century.* New York: Warner Books, 1997.

Donaldson, Michael C., and Mimi Donaldson. *Negotiating for Dummies.* Foster City, CA: IDG Books Worldwide, 1996.

A Volatile Environment

*T*oday's business world is as volatile as Kilauea on a bad lava day. The only defense against being swept up by the negative flow is to be prepared. This doesn't mean quaking in fear of the next layoff. Worry is a waste of energy. Take a proactive approach to your career and be prepared to make a change if you need to.

Today's job market has all the stability of a Jell-O mold. For some, that is a source of fear. For you, it's a source of opportunity.

What? Opportunity? When my company is floating belly-up in the economic pond?

Yes, opportunity. Maybe not the safe, secure, work-in-the-same-office-until-the-plaster-cracks job of the '50s you'd like to have. This opportunity is more like hopping in a Formula I race car and entering the Grand Prix at LeMans: speed, risk, challenge, curves and twists, competition sneaking up behind you, accidents to avoid, and an occasional pit stop for new tires and a gulp of Gatorade. It's exciting, energizing, and, admittedly, awe-inspiring. You know that in today's workplace there are going to be shining stars, and one of them might as well be you.

Darrell Simms, in *Black Experience Strategies and Tactics in the Business World,* offers his view of what's in store in the year 2000: "We are now on the brink of something big! What is it? Opportunity! From now until the year 2000, the U.S. work force is going to turn to the African-American professional as well as to other minorities and women to bolster the work force. These jobs will demand high skill levels."

Service industries, such as health care, foodservice, computer service and outsourced "corporate" departments (accounting, benefits, personnel, information management) are the job base of the future. If you are currently in a service-based position, develop job-related skills to their maximum. If you are not, look at service-based jobs that parallel your present position and work to build a service orientation into your profile.

For an entire generation we sneered at skilled tradesmen as blue-collar jobs that required manual labor. Plumbers, electricians, carpenters, and other craftsmen sent their children to college to "escape" from the stigma of working with one's hands. Those skills are service-related, and, for those who think they don't pay well, guess again. Today, lawyers are a dime a dozen, you can get a doctor's appointment within an hour or two of calling, but a plumber has a waiting list. If skilled trades are open to you, don't frown on getting your hands dirty. It's honest work and can lead to big success.

Back at the corporation, keep on top of company politics, understand the need for mergers and acquisitions (and their effect on employees), and rise above adverse situations; these are key elements of getting ahead—SuccessThink. To succeed in a volatile environment, you must keep in touch with the ebb and flow of today's business trends.

TODAY'S JOB MARKET

Here are a few facts that characterize big business in the '90s:

- In early 1994 more than 3,100 workers were dismissed each day across the United States. Eighty-five percent of Fortune 500 firms cut twenty-five percent of their workforce.

- Headlines from major US newspapers:

  "AT&T Offers Buyouts to 78,000 Managers, Half of Its Supervising Work Force"

  "GM Plans Layoffs of 74,000 Workers over Four Years"

  "Ford Announced 9000 Layoffs, Ranging from One Week to Indefinitely"

  "Boeing Fires or Retires 51,000 since 1989"

- Between October and December 1996, there were 1,802 mass layoff actions by employers, resulting in the separation of nearly 400,000 workers. *Bureau of Labor Statistics, "Mass Layoffs Summary."*

- Total layoffs in 1996: roughly 1,108,000 employees. *Bureau of Labor Statistics, "Mass Layoffs Summary."*

- States with the largest numbers of layoffs: California, Wisconsin, Illinois, Pennsylvania, Ohio, Texas. These states accounted for 64% of all layoffs. *Bureau of Labor Statistics, "Mass Layoffs Summary."*

- Firms increasing training budgets after announcing layoffs were twice as likely to report improved profits and productivity as ones that didn't. Study by *Money Magazine, 1996*

Ouch! Buzzwords fly—downsizing, right-sizing, restructuring, re-engineering. Jobs are cut to "trim the fat."

You are on your own. This point can't be emphasized too strongly—the only person really watching out for you and your career is you. So, what do you do?

THE WAYS AND MEANS OF BIG BUSINESS

The primary trends affecting businesses today are merging and divesting; international marketing and manufacturing; just in time inventories; low-cost production; cash flow and financial management; and reducing overhead, personnel, and benefits expenses.

- *Merging and divesting.* Sara Lee Corporation has sewn up the U.S. market on hot dogs and pantyhose. You buy dog biscuits, Lifesavers, and Oreos from the same company. At the same time, corporations divest themselves of unprofitable companies like pawns sacrificed on a chessboard. This trend will continue into and beyond the year 2000. You can not count on the company you work for even being in existence five years from now. What you can count on is that if have the skills and talents needed in the future, you will be employed.

> IBM'S BASIC BELIEFS:
>
> *Service: The best service organization in the world.*
> *People: Respect for the dignity of the individual.*
> *Excellence: Set high standards and strive for superior performance in all undertakings.*

- *International manufacturing.* There is no such thing as a local or regional corporation anymore. Your Japanese car is assembled in Kentucky of parts manufactured in Mexico. Major U.S. corporations have plants in Vietnam, Thailand,

Argentina, Brazil—just about anywhere where labor is inexpensive. It is cheaper to produce a pair of sneakers in Vietnam and ship them to Los Angeles than it is to make them in L.A. and truck them across the street.

- *International marketing.* The corporate defense against the imbalance of trade is to sell whatever the global market loves about America to non-Americans. You can buy a Coke and a Big Mac and settle back to catch a three-year old episode of Baywatch in Moscow or Sri Lanka or South Korea. Even the worst film put out this year by American filmmakers will be sold internationally for as much as half a million dollars. Your own company may want to take its products to the international marketplace. If so, be prepared to take part in the move. Take a Berlitz course in Japanese, Thai, or Hindi. Keep your passport up to date.

- *Just-in-time inventories.* No manufacturer today has a big inventory just sitting in hopes of being sold. At least, no profitable manufacturer. Consider BMW's premier American plant in Greer, South Carolina. BMW electronically transmits its order for axles to Lemforder, a German corporation with an American plant only three miles from BMW. Lemforder immediately makes the axles required in the sequence required (there are almost a dozen varieties of axle available) for BMW's line. A few hours later, BMW sends a truck to pick up the current batch of axles. Later in the day, they are already being installed in the cars. No inventory is stored at either location. If your company is plagued by high inventory levels, this may be an area you can address to help increase profitability.

"Mergers will work only when a Goliath learns to operate like a David—without becoming one."

—Deb Talbot,
Talbot and Associates

"Headhunters don't find jobs for people; they're paid to find people for jobs."

—*Nick A. Corcodilos,*
"The Secret to Finding a
Good Headhunter"

- *Low-cost production.* Low-cost production is not "cheap" production. This simply means getting the appropriate ingredients, supplies, or parts at the best possible price to make a product to be sold at the optimum, competitive price point.

- *Cash flow and financial management.* You work in Georgia and your paycheck is cut from Oregon? You purchase goods that are delivered within three days, and the supplier's invoice sits in accounts payable for 60 days before being paid? One way corporations add to their bottom line is by keeping their cash flow under control. It's all very logical: Soybean futures drop to an all-time low. You purchase three times the amount of mayonnaise your company normally sells in two months. It's delivered on Monday. You run a buy-one-get-one-free sale, and all the product is sold within two weeks at a substantial profit. Before you pay for that mayonnaise, you can put those profits to work for you for a good 45 days. Those MBAs are clever, aren't they?

- *Reducing overhead, personnel, and benefits expenses.* There is nothing quite like sitting next to the VP of Whatever during the annual benefits meeting. He tells you about his trip to Aruba. You listen to the HR rep explain that only 40% of your medical and dental insurance will now be covered by the company—your share of the premium will jump to $112 per month. VP tells you about his new Lexus

---

STALKING HEADHUNTERS

Not used to dealing with headhunters? Here are three rules that will help:

1. *The first rule is never say never to headhunters. Business is changing so fast that the job you love today may be entirely different tomorrow. Talk to them—nicely.*
2. *Second, get your resumé into the headhunting firm's databank. This way the searchers—and their clients—will know you.*
3. *Third, and most important: Actively manage your career and don't count on your employer to do it for you.*

(Source: Marshall Loeb, "What to Do When a Headhunter Calls")

company car, while HR explains that the company's had a bad year and, unfortunately, a major layoff will take place on the first.

When Downsizing Doesn't Work

The funny thing about all these layoffs, cost-cutting and belt-tightening is that it doesn't always work. According to studies reported in the May 1996 issue of *Money*, the average downsized company's stock was up only 4.7% after three years. Similar companies with fewer job cuts typically reported 34.3% increases for the same time period. A second study reported in the same issue found that firms increasing training budgets after announcing layoffs were twice as likely to report improved profits and productivity as ones that didn't.

Gauge Your Company's Financial Health   EXERCISE

Investigate your company's past financial history and see how earnings are trending. If you are working for a publicly traded company, check out the previous five years' annual reports. Gather information on number of employees, net earnings, stock values, mergers, and acquisitions. Is your company financially healthy? If not, don't wait to be the last rat left on the sinking ship. If your company is financially stable, and you're happy, rest easy.

How Headhunters Fit into Your Strategy

Be prepared to jump on any opportunity, particularly if it comes from a headhunter. The question is, how do you get noticed by a headhunter? According to Marshall Loeb, "You have to get in a position where you run something, where you can show demonstrable results. If you can't make the next step up, you have to agitate for your company to move you around to new jobs—the trendy term is broad banding."

You need to understand the headhunter's role in finding you a new job. He doesn't. He's got a job that needs filling, and he's hoping you might be the one to fill it. He also serves as a link between the employer and the hoping-to-be employed. Gary Ethan Klein explains, "Headhunters can, and often do, explain and add to the information contained on resumés and see to it that the proper person reviews the submission. Perhaps your resumé needs to be tailored to the specific needs of a particular search; emphasizing work you have done that you neglected to include."

IF THE WORST HAPPENS

The CFO of PCA, Inc. once said that in the 70s, he could count the number of people he knew who'd been laid off on one hand. By the mid-80s, he said he could now count those who had never been laid off on that same hand. Considering the statistics, it's highly likely that at some point you'll be faced with the opportunity to find other employment. There are two sides to "the worst." First, there are those who have to find a new job. Second, there are those who, in addition to the job they already have, will be doing the work you just left. Both sides are difficult, and, if you manage a department of those who were kept, don't expect a smooth ride. The pink slips have gone out; the survivors are still shaking.

David Noer points out the emotional component of these changes: "The harsh reality of the new psychological contract is that many 'family' members are no longer cared for and are treated as dispensable commodities. . . . Survivors of corporate layoffs—managers and employees alike—need to recognize their feelings of anger, fear, guilt, depression and distrust."

As a manager, what should you do to reassure your people? Survivors strive to get their work lives back under control. They want to know that the lunch in the cafeteria will still be served next week, and that their paychecks will still come on Thursday. They realize that changes have been made. Just because they didn't get the ax doesn't mean they are not affected.

There are several important internal steps managers should take after a layoff: Communication, assurance, reassignment of tasks, and management visibility.

Communicate all information you have that's accurate. Ask department personnel to come to you about rumors, concerns, and questions. Have regular meetings to keep personnel abreast of anything new or different. Let everyone know that Kathy will handle Sam's workload, Angela now reports to Frank, and any other changes that affect the smooth operation of the department.

Assurance is essential for people whose security has been given a jolt. Explain the reasons behind the layoff, what the company hopes to accomplish, and that you know (if it's true) that they are safe in their jobs.

Re-assign workloads immediately. People need to know what their responsibilities are, and you need to know that nothing is falling between the cracks. Ask department members to update you on any projects in the works.

Visibility is a key element of stability. When people are under stress, they need to know that management is forging ahead. You need to be there for your people. Keep your door open and a smile on your face.

What to Do When You've Lost Your Job

- *Calm down.* It could be worse. You could still be working for those people who don't want you.

- *Call unemployment* and learn your rights regarding Unemployment Compensation. In some states, you

"Humans must breathe, but corpora-tions must make money."

—*Alice Embree, "Media Images I: Madison Avenue Brainwashing— the Facts," from* Sisterhood Is Powerful, *1970*

can collect unemployment and severance pay at the same time. If so, bank the unemployment for future lean months. And, don't forget: you have to pay income tax on that money.

- *Read over every piece of paper handed to you by HR*—after you've calmed down and before you sign anything. Don't automatically assume that the deal you've gotten is the final word, and don't sign unless you are comfortable with what's been offered.

- *Check on all forms of insurance* you have through your company: LTD, Life, Health, etc. Can you continue them, and at what cost? Do some comparison shop-ping. If you get a better deal through the company, then keep up the payments on your own or negoti-ate the insurance into the package.

- *Ask for what you want.* Consider what's impor-tant to you: longer severance, outplacement, retraining, etc.

- *Call other people* who've been laid off by your com-pany in the past couple of years and ask them what kind of deal they got. Make sure in a situation where you get apples that the other guys didn't get the plums.

- *Ask what other services* your company might provide: resumé writing, printing or copying, long distance phone.

- *Check references.* You may be asked to sign a sheet giving permission to the company that just let you go to give a reference to future employers. Think very carefully about whether to agree that your for-mer company can give a reference about you. Usually, you'll be asked to authorize tenure of job, performance, attendance, etc. Only allow tenure of job. Get your own references about your performance and be selective in whom you choose.

- *Start making a list* from your Rolodex, club associations, professional organizations of people you know and can contact.

- *Have a business card printed* with your name and phone number. This can be done cheaply at any quick-print company. Keep a supply of cards with you wherever you go—including the barbershop, the supermarket, and the hardware store. When you meet people, give them your card and tell them you are looking for a new position.

- *Arrange to have family medical and dental care* attended to while your insurance is still in effect.

- *Smile.* You've just been given a chance to succeed where you might not have before—and if you have good severance, you are doing it at someone else's expense.

Keep Your Eyes Open

It is impossible to be blindsided if you are keeping a close eye on how your company's performance matches up to its competition. Whether you are a man or woman, be a Boy Scout. Be prepared. Then, it won't matter whether you are laid off or kept on, you'll handle the situation professionally.

CHAPTER RECAP

- Even the most dismal economic profile has opportunity for the person who looks for it.

- Today's business environment is rife with mergers, acquisitions, downsizing, international marketing, and other means of creating larger profits.

- Downsizing doesn't always land a company in the black.

- Never, ever tell a headhunter you are not interested.

- If you lose your job, all is not lost. There are a dozen things for you to do to get yourself back in the ranks of the employed.

Recommended Reading

Celente, Gerald. *Trends 2000: How to Prepare for and Profit from the Changes of the 21st Century.* New York: Warner Books, 1997.

Fisher, Lionel L. *On Your Own.* Englewood Cliffs, NJ: Prentice Hall, 1995.

Frost, Ted S. *The Second Coming of the Woolly Mammoth.* Berkeley, CA: Ten Speed Press, 1991.

Gibbons, Barry. *This Indecision Is Final.* Burr Ridge, IL: Irwin Professional Publishing, 1996.

Hochheiser, Robert M. *If You Want Guarantees, Buy a Toaster.* New York: William Morrow, 1991.

Pascale, Richard Tanner. *Managing on the Edge.* New York: Simon & Schuster, 1990.

Resumés, Interviews, on the Hunt

*W*hy bother to keep your resumé up to date? The answer is simple: You never know where the next opportunity is going to come from. Be prepared—an up-to-date resumé could be the key that opens that next door to success.

Besides, rewriting your resumé is like doing a job evaluation. You consider your accomplishments, weigh their importance and get a comprehensive picture of your triumphs. If nothing else, it should be an ego boost. It could also be an eye-opener if you haven't revamped your resumé in three years and have little new to add—get busy! You're in a rut and need to restructure your outlook and efforts.

Resumés, like ties, go in and out of style. Today's resumés must be focused, disciplined, and targeted. Today's job market is intense, and a top-notch resumé is a prerequisite for daily business living—even for those who are not looking for a job. Resumés are a "first contact" tool; crafted wisely, they can lead to a "second contact" or even a job.

IN THIS CHAPTER:

- *Tips on how to write a good resumé*

- *Resumé presentation ideas*

- *Keyword, functional, and targeted resumés*

- *Identifying job alternatives*

SAMPLE RESUMÉ

Alice Barr Cole
103 Deadwood Drive
Everywhere, NY 10101
914-555-8662 FAX: 914-555-2610

Summary

Creative, cost-effective, targeted writing and editing with 20+ years experience in all forms of written communication. Principal focus on education and training. Extensive background in primary and secondary education, curriculum development, corporate and small business training and marketing, and magazine editing/publishing.

Experience
1994–present

Cole Inc., Everywhere, NY
Video scriptwriting, magazine journalism, modular education programs, brochure copy, public relations, marketing plans, promotional materials. Scriptwriting principally for education, healthcare, and corporate/small business clients.

1988–1994

King Dairies, Inc., Someplace, NY
• Editor and publisher of The Big Cheese, a 6x yearly, full color dairy industry magazine, generating a $200K profit annually.
• Initiated and managed in-house agency which produced 100+ advertising/merchandising/marketing projects yearly—all on time and on budget.

1986–1988

Caraglow, Inc., Greenville, SC. Textile Manufacturer.
Produced copywriting, public relations, product introduction materials, trade show planning and execution, and sales support materials; all projects on time, on budget, and on target for double digit sales increases.

1985–1986

AdMakers, Inc., Topeka, KS. Advertising Agency. Copywriter.

1974–1985

Freelance investigative journalist in Sydney, Australia.

Education

Upstate University, Catskills, NY. BA/English
New England School of Marketing, Middle, MA. MA/Journalism

Professional
Affiliations

NAFE, Who's Who in American Women

References

References will be provided on request.

HOW TO WRITE A RESUMÉ

There are dozens of good books on the market explaining how to write a standard resumé. If you're not sure how to go about it and need a detailed version, pick up a manual at your public library. The basic, traditional format is chronological, showing your most recent job first. The resumé should include:

- Your name, address, and phone number, placed at the top and usually centered.

- Next, write your objective or summary, the type or style of job you are seeking. This is left justified.

- Next follows job experience: the dates of employment, the job title, employer, location and a few brief comments covering accomplishments achieved during your tenure. Entries are in chronologically descending order.

- Add education, professional affiliations, honors, and pertinent training.

- Follow that by "References will be provided upon request."

While this information provides the format, it doesn't include the pizzazz you'll need to separate your resumé from the hundreds of others sitting on the HR director's desk. You want to punch up your resumé so that you'll make the short list and get an interview. To do this, fine tune your written material to meet these criteria:

- Choose a fine quality paper—25% cotton bond, heavy weight, bright white, white, or ivory. Don't use a colored or textured paper.

- Use a common, readable type font—Times Roman or Century Schoolbook are common. If you prefer a *sans serif* font, use something like Helvetica or

"Two words describe a good handshake: brief and firm. It is a clasping of hands and holding of that position for a brief moment. . . . That second or two, is extremely significant."

—*J. Robert Parkinson,*
How to Get People to
Do Things Your Way

Ariel. Do not use cursive, ornate, or decorative fonts. If you don't have a computer or laser printer to create a quality look, go to a quick-print shop like Kinko's and have them typeset your resumé for you.

- Your resumé must be accompanied by a cover letter. In the letter include how you heard about the position, why you are interested, a few lines about your qualifications, and close with a commitment to follow up your letter. The letter, envelope, and resumé should all be on the same paper stock. Have your resumé printed (or copied) in black ink.

- Follow a standard, easy to read format. This is not the time to show your creativity. Boldface type, italics, illustrations, and underlining should be used sparingly if at all. Do not use all capital letters except in single- or two-word headers.

- If you have a laser printer and word processing capabilities, revamp your objective every time you send a resumé. While you might think this is cheating, it isn't. Mark has five different resumés and matching project lists that he sends to potential clients. Educational publishers want to know his education experience; business publishers want to know his business experience. They want to buy bananas, and he sells what they want. That doesn't mean Mark doesn't also have apples, pears, and the occasional papaya for sale. Hone your resumé to suit the prospective employer and the job available.

- Make sure the employer understands the job you want and why you should be hired.

- Punch up the verbiage with active, positive, promotional words. Your resumé is your advertisement. Sell yourself with dignity, but sell yourself, nonetheless.

Remember, you don't sell the steak, you sell the sizzle. Support your information with facts, data, and details. Don't say: Responsible for a large sales territory. Do say: Expanded sales within my territory to $4.6 million, an increase of 18% over the previous year.

- Send the cover letter and resumé to a specific person. If you don't know a specific name, call the switchboard and ask who's in charge of XYZ.

- Make sure your package is totally professional, polished and error-free. It should be neat and readable and no longer than two pages. One page is ideal, two are acceptable, and three keep you on the unemployment line.

RESUMÉ TIPS FROM THE PROS

Here are a few extra tips from a variety of knowledgeable sources:

- *State specific objectives.* Employers like to know what you want from a career and where you expect to go. Stating specific objectives lets them know you are following a plan, not just waffling.

- *Make a good first impression.* Your resumé is you on paper. This is the first chance you have to say, "Hello, I'm Dave." Make your first impression a good one.

- *Emphasize skills, talents.* In today's frenetic job market, employers want to know you are multi-talented, versatile, flexible, competent to handle more than one task. Make sure your resumé covers your primary skills.

- *Use industry jargon.* Let the employer know that you are conversant with the industry, product, and workings of your job.

*"Believe in life!
Always, human beings
will live and progress
to a greater, broader,
and fuller life."*

—*W. E. B. DuBois*

- *Show consistency in your work history.* If you have major gaps that you filled with small, part-time jobs, give a quick list of those jobs so the employer knows you weren't just sitting around watching *Oprah* for seven months.

- *Choose the resumé format that will give best results.* Work up several styles of resumés—chronological, functional, targeted—and send the one that best suits the job offered.

- *Bypassing HR actually works.* Although HR departments grit their teeth when circumvented, do it anyway. The VP or director of your future department will be the one who actually says "yea" or "nay," so make sure you are known to her.

- *Salary requirements.* Here's employment quicksand! You're too high, you have no chance. If you're too low, you cheat yourself. It's best to give no price, and just say in your cover letter "salary is negotiable."

- *You must market yourself.* Sell yourself aggressively in your resumé.

- *Words and phrases to use.* High-profile, high-visibility, catalyst, high-caliber, proactive, pioneered, created, transitioned, orchestrated, redesigned, drove, improved.

- *Present your best side.* Be assertive. Be confident. Be focused. Be honest.

KEYWORD, FUNCTIONAL, OR TARGETED RESUMÉS

The standard resumé may work well if you move from one job to another job in the same town. It no longer meets the demands of the computer age, where resumés are scanned for placement on a database. Once on-line, searchers review resumés by sorting through keywords that sift viable candidates from the slag heap.

"In order to satisfy the idiosyncrasies of the scanning process, a new resumé style, utilizing keywords, has developed. Key Words refer to those words or phrases that are used for searches of databases for resumés that match. This match is called a hit and occurs when one or more resumés are selected as matching the criteria used in the search," says Wayne M. Gonyea, author of "Keyword Resumés— Your New Hi-Tech Way to Get a Job!"

Keywords are usually nouns or noun phrases: Quality Circle Leader, UNIX, Financial Analyst, Researcher, Credit Manager.

You'll need to have two resumés: the kind that goes on the Internet (Keyword) and the kind that gets read by

KEYWORD RESUMÉ SAMPLE

JANE SMITH JONES—INFORMATION SYSTEMS MANAGER
432 Maple Dr.
Smalltown, SC 29666
864-555-3579

SYSOP, SYSTEMS ADMINISTRATOR, MANAGER INFORMATION SYSTEMS, SYSTEMS ANALYST, UNIX, DATABASE FORMULATION, PROGRAM ENGINEER, SYSTEMS ENGINEER

Summary: Results-oriented professional with administration, analysis, and management experience with mid-sized to large corporations.

Supervising: operations; programming; program analysis; systems analysis; program design; computer engineering; strategic planning.

Excellent interpersonal skills, team player, leadership skills. High-caliber presentation skills, project management, trouble-shooting, and mentoring.

(The remainder reads much like a standard resumé, detailing job history, dates, and accomplishments.)

the average HR department or business executive (Chronological, Functional, Targeted). In addition to the standard time-oriented format, functional and targeted resumés may give you an advantage in the job market.

A functional resumé highlights the tasks, skills, and abilities of an applicant, rather than relating job experience in chronological order. One reason to use a functional resumé is to play down any gaps in the chronology of your employment history. Another reason is if you are trying to change careers. If you are an English teacher and want to get a job as an advertising copywriter, a functional resumé will work better for you.

A functional resumé format is set up as follows:

- Name, address, phone number at the top of the page, either centered or left justified.

- The functions or tasks performed, all caps, left justified.

- Below each function, list related experience. This experience does not have to be linked to a specific employer or time frame.

- Include education, additional training, additional skills, and employment history toward the bottom.

EXERCISE   *Writing a Functional Resumé*

Write a "Functional" resumé for yourself. You will need a minimum of three functional areas, with supporting facts for each. Follow the format in the sample.

Targeted resumés identify the exact job you are looking for as part of your resumé. They feature a series of capabilities, skills, and achievements. These are things you can do, whether you can back them up with the specific job or not. A targeted resumé format is set up as follows:

FUNCTIONAL RESUMÉ SAMPLE

Jane Smith-Jones
432 Maple Dr.
Smalltown, OR 89898
555-555-3579

TEACHING:

- Developed and implemented anti-drug curriculum in five regional elementary schools.

- Instructed community volunteers in anti-drug program presented at 73 regional elementary and middle schools.

- Ran workshops for parents on drug abuse among children.

- Instructed public school teachers on recognizing signs of drug abuse among elementary students.

ORGANIZATION:

- Coordinated actions of forty volunteers for Just Say No week.

- Enlisted support of over 100 community businesses for Just Say No week.

- Developed proposal to local government for working with police and social service agency in dealing with local drug-related crime.

VOLUNTEER WORK HISTORY:

1993–Present	Small County Drug Abuse Hot Line
1990–1996	Southeast Oregon Parents Against Drug Abuse, Coordinator
1986–1997	Small County Parents & Teachers Against Drug Abuse, President, 1992–1995

EDUCATION:

1983	B. S. Psychology, Saint Lawrence University, Canton, NY

- Name, address, phone number at the top, centered or left-justified.

- The exact job target you are aiming for.

- A list of your capabilities, headed by CAPABILITIES in all caps.

- A list of your achievements, headed by ACHIEVEMENTS in all caps.

- Chronological work history, from most recent to the past.

- Education.

HI-TECH TECHNIQUES FOR KEEPING ABREAST OF OPPORTUNITIES

Using the Internet to investigate today's job market is too new to be documented as successful. However, it must work—everybody's doing it. You can—and should—access the job-surfing network. The jobs available cover all fields, all regions, and even international business opportunities.

When using the Internet, you will have to either enter your resumé into the computer or have it scanned. Either way, it will become part of one or more databases, and you will need to produce a keyword resumé. To enhance scanability, follow these tips:

- Don't use lines or borders.

- Don't use boldface, italics, underlining.

- Use a large, clear, sans serif type style like Avant Garde or Helvetica Regular.

- Leave big margins, 1" to 1.25" should do it.

- Use white or ivory paper—no colors.

TARGETED RESUMÉ SAMPLE

Jane Smith-Jones
432 Maple Dr.
Smalltown, OR 89898
555-555-3579

JOB TARGET: Administrator, Small County Drug Rehabilitation Program

CAPABILITIES:

- Instruct large groups.
- Plan and implement long-term programs.
- Recognize and handle drug-related situations.
- Manage an extensive budget.
- Coordinate public and private sector efforts.

ACHIEVEMENTS:

- Developed and implemented anti-drug curriculum in five regional elementary schools.
- Instructed community volunteers in anti-drug program presented at 73 regional elementary and middle schools.
- Ran workshops for parents on drug abuse among children.
- Instructed public school teachers on recognizing signs of drug abuse among elementary students.
- Coordinated actions of forty volunteers for Just Say No week.
- Enlisted support of over 100 community businesses for Just Say No week.
- Developed proposal to local government for working with police and social service agency in dealing with local drug-related crime.

VOLUNTEER WORK HISTORY:

1993–Present	Small County Drug Abuse Hot Line
1990–1996	Southeast Oregon Parents Against Drug Abuse, Coordinator

EDUCATION:

1983	B.S. Psychology, Saint Lawrence University, Canton, NY

- Use black ink.

- Left justify document.

- Avoid tabs and hard returns.

- Avoid parentheses and brackets.

- Do not fax.

EXERCISE	*Writing a Keyword Resumé*

Write a keyword resumé for yourself. Follow the sample in the previous section. Use the formatting tips given earlier.

Be aware that job seeking on the Web has its drawbacks. Your resumé, once on-line, is fully public and can be accessed by thousands of people. Don't put anything in it that you don't want everyone to see—like your salary.

THE HUNT

You're in the hunt, either by choice or necessity. You've worked up both keyword and chronological resumés. You have your paper stock for cover letters. You're surfing the net and pounding the touch-tone buttons. And you still have no luck. How is this possible? Here are some job hunting facts you should know:

- *Over 85% of job vacancies are not available through traditional resources* like newspaper ads, civil service notices, or employment agencies. You have a better chance through networking. Answer all the ads you like, but also call at least five people each day to network for a new job.

- *Outplacement services don't find a job for you.*
  They help you prepare to find your own job.
  They'll give you resumé tips, interviewing tips,

support staff, and all the materials you need to do your own job search. If outplacement costs are coming out of your own pocket, evaluate what you are really getting.

• *Less than 7% of all professional, managerial, and executive positions are listed with employment agencies.* That doesn't mean that promotions all come from within. Many upper management types are hired away from other companies, which explains why you need to keep your industry network buzzing.

• *Employment agencies, recruiters, and headhunters are not working for you.* They are working for a company to fill a specific job. They are paid by the company to find the right person and will be interested in you only if they have a position that you can fill.

• *The chances are good that you'll lose your job.* In the past ten years, more than half a million middle and upper managers lost their jobs. Don't wait until you do to get yourself out in the job market. It's always easier to get a new job if you have a job than if you're unemployed.

• *Be patient.* If you are unemployed, it takes roughly one month per $10,000 salary to find a comparable job. Recent studies show that a middle management job search lasts 7.4 months on average.

• *Use temp agencies.* Providers like Manpower, Adia, or Kelly, for example, are an excellent way to try on a job and a company without being permanently committed. It's also an superb "in" with the employer if you perform well. And, yes, they do have management-level temp positions.

ALTERNATIVE JOB SOURCES

The federal government is a massive employer. True, the pay isn't as great as in the private sector, but the benefits are terrific. You must pass a Civil Service test to be employed. Once you are eligible to be hired, you will be ranked according to regulations and referred for appointment to a position. For the real world, this is a candidate list. The feds call it a certificate. You will also be given bio-data testing—a personnel measurement technique that is useful in tapping motivational, attitudinal, and intellectual characteristics.

While all this seems tedious, Civil Servants get lots of holidays, good vacations, health packages, retirement plans and, usually, job security. There are also what the feds call Critical Shortage Occupations—occupations where there are too few qualified candidates to fill vacancies. If you qualify, you are pretty much guaranteed a job. Then, you can legitimately say, "Not bad for government work!"

Working as a temp is another alternative to a "regular" job. Temping is a great way to start working immediately after moving. Manpower and other temp agencies now take on professionals, and there are agencies specifically designed to place tech-temps (technology temporaries). You may get a three-month, six-month, or three-day position. One advantage of going the temp route is that you can check out the local job market as well as any company you get assigned to. Many temp appointments lead to permanent employment, and you have money on which to live in the meantime.

In "Future Resumés and Diversity in the 21st Century Workplace" Pat Heggy says, "At least one study estimates that contingent or non-regular employees will constitute as much as 50% of the work force within ten years." You may need to join the fluctuating work force until a better opportunity comes along.

Avoiding Job Hunt Mistakes

The job hunt is like a SEALS obstacle course: swamp underfoot, bullets flying overhead, and plenty of hard work. You can make the hunt easier if you avoid some of the more obvious pitfalls:

- *Know what kind of job you want* or a direction for your career. You are too old to be saying, "I don't know what I want to be when I grow up." Would you hire anyone who had no idea what to do with himself?

- *Never rely solely on classifieds, executive searches, or direct-mail campaigns* for a job opportunity. It's tough to ask friends, colleagues, and even mere acquaintances to pass the word that you are looking, but that's the most likely path to a new job, so do it.

- *Research the company, job, and industry* before you go for the interview. Go to the library and look up information in the local paper about the company. What is its financial history? What about employment? You should know the principal people and products a company produces before you go for an interview. Otherwise, why are you interviewing with them?

- *Create a resumé that targets the company you want to hire you.* This is simply honing or slanting the material to provide what the customer wants to buy.

- *Don't take a job you don't want.* Life is too short to take a job you will hate or to work for a company you can't abide. Many people struggle for years in dead-end jobs with deadbeat companies, only to discover there were other opportunities they could have taken.

- *Negotiate your hiring package.* Nothing is set in stone except your epitaph. Tell your prospective employer what you want. Be reasonable. When the negotiations reach an end, give your answer.

TRENDS IN INTERVIEWING

Whoopee! You've got an interview for a big job with a huge salary boost. Get the suit pressed. Polish those shoes. Bring a hanky to dry your sweaty palms. Now, prepare to sit and be bombarded with questions you never imagined anyone would ask. Don't waffle, don't lie, don't be nervous, don't giggle, don't defend. And you still think you're getting this job? You will—with some interview tips from the pros!

In an interview, consider all the aspects of your body: your posture, your smile, your eye contact, your handshake, how your speak, what you say, your attention when you listen. You can control an interview by your body language, your attitude, and your personality. Says J. Robert Parkinson in *How to Get People to Do Things Your Way,* "knowing how to control situations and encounters, you'll be able to recognize techniques being employed by others attempting to manipulate and control you. Your movements should be controlled in such a way that you can communicate that you are attentive, active, alert and aggressive."

Here are some tips on successful interviewing:

- *Dress for success.* Suit, tie, shined shoes, and a smile.

- *Relax.* Thumbscrews are out at interviews, so there's nothing to fear. Make the interviewer feel you are enjoying the process, not dreading it.

- *Think first, speak second.* Don't be afraid to say "I don't know" or "I'll have to think more about that before answering."

- *Don't blast your listener* with fifty-cent words. Don't fill your conversation with jargon.

> *"It is better to know some of the questions than all of the answers."*
>
> —*James Thurber*

- *Develop a 60-second sound bite*—and use it. This is a brief synopsis of who you are, what you want, and what you can do. It is a mixture of personal and business information. Practice your sound bite by taping yourself. You'll learn a great deal about yourself.

- *Clean out your ears—then, listen, listen, listen.* An interview is as much for you to learn about the company and people you'll be working with as it is for them to learn about you.

Developing a 60-Second Sound Bite	EXERCISE

Develop a 60-second sound bite. Talk about your work style, the skills you have, and those you want to acquire. Mention your future plans for your career. Bring in your personal life to give yourself a more rounded profile. Sixty seconds is about two-thirds of a page of typed material. Practice your sound bite in front of a mirror. Time yourself. How close did you come to 60 seconds?

Today's business interviewer asks some pretty strange questions. No matter how prepared you are, you'll find yourself wondering what planet you're on when the interviewer asks you how long it would take you to move Mount Everest, how you might sell an Uzi to an old lady in Wichita, or to design an ad selling yourself. According to Nina Munk and Suzanne Oliver, "The gentle job interview is dead. Basing hiring decisions on IQ tests—which the politically correct claim are culturally biased—leaves an employer open to lawsuits. . . . These days companies ask applicants to solve brainteasers and riddles, create art out of paper bags, spend a day acting as managers of make-believe companies and solve complex business problems."

So, how many times would a ping-pong ball bounce if you dropped it off the Empire State Building? The answer to this and other absurdities just might land that next big promotion.

SURFING TO FIND IT

The hiring wave of today and tomorrow is on the Internet. Check out these job-hunting Web sites for tips on resumés and job leads.

The Monster Board: A searchable index of over 40 companies, primarily in the computer industry. On-line resumé, e-mail, employer profiles, job postings. http://www.monster.com

Career Mosaic: A group of 20 large employers with openings listed in a searchable database. Info for job seekers. http://www.careermosaic.com

Jobtrak: Approximately 500 new job listings daily, used by 150,000 employers. Emphasis is on recent college grads or soon-to-be grads. http://www.jobtrak.com

JobBank USA: Database for seekers, recruiters, and employers. On-line resumés, largest job search database. http://www.jobbankusa.com

CareerPath: Job listings from major U.S. newspapers. Search by city, state, or category. http://www.careerpath.com

Career Net: Link to 15,000 jobs, links to career Web sites, regional career resources. http://www.careers.org.

America's Employers: Thousands of job opportunities. Easy to use. http://www.americasemployers.com

CareerWEB: Global recruitment and resource center. Job listings and info from the National Business Employment Weekly. http://www.cweb.com

CHAPTER RECAP

- There are dozens of books about writing resumés. Check out recently published books for current resumé trends.

- Print your resumé on good quality white paper in a neat, readable type font.

- Tailor your resumé to suit the company you are applying to.

- A resumé is you on paper. Make a good first impression.

- Pursue Internet job hunting.

- No matter how abhorrent, use networking to locate jobs. Less than 7% of all professional, managerial, and executive positions are listed with employment agencies. The same goes for newspaper classifieds.

Recommended Reading

Bell, Arthur H. *Great Jobs Abroad.* New York: McGraw-Hill, 1997.

Gonyea, Wayne M. *Keyword Resumés.* On-line Solutions, Inc., 1997.

Heggy, Pat. *Future Resumés and Diversity in the 21st Century Workplace.* Heggy Leadership Enterprises, 1997.

Keying in on Future Work-Related Trends

Not only are jobs changing, the way we work and the places where we work are changing as well. More people work from their homes, their cars, and even their private planes. Technology has changed the need for everyone to be in the same place at the same time. Meetings are convened by video-conferencing; laptops are "standard equipment" in many sales-oriented companies. Welcome to the 21st century.

Muhammed Ali once said "The man who views the world at fifty the same as he did at twenty has wasted thirty years of his life." New viewpoints lead to new directions, and more people are choosing to realign their work lives by employing their business skills in areas that were formerly considered "non-work." Success and opportunity don't only come in a gray pinstriped suit with a Jerry Garcia tie. LINK, a NY-based data group estimates that 39,000,000 Americans currently work alone:

- 12.1 million full-time self-employed homeworkers

- 11.7 million part-time self-employed homeworkers

IN THIS CHAPTER:

- *Identifying alternative work-places and styles*

- *Tips on setting up job sharing*

- *Family v. work—which side is winning*

- *Non-profits—a viable work alternative*

- *Turning hobbies into jobs*

- 6.6 million telecommuters

- 8.6 million corporate after-hours homeworkers.

For those of you who can't imagine not rising at 5:45 a.m., dressing in suits and ties or pantyhose and heels, and commuting for an hour-plus each way to work, here's a surprise. There is another world out there, and you just might like it better than the one you're in right now.

"Beyond talent lie all the usual words: discipline, love, luck— but, most of all, endurance."

—James Baldwin

TELECOMMUTING, FLEXTIME, FLEXSPACE

Flexplace/flexspace could be the answer to burn out. The saying, "A change is as good as a rest," applies to even the most fulfilling career. Also called telecommuting, flexplace gives more and more people the option to work away from the regular office in a home office. This is an alternative to the 8-to-5, in-your-cubicle world of the past. It allows for flexible hours and flexible locations. Some rules and reasons for setting up flexplace/flexspace agreements:

- *Be flexible.* Considering the cost of replacing a quality person, giving latitude about where and when they work makes sense. A new mother or father, an elder-caregiver, or a person with a long-term disability can still contribute.

- *Working at home is quieter,* less hectic, and offers fewer disruptions to the workload. Workers become more productive in a shorter period of time.

- *Management will have to rethink definitions.* It will have to give up the idea that being at work means actually working, while being away from the office is non-productive. Management will look for results, met deadlines, and quality of work rather than an attendance policy.

- *A flex plan that allows two or more people to share one workspace saves money.*

- *Phone, fax, FedEx, or Airborne expenses will have to be covered,* and policies on submitting expenses will have to be spelled out clearly. Will the company pay for fax, extra phone lines, an at-home computer workstation? Make these decisions in advance.

- *Not everyone can be eligible for flexplace work.* Two factors to consider are (1) the employee's ability to work effectively off-site and (2) the employee's connection to the company.

- *Flex people will need to spend time in the office,* attending meetings, updating their supervisors, and so on.

When Craig accepted his job as an editor for a major trade publisher in Boston, he knew that some day he'd be telecommuting. He wouldn't have

SUCCESSTHOUGHTS

Talk to your supervisor about your potential for working in a flex situation. Changing the times you work and/or the place you work can make you more productive and enhance your personal life.

taken the job otherwise. The decision was simple for Craig. New Hampshire offered a better lifestyle and affordable housing; Boston did not. For just over two years, Craig paid his dues, commuting an hour and a half each way, five days a week. Then, it was time for the transition. Now, he goes in once or twice a week, and works out of his home the rest of the time.

Lionel Fisher says, "The virtual office has burst onto the scene. It's not really a place, notes Phil Patton of the *New York Times,* but a nonplace. More of an idea, actually a work style whose time has come. It is the 21st century office, with no particular address, not even parameters."

Telecommuting requires a give and take from management and employee. It also requires equipment—fax, laptop or other computer, modem, extra phone lines into the home, an answering machine and extra phones.

Not everyone can work this way, but perhaps you can. Answer these questions:

- *Does your job require you to interact* regularly in conjunction with other people or are you mostly working by yourself?

- *Is your job location-dictated, time-dictated, or project-dictated?* A secretary, car salesperson, or assembly line worker cannot work away from the office. A writer, graphic designer, or sales representative can.

- *Are you willing to sacrifice office interaction* for peace and quiet? Don't laugh. Some people can't stand the thought of not being around people.

- *Is your company flexible?*

- *Does your supervisor trust you* enough to allow you to telecommute two or three days a week?

Technical innovation may make telecommuting an option for you, but your work style may not. Remember, telecommuting isn't getting paid to stay home with the kids, it's *working*—producing the same amount or more work of the same or better quality than you complete in the office environment.

SHARED JOBS, SHARED RESPONSIBILITIES

At one point shared jobs seemed the ideal situation for young mothers who wanted to work. Today, the concept of a shared job, although a hard sell in some corporations, makes sense for a variety of pairings. Sharing a job would be ideal for senior citizens on social security where each person could work up to the maximum amount allowed by social security.

Setting up a shared job situation requires some adjustments:

- Both parties have to work well together and accept the quality of work turned out during their absence.

- Both parties have to make adjustments in time worked to attend meetings together and to have an overlap that covers work in progress.

- The employer has to be flexible and expect some glitches at the start.

- Benefits, salary, vacations, work hours, and so on, will need to be carefully monitored.

The one major benefit, besides the time situation, is that two heads really are better than one. With a shared job, two people will be considering a project from all angles. Their solutions will be greater than either one would have come up with on his own.

"You can get by on charm for about 15 minutes. After that, you better know something."

—H. Jackson Brown Jr.

On-site Daycare

It is ridiculous to assume that childbearing and childrearing don't impact businesses of all sizes. In Greenville, South Carolina, a female ad agency owner found a practical solution to childcare. Both she and one of her employees were due to deliver within weeks of each other. Neither wanted to give up her job, yet it was hard to leave a new baby at daycare. So, she made space in her workplace for a nursery and hired a nanny. Now, both mothers could be with their infants and still be at work.

SAS, the software company, offers on-site daycare for its employees' children. In today's society, both spouses must work to meet financial needs. However, parents want to raise their children and participate in their children's lives. On-site daycare will gain in significance for choosing a place of employment in the near future, as parents realize they don't have to sacrifice family for work.

Family Leave, Family Options

Family leave is a controversial concept at best. However, employers will need to recognize that employees with children and responsibility for elderly parents can't manage without family leave options. Business writer Keith Hammond says, "Disbelievers, working stiffs, take note: Work-family strategies haven't just hit the corporate mainstream—they've become a competitive advantage. The exclusive province of working mothers a decade ago, such benefits now extend to elder-care assistance, flexible scheduling, job-sharing, adoption benefits, on-site summer camp, employee-help lines, even—no joke—pet care and lawn-service referrals."

Hammond offers First Tennessee National Corporation as an example. In a revolutionary program, they started taking family issues to heart, treating these issues as strategic business issues. The bank got rid of many of its work rules and allowed its people to set their own work schedules. Surprise: Productivity and customer service showed clear gains. First Tennessee offers such benefits as on-site childcare, job sharing, and fitness centers.

In other pioneering moves, companies have found that extending parental leave periods to new mothers has paid off in cutting resignations. Aetna Life & Casualty Company halved its new mother employee loss by extending unpaid parental leave to six months. Says Hammond, "a raft of family programs introduced en masse at Johnson & Johnson in 1992 reduced the number of days absent among all workers."

Family support is an employment issue. If your company battles for future stars, consider offering the benefits that will bring those stars to work with you. If those benefits appeal to you, make sure you ask about family programs before you hire on. You just might want to shop around to find the best value for your time.

CONSULTING FOR A LIVING

Harry worked for a mega-giant insurance corporation in the business insurance division. For almost twenty years he inspected buildings for potential problems, suggested areas in which corporations could improve building safety, and assessed the value on damaged buildings. Essentially, Harry knew facilities management from the inside out. When his employer cut back, Harry found himself over fifty and out of work. He immediately set up his own consultancy. Using the outplacement service provided by his former employer, Harry sent letters and announcements about his new job, facilities management consultant, to everyone he'd ever served. His phone rang off the hook, and Harry was back in business almost as soon as he was out of work.

Consulting is simply selling a service that other people need to do their business better, safer, more efficiently. The greatest job growth in the next millennium will be in service-related businesses. If you know something others will buy, sell it at a profit.

> **FUTURE TRENDS IN THE WORKPLACE**
>
> - *Added pressure, added stress, added responsibility—same or slightly higher pay.*
> - *Budget, cost-control, low cost producer are key elements of companies. This will translate eventually to benefits, retirement packages, etc.*
> - *Teamwork will rise again because there are too few employees with too many responsibilities for any one to be an expert over all areas of work.*
> - *Education, learning, upgrading skills is paramount, even if you have to pay for this education yourself.*
> - *You are responsible for your own career, your own lifestyle, and, ultimately, your own retirement, as vested pensions, Social Security and ESOPs become less secure.*

One way to jump into consultancy with little fuss and effort is through a temp agency like Manpower. *Business Week* reporter Richard Melcher says, "Manpower . . . is filling high-paying temporary engineering, consulting, and computer jobs, where the growth rate is 20% annually. . . . As corporate restructurings have left many companies searching for cheaper ways to meet staffing needs, more are turning to temp companies to fill the gap."

Keep your eye on trends in your area of expertise. Human resources, benefits administration, hiring and outplacement—all formerly in-house projects—are going to consulting firms, as are computer programming and information services, accounting, purchasing, and even training.

Working for Nonprofits

In the fifties and sixties people were free to volunteer for nonprofit organizations. Today, there are fewer people home and fewer to handle the enormous amount of work involved in running an association or nonprofit group. Here is an opportunity to use business skills you've already acquired without worrying so much about the profit margin, sales force, and bonus ratios.

Nonprofit work is mostly in the arts, education, social services, health, and religion. These groups need managers who can plan strategies, raise funds, promote the group, market and administer programs. The pay may be lower, but satisfaction in many nonprofit jobs is high.

REVAMPING EXPECTATIONS

The career scene is in a constant state of flux. Today's top executive may become tomorrow's gardener. However, there are some areas that will grow in the future and will need more employees.

- There is hardly a single business today that does not rely on computer technology. Keep current with technological advances in your field to keep yourself employable.

- The U.S. Department of Labor estimates there will be one million new construction-related jobs within the next ten years. Many of these jobs will involve revamping or replacing infrastructure, others involve environmental issues. Keep up on issues in your construction area. Take courses in environmental materials handling at your local community college.

- Sales—once the purview of the hard-sell fanatic—is taking on a kinder, gentler profile. The focus has switched from closure to building long-term relationships. Sales reps now listen to their customers, identify their needs, and resolve their concerns. Strong-arm sales tactics went out with the Edsel.

"You see things;
and you say, Why?
But I dream things
that never were,
and I say, Why not?"

—George Bernard Shaw

Business Savvy in the Home

According to a 1993 *Home Office Computing* magazine survey, most people have both positive and negative reactions to working from their home.

What people say is positive: I feel more relaxed. I have a healthier diet. I take more time off. I exercise more often. I have a better marriage and sex life.

What people say is negative: I have no paid benefits. I miss office socializing. I have no staff or support. I don't get regular raises and bonuses.

Despite the pros and cons, home business options, like telecommuting, are growing. Some are forced into home business by layoffs, while others choose the option due to family needs or personal habits. There are as many Horatio Alger stories that come from home businesses as anywhere else.

Turning Hobbies into Jobs

Pauline had baked bread for years. Some she fed to her family; some she gave away as gifts. At one point her hobby turned into a business venture when a friend suggested she sell her baked goods. Mom's Kitchen began as a small venture, providing business lunches on homemade bread, delivered to the office. Today Pauline is on her third successful restaurant—and still baking her bread.

Jeff was a teacher from September to June, but wanted a break from the classroom during the summer months. He started a lawn service, which he built by hiring his better students to mow-for-money. After twenty-five years teaching, Jeff retired and expanded his lawn service to an all-year venture.

Annette was an avid quilter and seamstress making all her own clothes as well as decorating her home. When her husband was transferred to Ohio, she decided it was time to turn her hobby into a profit maker. She opened up a shop where she gave sewing and quilting lessons.

Whether you are retired or laid off or just need a change in your life, your hobby can become your work. Success may come to you in unusual forms: less stress, greater contentment, better work hours, and a smile on your face.

CHAPTER RECAP

- Telecommuting keeps in touch with the office and eliminates time-wasting commutes.

- There are over 23 million part-and full-time self-employed homeworkers.

- A shared job is ideal for seniors and young parents.

- Family options are a key element in the workplace, with family considerations becoming a primary benefit.

- You can turn hobbies or volunteer projects into actual jobs.

Recommended Reading

Barker, Robert. "Securing Your Future: A Self-Help Guide," *Business Week,* July 21, 1997.

Fullerton Jr., Howard N. "Tomorrow's Jobs," *Occupational Outlook Handbook,* Bureau of Labor Statistics, March 7, 1996.

Geller, Robert E. *How to Survive in the Nonprofit World.* Sacramento: California State Library Foundation, 1990.

Hammonds, Keith H. "Balancing Work and Family," *Business Week,* September 16, 1996.

Jeffers, Michelle. "Here Come the Consultants," *Forbes ASAP,* April 7, 1997.

Lee, Tony. "How to Change Careers," *National Business Employment Weekly,* February 1, 1996.

Lee, Tony. "It's Never Too Late to Find Your Perfect Career," *National Business Employment Weekly,* June 1, 1995.

Peters, Tom. "Opportunity Knocks," *Forbes ASAP,* June 2, 1997.

In the New
Millennium

*T*he career a person who trained in the seventies, worked in the eighties, and lost in the nineties may well not exist in the new millennium—there will be dramatic changes. New technology, archaic business practices, downsizing, merging, and global influences account for many changes. How will these changes affect your road to success?

It used to be that the job was everything; the paycheck a pagan god. But business is changing. People cherish their free time more than in the past. Americans, stuck with two weeks vacation each year, turn green with envy over the six to eight week vacations of many European employees. Employees are shifting from being grateful to have a job to expecting their employers to show gratitude and appreciation for the fact that they show up for work at all.

The new millennium will bring changes we can't even imagine, new jobs and job titles, new workplaces, greater personal responsibility, and more opportunity. Are you ready?

IN THIS CHAPTER:

• *New jobs, new titles, new work places*

• *Tips on locating 21st century jobs*

• *Addressing future skill needs*

CAREER TRENDS—HOW WILL YOU BE EARNING IN 2010?

The number of small, entrepreneurial businesses will increase, while mega-corporations, already slimmed down to anemic proportions, will endeavor to do more with less. With fewer employees, corporations will need to become more flexible, less bureaucratic, and work with fewer rules.

Among the changes you can expect are new business strategies and new organization plans. Management will have fewer levels. The massive organization tree, listing who reports to whom with dotted lines in every direction, is a thing of the past. Corporations have already cut out the middle managers. Leaders will emerge as the new heads of companies, while employees will learn to manage their work, their projects, and themselves under team programs.

The customer will continue to be the prime focus in the future. Service, price, and product performance will center on consumer demands, particularly as imports of every imaginable sort will continue to flesh out the supply.

Computers and technology, already controlling much of our lives, won't release their hold. We can only pray that people will revert to answering telephones again, so that we no longer follow the frustrating path of "press one for customer service, press two. . . ."

Business culture should change to match the changes in management. Power mongers and management bullies will soon retire, hopefully leaving enlightened managers in their stead. Employee management will empower workers to act, be quick to make decisions, become ethical and open, share information, and tolerate risks. Having said all that, there is one caveat: This won't all happen tomorrow.

One area in which people will find more employment opportunity is with nonprofit organizations or associations that need management skills to compete. According to Peter Drucker, "The Girls Scouts, the Red Cross, the pastoral churches—our nonprofit organizations—are becoming

"The year 2000 will mark the end of what has been called the American century. The last years of this century are certain to bring new developments in technology, international competition, demography and other factors that will alter the nation's economic and social landscape."

—*William B. Johnstone,* Workforce 2000: Work and Workers for the Twenty-First Century

America's management leaders. In two areas, strategy and the effectiveness of the board, they are practicing what most American businesses only preach. And in the most crucial area—the motivation and productivity of knowledge workers—they are truly pioneers, working out the policies and practices that business will have to learn tomorrow."

"A consultant is someone who saves his client almost enough to pay his fee."

—Arnold Glasow

Where's the Job?

"Anyone planning to join the work world or already in it will need to constantly gain new skills and update antiquated ones. Training, in other words, is constant. Anyone in school now should cut a wide swath through the course catalogue—major in business, perhaps, but minor in psychology. The ability to understand and manage personnel or customers is crucial in today's workplace—and it will enhance your life," says business writer Laura Sharpe in "Hot Tracks: Cool Tips for Finding the Hottest Jobs Around."

Combined skills will become more important toward getting a new job: business and education, business and technology, marketing and political science, technology and journalism or writing skills can make you more appealing to an employer.

> ### SUCCESSTHOUGHTS
> *If you have no computer skills, you are about as employable as a wainwright or an alchemist. Trot over to your local community college and sign up for night courses.*

Just where are the jobs going to be found?

- *Computer or technology skills* will increase in importance. Technology, already in the $300 billion per year range, will continue to grow as emerging nations take a giant step into the technological age.

- *Health care services,* already suffering from too few trained workers, need caregivers: Elder care, senior services, child care, primary care physicians, medical technologists, subacute or long-term care givers, physical therapists, nurses, nurse practitioners/physicians assistants. Reports Laura Sharpe, "Each graduating physicians' assistant from the nation's 51 programs this year had an average of 6.3 job offers. The average salary? $56,568 per year."

- *Construction, agriculture, forestry, and fishing should increase,* while manufacturing and mining will decrease, according to the Bureau of Labor Statistics (BLS). We will need: skilled workers— electricians, plumbers, cabinet makers, and crafts-men, including auto technicians who can deal with today's computer-enhanced cars.

- *There will be a decrease in operators, fabricators, labor-ers, and precision production according to the BLS.* Those jobs will either become automated or go to emerging nations where labor is cheap.

- *Twenty occupations will account for half of all job growth* in the 1994–2005 period. Three health occupations and three education-related occupa-tions are in the top twenty. Employment of com-puter engineers and systems analysts is expected to grow rapidly.

Will Your Skills Still Be Needed?

In *Business Week,* Stephen Baker reports, "The Information Revolution is racing ahead of its vital raw material: brain power. As demand explodes for computerized applications for everything from electronic commerce on the Internet to sorting out the Year 2000 glitch, companies are finding themselves strapped for programmers. In the U.S. alone, which accounts for two thirds of the world's $300 billion market in software products and services, some 190,000 high tech jobs stand open, most of them for programmers, according to the Information Technology Association."

Looking for a career? Programmers now earn about $70,000/year with salary increases in the 12–15% range yearly. Compare that to many corporations where pay increases range between 2% and 5%. For many programmers, signing bonuses—$10,000–$20,000 just for agreeing to work at the company—are not uncommon.

The BLS reports that services and retail trade industries will account for 16.2 million out of a total projected growth of 16.8 million wage and salary jobs. Business, health, and education services will account for 80% of the growth within service-related jobs.

Specifically, healthcare services will account for almost 20% of all job growth from 1994–2005. Patients will increasingly be shifted out of hospitals and into outpatient facilities, nursing homes, and home healthcare in an attempt to contain costs. Care providers will have their choice of jobs as Americans age.

And you can expect some changes in business culture. Corporations will have to stop downsizing or there won't be anyone left to answer the telephone. As a result, many corporations will change their approach toward employees and develop a greater respect for employee knowledge, creativity, and skills.

NEW FIELDS FOR THE NEW MILLENNIUM

- *Cybrarian management (data)*
- *Computer programming*
- *Construction*
- *Human resource administration and training*
- *Education*
- *Marketing/ Communications*
- *Nonprofit or association management*
- *Technical writing*
- *Meeting planning*
- *Tourism*

Where You Fit In

Where do you fit in? Where do you want to fit in? You can either stay within the structure you know, working your way up the ladder, or you can step away. Once away, you can work for someone else or yourself. There are plusses and minuses to being your own boss. However, there is one self-employed option that falls under trends: consulting.

Consulting is big business and big bucks in the pocket if you can get the assignments. Corporations willingly pay outsiders to come in and sort the wheat from the chaff. The theory is that the outside observer sees more clearly and objectively than those working within the company.

Oddly enough, consultants are often hired to determine the "intellectual capital" of the company. These consultants decide who is creative, who is innovative, and therefore valuable. In "Here Come the Consultants," *Forbes* writer Michelle Jeffers says, "Most corporations remain unclear on the concept of intellectual capital and how to make the most of the internal knowledge they may have. A tab of $2 million to $3 million is typical for Ernst & Young's four-pronged approach to mining corporate intellectual capital—prongs known at the consultancy as *culture, infrastructure, knowledge content,* and *stewardship.*"

> We can't always see beyond the present to the future. Aren't you glad you weren't the one to say:
>
> - "The earth is flat." Almost anyone alive before Columbus' voyage.
> - "Man will not fly for another fifty years." Wilbur Wright, 1901.
> - "Who the heck wants to hear actors talk?" Harry M. Warner, Warner Brothers, 1927.
> - "A woman's place is in the home." Almost any man in the 1950s.
> - "There is no reason for any individual to have a computer in their home." Ken Olsen, Digital Equipment Corp., 1977.

You'll never be more valued than when you leave. While you might not get the chunk of change of Ernst & Young, you can return as a consultant and charge five times your previous salary—which your previous company will pay without question.

Overall, you will most likely have a job if you (a) want one and (b) look hard enough. According to the BLS:

- Over the 1994–2005 period, employment is projected to increase by 17.7 million jobs or 14%.

- Wage and salary worker employment will account for 95% of this increase.

- Self-employed workers should increase by 950,000 to 11.6 million by 2005.

- Jobs requiring the most education and training will be the fastest growing and highest paying.

- Eight occupations will dominate new job hires: registered nurses, systems analysts, blue-collar worker supervisors, general managers and top executives, and four teaching occupations (elementary, secondary, college, and special education).

> **CHANGES FOR WOMEN IN THE NEW MILLENNIUM**
> - *Narrowing of the wage gap between men and women*
> - *Corporate subsidies for child and elder care*
> - *Child and elder care provided at or near work sites*
> - *Flextime, flexplace, telecommuting*
> - *Shared jobs, part-time jobs with benefits*
> - *Technological changes to ease work load*
> - *Parental leave, shared parental load*
> - *Small business ownership*

CHANGING DIRECTIONS MIDSTREAM

Los Angeles Times business writer Stuart Silverstein says, "Older workers, often pushed out the door amid the corporate layoffs of the 1980s and 1990s, are likely to emerge in the coming years as hot prospects in the job market."

He adds, "*Workforce 2000* . . . predicts that the portion of the work force consisting of minorities will edge up from 23% in 1994 to 26% in the year 2005. Likewise, the percentage of women is expected to inch up from 46% to 48% over the same period."

One answer for the future is to re-train. People are regularly retiring after 20 or 25 years service with one company or career and starting a second career in their mid- to late-forties. If you are with a company, ask them to reimburse, partially or fully, any advanced education courses you take that will enhance your performance on the job. Keep educating yourself if your company won't.

Where will you find work? Wherever you want to! Remember: The choice is yours.

CHAPTER RECAP

• Jobs will be available in computer technology, services, and skilled trades.

• Jobs in nonprofit organizations will be an excellent opportunity to use management skills.

• Having a broad combination of skills will help you land a position.

• Flexible hours and workplaces will increase as offices grow smaller and meetings are held via conference calls.

Recommended Reading

Celente, Gerald. *Trends 2000: How to Prepare for and Profit from the Changes of the 21st Century.* New York: Warner Books, 1997.

Drucker, Peter F. *Managing for the Future.* New York: Truman Talley Books, 1992.

Gonyea, Wayne M. "Keyword Resumés—Your New Hi-tech Way to Get a Job!" On-line Solutions, Inc., 1997.

James, Jennifer. *Thinking in the Future Tense: Leadership Skills for a New Age.* New York: Simon & Schuster, 1996.

Toffler, Alvin. *Powershift: Knowledge, Wealth, and Violence at the Edge of the 21st Century.* New York: Bantam Books, 1991.

Going Global

*W*ith more and more corporations going "global," there's no reason for you to feel tied to the American job market. Can't stand Peoria anymore? Try Argentina or Thailand.

Want to move up in your corporation? Hone your multi-cultural skills. Learn a second language (Japanese, Chinese, or German would be handy). Do you want to become your company's rep to Hong Kong? Madrid? Turkey? Then, learn everything you can about the culture, habits, and traditions of the country you may become involved in—and let your supervisor know you want this opportunity.

There are immense opportunities involved in the global market, and some come with exotic pitfalls that lure unprepared business Vikings. The food you'll eat, the style of housing you'll live in, the heating and cooling, and just about every other aspect of life differs from country to country. Don't expect living in Tokyo to be like living in Topeka. It isn't. On the other hand, if you are a modern day Magellan and learning about other cultures turns you on, the overseas market may chart your map to success.

GLOBAL BUSINESS PRACTICES

In today's world international markets offer plenty of opportunity. There is the English speaking world—the UK and associates. There is the Euromarket. Japan is pretty much a market unto itself. Then you have Asia, Southeast Asia, South America, the Middle East, and Africa. So many markets, so many different ways of doing business, so many different cultures to deal with, so many obstacles to success.

SUCCESSTHOUGHTS

For women, international assignments may prove valuable. In Working Woman, *Patricia M. Carey says, "Career experts say that the cross-cultural and cross-functional skills developed during an assignment abroad may help women crack the glass ceiling back home." Women are expected to make up roughly eighteen percent of American employees assigned to foreign positions.*

"From the earliest times, international business has been fraught with problems including wars, civil strife, piracy, economic upheavals and cultural barriers. Despite this, there has never been any doubt of man's desire—even imperative—to trade across international borders," say James Taggart and Michael McDermott in *The Essence of International Business.*

There are few corporations that have restricted their reach to American borders. Sara Lee sells coffee in the Netherlands, pantyhose in France, and frozen desserts in Australia. Alaskan fisherman sell part of every year's crab catch to Japan, while Florida's citrus growers send prime produce to the same place. Your GM car is assembled from parts made in Mexico, and your CD player is Japanese. There is no product, service, or industry that doesn't have international counterparts. Whatever you are doing, you can do it elsewhere.

However, don't confuse international work with a vacation. Yes, you get to see the world, between meetings, plane trips, and airports. You get to eat in exotic places, bring back souvenirs and cultural savvy, and you may find when you get back to the U.S., no one cares but you. A survey by Berlitz International and HFS Mobility Services indicates that 39% of 184 employees returning from abroad would not take another overseas assignment. Roughly two-thirds, both men and women, said they used their skills from their international experience in their current job.

What exactly is international business? It is . . .

- importing and exporting of goods and services;

- financial investments in goods, services, infrastructure, programs;

- providing skills and services to developing countries;

- marketing, advertising, and merchandising American products and services abroad.

Services can be anything from computer programming to legal advice, banking to birth control clinics. Many emerging nations have a need for American infrastructure—roads, communications, utilities—all of which require advanced technology in today's world. However, an attorney in Tacoma and an attorney in Tokyo will find their working environments vastly different. It's not just the location: it's tradition, culture, and style.

Robert M. March, author of *Working for a Japanese Company*, explains, "One of the most common concerns of Westerners is the lack of a job specification or description, which they are accustomed to receiving when accepting employment by a Western company. This is not a practice of Japanese companies." Japanese corporations have a looser, less structured entrance plan, with little formatted when you start work. Later, you may have a more structured job, but not in the beginning. Some people will find this disconcerting; success-seekers will consider it a challenge.

"While you are negotiating for a 35-hour week, remember they have only just gotten 66 hours [per week] in Taiwan, and you're competing with Taiwan."

—Victor Kiam, Remington Products

Management maven Peter Drucker sees a need for more than just mega-corporations in the world business arena. He says, "Many middle-sized and even small businesses will have to become active in the world economy. To maintain leadership in one developed market, a company increasingly has to have a strong presence in all such markets worldwide."

WHAT'S HOT OVERSEAS

What does the international market want from the U.S.? Products, manufacturing jobs, technology, and the staff to make it all work, infrastructure, and entertainment. Yes, as dreadful as our television programs may appear to us, remember that *I Love Lucy* reruns are still viewed throughout the world.

Marketing abroad requires some adjustment as foreign markets have their own uniqueness. Sam's Club would never survive in most European countries where shopping is a daily event, and refrigerators are the size of a large Samsonite suitcase. Companies planning to push their products abroad should consider using international marketing research to identify the potential for their product or service. They will also need international marketing to spell out the demographics in order to approach target groups.

You may find yourself thinking, "What's wrong with good, old American know-how?" David Ricks offers this example that should change your perspective: "When the Coca-Cola® Company was planning its strategy for marketing in China in the 1920s, it wanted to introduce its product with the English pronunciation of 'Coca-Cola.' A translator developed a group of Chinese characters that, when pronounced, sounded like the product name. The characters were placed on the cola bottles and marketed. Was it any wonder the sales levels were low? The characters used actually meant 'bite the wax tadpole.'"

It is a good thing to remember that consumers throughout the world are looking for many of the same things in products and services. People want quality, affordability, up-to-date design elements, timely service, and state-of-the-art technology. Consider these elements and how you can bring your expertise to leading your company's products or services into international markets.

CULTURAL DIFFERENCES, NECESSARY ADAPTATIONS

"Cultural differences are the most significant and troublesome variables encountered by the multinational company. The failure of managers to comprehend fully these disparities has led to most international business blunders," says David Ricks in *Blunders in International Business,* a must read *before* you leap into foreign markets.

He explains, "All nationalities possess unique characteristics that must be understood. For example, Arabs typically dislike deadlines. An Arab faced with a deadline tends to feel threatened and backed into a corner. Many Americans, on the other hand, try to expedite matters by setting deadlines."

Rebecca, a purchasing agent for the Air Force, was stationed in Italy where she frequently met with foreign sales representatives. In the United States, the meeting would be quick—about an hour. Then, you shake hands and say good-bye. In Italy, she found supplier meetings to be a completely different matter. The Italians wanted to chat for a while—an hour or two—over a bottle of wine. Lunch or dinner wasn't unusual as part of the meeting. A one-hour American meeting took all day—just to buy forty cases of toilet paper. Ah, but the wine was excellent and the pasta superb.

> *"Many people dream of success. To me success can only be achieved through repeated failure and introspection. In fact, success represents 1% of your work which results from the 99% that is called failure."*
>
> —*Soichiro Honda, Honda Corporation*

If you are going to be in Rome or Rangoon, you'll need to adjust to local business practices. However, don't limit your focus to the differences. People are people all over the world, as the song goes. We all have inner similarities such as compassion, appreciation of beauty, sexuality, a sense of humor, an interest in others, and love for our families. Find common ground for personal discussions and adapt your business practices to the pace, style, and customs of the people you are dealing with.

Communication is a key issue in business as well as politics. In most Asian countries respect, honor, and "saving face" are all part of business communications. You may win the argument but lose the account. Germans, Swiss, and Austrians are notably candid, so much so many Americans find their efficiency and business zeal off-putting. As a contrast, Spaniards and Portuguese work at a slower, more leisurely pace. In Italy, a bottle of wine is a key element of a business meeting; in Saudi Arabia, a bottle of wine is an offense against religious custom.

It's not only how you say it, it's also what you say. Idioms vary from place to place. Caroline, an American newly arrived in Australia, started work at the government mental health clinic in Canberra. On her first day of work, she was told by one of the psychiatrists to go to the supply cupboard and get a box of rubbers. She looked all over for condoms; he wanted erasers.

In *International Business*, Asheghian and Ebrahimi give a useful checklist for multinational employees to help with international differences in culture:

- *Be culturally prepared:* forewarned is forearmed.

- *Learn the local language* and its non-verbal elements.

- *Mix with host nationals,* including socially.

- *Be creative* and experimental without fear of failure.

- *Perceive yourself as a culture bearer* and ambassador.

- *Be patient, understanding, and accepting* of your hosts.

- *Accept the challenge of intercultural experiences.*

Marmite, Lutefisk, and Dolmades: Outside the Workplace

Don't go abroad expecting to live like an American. You'll be miserable. People in other parts of the world shop differently, eat differently, and live differently. Part of the experience is to blend into the country.

Food will be the first and most obvious change. Before you go, try out recipes of the local cuisine, or eat at an ethnic restaurant that serves authentic dishes. For those who find eating ethnic foods a burden, please follow this well-meant advice: Stay home. You can buy a Big Mac in Tokyo, but it will cost you Big Bucks. For those who don't already know: Marmite is a yeast extract spread on toast. Lutefisk is a boiled fish course. Dolmades are stuffed grape leaves.

Andy was in Fiji on business and decided to use the local bus system to get back to his hotel. The bus was open-sided, a fact that didn't concern Andy until it started to rain. Those sitting next to the windows were expected to roll down the bamboo curtains, a task that Andy performed with alacrity once he realized his responsibility. About a mile outside of Nandi, the bus pulled off the road onto a field. Several people got off, bought taro from an old man selling from his wheelbarrow, then returned to the bus. The woman sitting next to Andy smiled and said, "It's hard to find good taro anymore." Andy nodded in agreement, completely ignorant of why anyone would want taro to begin with. As the bus moved back onto the road, Andy noticed his seatmate had a live chicken in her string back. "A pet?" Andy asked naively. "Dinner," replied his seatmate. Life in a foreign land is always an adventure.

When you go, bring an ample supply of any prescription medicines you are taking, any over-the-counter medicines you normally use, and a cache of toilet paper and facial tissue. You'll be glad you planned ahead.

THE GLOBAL JOB SEARCH

Arthur Bell, author of *Great Jobs Abroad,* offers practical tips on how to secure a foreign post:

- *Investigate companies,* organizations and job descriptions that interest you.

- *Prepare a persuasive application letter* and compelling resumé.

- *Interview for the position with confidence.*

- *Obtain the necessary visas and work permits* you'll need to work in the country you've chosen.

You should have no trouble finding work opportunities abroad. If you are not sure where to look, check out the Web sites on the following page.

You do not need to speak a foreign language to get a foreign job. In most countries English is the second language, and certainly the primary language of international business. Nonetheless, fluent language skills help, and a quick Berlitz

---

ARAB PROVERB

He who knows not and knows not that he knows not is a fool. Avoid him.

He who knows not but knows that he knows not is ignorant. Instruct him.

He who knows but knows not that he knows is asleep. Awaken him.

He who knows and knows that he knows is a leader. Follow him.

course can make the difference between ordering fillet of flounder or sautéed sea slug.

If you know someone involved in foreign business, contact her. Networking is always a good way to find and get jobs, whether at home or abroad. The key is not who you know, however, but how willing you are to pursue the opportunity. If you persist, you will succeed.

Don't take a job just because it will move you to your country of choice. A job you hate is the same regardless of where you work.

CHECK OUT THESE INTERNATIONAL JOB SITES ON THE INTERNET

- *http://www.camrev.com.au/share/jobs.html International academic jobs*
- *http://www.espan.com International jobs, all ranges*
- *http://www.jobsource.com International jobs, all ranges*

Most European countries are expensive to live in, so check out the salary and cost of living before accepting a position that may put you on the poverty line.

Obtain a visa. This is a time-consuming process, so don't consider it an automatic you needn't worry about until the week before you leave. As soon as you know where you are going, research the visa requirements, get your passport in order, obtain a visa application and get started. Information on visa requirements can be obtained from the U.S. Consumer Information Center, Pueblo, CO 81009. Ask for the free pamphlet entitled "Foreign Entry Requirements."

Obtaining a work permit. Just because you have a passport and a visa, you don't have a right to work in a foreign country. For details on work permits in foreign countries, contact the embassy of the country to which you are going and ask for an application. You can find embassy addresses in the research section of your public library or in *The New York Public Library Desk Reference*, published by Prentice Hall.

Get in touch with your U.S. embassy. Once you've landed the job and arrived, go to the nearest U.S. embassy or consular office and introduce yourself. You'll feel much more comfortable knowing someone there in case you have trouble, lose your passport, etc. Embassy types can also recommend English-speaking doctors and dentists, schools, and places you should or should not look for housing.

And finally, don't forget to send a postcard. Those of us still slaving away in Buffalo or Birmingham would love to hear from you. *Sayonara!*

CHAPTER RECAP

- When accepting a position abroad, expect the lifestyle to be different from the United States.

- You need a visa, a work permit, and a passport to work outside the United States.

- Contact with someone who is already working for an international company can help locate a good job abroad.

- Learning a second language is helpful, but not essential.

- Learn as much as you can about the people and culture of the country where you will be working. It is one way to avoid business blunders.

Recommended Reading

Asheghian, P., and B. Ebrahimi. *International Business.* New York: Harper and Row, 1990.

Bell, Arthur H. *Great Jobs Abroad.* New York: McGraw-Hill, 1997.

March, Robert M. *Working for a Japanese Company.* Tokyo: Kodansha, Inc., 1992.

Ricks, David A. *Blunders in International Business.* Cambridge, MA: Blackwell Publishers, 1993.

The Best Boss You've Ever Had—You!

*W*hen people say, "You're so lucky, you work for your-self," what are they thinking? Do they realize the worry involved in self-employment? Do they comprehend the stark terror of knowing that you have to deliver a $2500 payroll tomorrow, and you have only $567.92 in the bank?

Owning a small business may be the dream of some, but it has its nightmares too. Starting a small business, demands hours of dedication, family support, practical know-how, and talent. However this growing trend can be the springboard to personal and financial fulfillment. When it's successful, small business is perhaps the most rewarding event since the birth of your most recent child.

No one chapter can possibly take the place of the myriad books on this subject. This is a down-and-dirty, pithy view of the start-up process. On your mark. Get set. Go!

SELF-ASSESSMENT—THE FIRST STEP

Are you self motivated? A procrastinator? Can you meet new people easily? Will you work a project to completion without getting distracted? Can you handle both the creative and business side of things? Are you willing to do bookkeeping, invoicing, secretarial work, filing, and clean the bathroom? The first step in deciding whether you'll start your own business is determining if your personality and work style suits self-management.

Here is a general list of characteristics of a successful self-employed individual: self-confident, self-motivated, disciplined, flexible, demanding of yourself, perfectionist, extroverted, independent thinker, assertive, risk-taker, solid negotiator, competitive mind, market savvy, strategic planner, long and short range planning skills, like being alone, happy with yourself. To be blunt, you either fit this mold or you don't.

Personal Elements, Ideas, Sources, and Resources

No one decides to go into business today and opens his doors tomorrow. Here are just a few of the things you need to do/decide/act upon to start a business:

- *Select a business name.* If you want to trademark your name, you will have to do a legal search. This costs money. And you can't use 3M®, IBM®, Disney®, or Quaker®—they're all taken, and you'll get sued.

- *Decide on the form of business:* corporation, sole proprietorship, LLC (Limited Liability Corporation), partnership. Investigate the advantages and disadvantages of each.

- *Determine the nature and extent of the business.* What are you selling? To whom? How? Who will run the shop? What do you need to open up?

- *Draw up a plan,* including start-up costs, projected costs, and projected pay-off or break-even date.

- *Determine the purpose behind your business,* it's goals, future opportunities, growth plan.

- *Evaluate your current status,* financial and otherwise.

- *People: how many do you need,* what skills, qualifications? Also: what benefits, salary, demands, rewards will you provide?

- *Make a realistic budget* and arrange financing.

- *Access assistance* from the Small Business Administration, Chamber of Commerce Small Business Association, SCORE, etc.

- *Obtain tax info,* attend tax school by IRS (free), establish bookkeeping and accounting procedures, bank accounts, EIN (Employer Identification Number), state and local licenses, insurance, etc. Find out about regulations that cover your chosen field and which organizations govern your efforts.

- *Promote your business,* promote yourself.

- *Where do you find ideas on what businesses are needed in your area?* Try your family, friends, the Yellow Pages, small business owners in your area, opportunity magazines, the Internet, libraries, bookstores, "how-to" books, business opportunity fairs, trade and industry publications, and trade shows.

FINANCING, ACCOUNTING, AND TAXES

"If you would know the value of money, go and try to borrow some," said Benjamin Franklin. His point is still valid today. Until you try to borrow for your new business, you have no idea just how tight investment money is. If you are a woman, multiply the difficulty for borrowing by a factor of five.

Banks don't lend money to people unless they're pretty sure of getting it back. You will have to prove yourself to any lending institution, which you can do by producing a viable, practical business plan. No plan, no money.

When considering finances, take into account all start-up costs of the business and also all your personal living expenses. For example, business expenses: equipment, office rental, inventory, renovations, supplies, marketing, utilities, professional dues/licenses, personnel costs, insurance/bonds. Living expenses: rent/mortgage, food, car, utilities, clothing, credit card, medical expenses, day care, etc. You will need a minimum of six to nine months of living expenses to carry you until you can start making money. Any revenues received before that will most likely go into increased marketing, inventory, or surprises—and there will be plenty.

One last word about financing: Beware of entering into a partnership—it's more complex than you imagine. As Arnold Goldstein says in *Starting on a Shoestring,* "Partnership money is the most expensive money you can buy. If you want a partner for his money alone—consider it your last resort." You are jointly responsible for your partner's debts and difficulties. If he absconds with the payroll, you have to make good. And breaking up a legal partnership is

---

DETERMINING MONTHLY EXPENSES

Here is a list from the U.S. Small Business Administration's initial capital requirement worksheet:

Salary of owner-manager	All other salaries and wages
Rent	Advertising
Delivery expenses	Supplies
Telephone/fax/modem	Electricity/gas/water
Taxes	Social Security and Medicare
Loan interest	Maintenance
Legal and professional fees	Miscellaneous
One time start-up costs	Fixtures and equipment
Decorating and remodeling	Starting inventory
Deposits with public utilities	Licenses and permits
Advertising and promotion	Accounts receivable
Cash	Bad debt
	Other

more involved than getting a divorce. There's no quick solution for dissolving a partnership.

Accounting and Your Pal—the IRS

Before you venture into the business world, consider how well you like dealing with the IRS—they'll be in touch with you regularly when you first start. Call the IRS 800 number and get Publication 910, *Guide to Free Tax Services*, which lists all free services—you'll need most of them. Next, attend the IRS Small Business Tax School—it takes one full day and gives you an idea of all the paperwork, forms, and payments you'll be making. The one thing they always tell you at IRS school is to pay the government first. Believe them.

Once you've become kissing cousins with the IRS, you need to move down the food chain to state, local, and sales taxes. Yes, these also require paperwork, forms, and payments, which you fill out, duplicate, file and mail, and write checks for.

Tax Hint: If a bank is not your bank, it does not have to accept payroll tax deposits. When choosing a business bank, make sure it is a depository bank so you can make your deposits easily.

Here are a few tips you should keep in mind:

- People who have problems with the IRS should call, write, and plead to get their penalties back. Sometimes they give them back.

- Never spend tax money elsewhere. Uncle Sam has no sense of humor, and this is not your money, honey.

- Follow IRS tax rules for home businesses, deducting only legitimate expenses. Keep a record of everything! If you plan to deduct your office space (the former dining room), consider how

"It is not the employer who pays wages—he only handles the money. It is the product that pays wages."

—*Henry Ford*

much you'll enjoy being audited. Home office space deduction equals bull and red flag.

- If you are a corporation, you must pay yourself a salary. Don't have the money this week? Then you don't get paid. But—if you have the money, then you must pay yourself a salary and the appropriate taxes, Social Security, Medicare, and state withholding. Penalties are severe—so watch your step.

Pricing and Promotion

You will have to price your product or service, and then get out and sell it to someone. Pricing strategy depends on your target market, the nature and extent of the competition, the price charged by the competition, the value of your location to draw and keep customers, overhead, profit margin, and cost of initial goods and services. In general, retail price = cost + markup. Cost is the cost of the product to you, markup is the additional percentage needed to cover all other expenses and give you a profit.

When you first start out, you will want to advertise, but don't give in to the urge. You simply can't afford to penetrate the market sufficiently for your ads to pay their way. And don't buy a cable package and do your own TV commercial. Try one of these strategies instead:

- *Offer 50% off first servicing,* regular price thereafter.

- *Offer a 10–20–30 deal,* increasing the percent off the normal price of three successive services in order to establish a routine business pattern.

- *Use coupons* given with purchase.

- *Use a card for 1 free* with repeat purchases (usually 10 paid events = 1 freebie)

When promoting yourself, a good reputation is worth ten times more than advertising. Word-of-mouth from loyal customers will get you even more loyal customers. Ask your customers to help you grow your business.

Technology Can Help

New businesses—even those opening on a shoestring—can get some needed help from today's computer technology. If you want to use a packaged business plan maker, try BizPlan Builder (1-800-346-5426) or MultiMedia MBS (1-800-228-5609), or review other business plan software through PC or Mac magazines or catalogs. If you are not computer literate at this point, take a class. You will have a hard time surviving in business these days without a computer.

There are several excellent accounting software programs for small businesses: MYOB, Peachtree Accounting, and QuickBooks from Quicken. Read up on each program before buying the software and choose one with payroll, accounts receivable, accounts payable, and, for retail operations, inventory control. Once you know how to use your program, the amount of time saved and the accuracy of your reports will be a godsend.

One comprehensive package many small businesses use successfully is Microsoft Office. It includes a word processing program for letters and reports (and your business plan), a spreadsheet program, a graphics program for making presentations, Internet e-mail, and an Internet browser. Don't go overboard getting programs you don't need or can't use—they'll be outdated before you even open the manual.

YOUR HOME OFFICE

We've all seen the MCI commercial with the lady working in her pajamas, faxing over oatmeal, and networking while a slipper dangles from her foot. Yes, it could be you.

Here's a tip or two about setting up your home office on a budget:

- *Use plastic milk crate files.* Cost about $4.00 each, stackable, light weight, hold plenty of stuff.

- *Buy office supplies in bulk,* and only those things you really need.

- *Make a cheap desk* out of a sheet of plywood and two two-drawer file cabinets.

- *Newer, faster, bigger memories are needed to run current software.* Used computer equipment may not be the best buy. Clones are cheaper than the name brands and many are just as good.

- *Don't go overboard on software.* It's expensive and goes out of date quickly. Figure out what you need and buy it, then be discriminating about the upgrades.

- *Buy carefully.* Before you invest in anything, decide whether or not you really need it, where it will go, and what size item will do the job.

WRITING A BUSINESS PLAN

A business plan is a necessity if you want to borrow money. For people who can't write, hire a freelance business writer. For those who think they can handle it, here is what goes into a 40–50 page business plan:

- *Facts.* Do your research on market potential, materials costing, materials supplies, fabrication equipment (obtaining, training, maintaining), and packaging (costs, design, development).

- *Analysis.* If you are going to sell widgets, how many will you have to sell to make a dollar? What is the real profit? How will you address customer service? quality control? damaged goods? loss from theft? Will you be able to make enough with one widget maker to meet the demand?

- *Competition.* In a small market with heavy competition, can you make a profit? How?

- *Technical v. Practical.* While it's nice to let your potential investors know that you can debug four lines of code in three nanoseconds, don't expect anyone to be impressed. Jargon, techno-speak, and complex explanations of intricate details don't make it at the bank. They want to know what you intend to do and how you'll be able to pay them back.

- *Be Timely.* Most great ideas have two things going for them: They (1) provide a product/service (2) people want it.

- *Tune In.* If you can't focus your ideas well enough to (a) write them down in a cogent, concise manner or (b) explain them to lay people and potential customers, then how will you sell that concept/product?

Always remember Murphy's Law: Whatever can go wrong, will go wrong. Always have a contingency plan.

Now that you know what to write, you'll have to organize it into a clearly defined statement. Organize as follows:

- *Who* you are and what you want to do.

- *Where* you intend to open your business and your anticipated success rate. (How soon you'll make a profit.)

- *The "business" of the business:* knowledge of the business, how you intend to start/expand/grow the

business, the anticipated financial profile, marketing and merchandising, organization.

- *The basic elements needed* and what they cost: equip-
  ment/ furnishings/building requirements, "homework" on the competition and the demographics of
  the business.

- *Any partners, family participants, talents* you can call
  on to help (including the SBA [Small Business
  Association] and SCORE[Service Core of Retired
  Executives]). Preparations you have already made or
  are planning to undertake to learn what you need to
  know, such as building computer skills, attending
  IRS small business tax seminar, basic accounting
  classes, marketing classes, etc.

- *Basic approach to establishing financial stability:* a
  budget of costs, how the money is going to be spent
  and why, the amount you need to make a go of it,
  when it will be paid back, cash flow, collateral.

In starting your own business, you don't have to know
everything. There are outside consultants, financial consultants, accounting firms, and so on, that can provide the
missing links to your chain of business sense. Just be aware
that their expertise comes at a price.

Is it all worth it? "That's the thrill of it all. You want a
business of your own so you go for it. You connive, beg, borrow, hustle, and manipulate to get it together and keep it
together. You work you butt to the bone to make it happen.
In the process you thumb your nose at a world of non-
believers, skeptics, pessimists, and conventionalists with their
words of wisdom on why you can't or why you shouldn't, says
Arnold Goldstein. "No, it's never easy, but when you're
through and have the business off and running, you stand tall
and pat yourself on the back. You did it, and you did it on a
shoestring. In short, you made your own miracles."

CHAPTER RECAP

- Rule number one in running your own business: Always pay the IRS on time.

- A self-employed person must be committed, dedicated, self-confident, self-motivated, assertive, a risk-taker, and a dozen other things.

- You cannot borrow money without a business plan. There are software programs to help you write one.

- Don't spend a fortune setting up your office. Find inexpensive alternatives to fancy furniture and expensive computers.

- Know how much the start-up of the business will cost, including personal living expenses. You still have to eat whether the business succeeds or not.

Recommended Reading

Berner, Jeff. *The Joy of Working from Home.* San Francisco: Berrett-Koehler Publishers, Inc., 1994.

Davis, Will. *Start Your Own Business For $1,000 or Less.* Dover, NH: Upstart Publishing Company, Inc., 1995.

Edwards, Paul and Sarah. *The Best Home Businesses for the 90s.* Los Angeles: Jeremy P. Tarcher, Inc., 1991.

Goldstein, Arnold S., PhD. *Starting on a Shoestring.* New York: John Wiley & Sons, 1991.

Harper, Stephen C. *The McGraw-Hill Guide to Starting Your Own Business.* New York: McGraw-Hill, Inc., 1991.

Lovig, Brian. *Bright Business Ideas.* Oroville, WA: Bright Publishing Inc., 1993.

Paulson, Edward, with Marcia Layton. *The Complete Idiot's Guide to Starting Your Own Business.* New York: Alpha Books, 1995.

Sotkin, Joan. *Starting Your Own Business.* Laguna Hills, CA: Build Your Business, Inc., 1993.

Some associations that can give you more information about starting your own business can be found in the appendix.

Lifestyle Trends

*W*hen job demands change, lifestyles change as well. SuccessThink will never just mean success in the workplace. Movies, TV, music, entertainment, family life, housing —these things change constantly, along with what and where we eat, what we wear, and where we're headed. What changes will you see in the future? Like success, your future is in your hands. However, some knowledgeable people have made predictions based on yesterday's history and today's trends.

THE WORLD GROWS SMALLER

The Environment: In 1990, fewer than half of America's high school seniors had ever heard of the greenhouse effect. Roughly 70% could not identify Chernobyl as the worst nuclear accident in history. Rain forests have been devastated during the past decade to make way for our encroachment upon nature. The ozone layer has a huge hole in it; global warming is melting polar icecaps. Endangered species have a better chance of survival in zoos than in their natural habitats. Prediction? Environmental issues will expand as we discover the impossibility of living with the destruction resulting from past ignorance. Hopefully, schools will add environmental science as a requirement instead of an elective.

Health and Wellness. Despite advances in drug treatments, medicine is seeing airborne tuberculosis, meningitis, and highly drug-resistant illnesses sprout up all over. The ancient plagues of leprosy, cholera, and typhoid fever are joined by flesh-eating strep, ebola, hanta, AIDS and a host of other diseases still to be identified. Millions of children go to bed hungry every night while, in the U.S., roughly 42% of women and 36% of men aged 45-54 are overweight. Sexually transmitted diseases (STDs)—syphilis, gonorrhea, herpes, and AIDS—flourish as drug-resistant strains of STDs become prevalent. Prediction? Health and wellness, medical care in emerging nations, and controlling pandemic disease will be vital elements of the next decade.

Nuclear energy. Once the promise of endless power and the solution to fossil fuels, nuclear energy has left us with an untenable end product—radioactive waste. Along with other forms of pollution, garbage, and sewage, the disposal of waste products and the value of recycling efforts will continue to bear scrutiny. Prediction? A return to low-waste conservation efforts will become an imperative in the new millennium.

Finance. A single Eurocurrency is coming into existence. Although a few European countries have initially passed on adopting the Eurocurrency, you only have to look at the vitality of the Common Market to see that a unified currency will prevail. Emerging markets will continue to provide cheap labor. If you believe history repeats itself, then think of the mineworkers in the U.S., child labor during the Industrial Revolution, and slave labor throughout the

"Adventure is worthwhile in itself."

—*Amelia Earhart*

world. Prediction? Can unionism be far behind in emerging nations?

Life Expectancy. "In a culture in which 60 feels like 45 and 50 feels like 35, the reality about how we live, love, work, and play at a certain age is amazingly different from what we imagined or expected," says trend maven Faith Popcorn in *Clicking*. People are living longer, more vital lives. At the same time, death with dignity is an option being taken away by modern medicine. Fear of malpractice suits urges medical personnel to save everyone from 1.5 pound babies to 95 year-old Alzheimer's victims. Prediction? Living wills and "DNR"—do not resuscitate—demands will become more essential as life-sustaining efforts increase in success.

WORKPLACE CHANGES

"Predicting how the millennium will redefine business has become a favorite pastime of Corporate America, where hyperpaced competition has tuned the present, let alone the future, into a high-stakes craps game," says Kathy Balog in *USA Today*.

You already know that corporations seek ways to do more with less—less inventory, less management, and less permanent staff. Modified versions of teamwork concepts will flourish—there is no other way to get the work done.

According to Gerald Celente, author of *Trends 2000*, "As consumers shop by computer, malls will die out; video phones will become the hottest digital invention; clean food devoid of chemicals and processing will eclipse accepted farming and processing procedures; a new energy source will replace oil."

Faith Popcorn states that women will be "cashing out." This means that working women will question the

THE TEN MOST
TRUSTED
OCCUPATIONS

1. Druggists

2. Clergy

3. College teachers

4. Medical doctors

5. Dentists

6. Policemen

7. Engineers

8. Funeral directors

9. Bankers

10. Journalists

(Source: Gallup Poll, December, 1996)

intrinsic value of a high-powered career. Women will weigh giving up family and home for the workplace. This is another area where telecommuting will come into play, as mother decides that she can have both children and job.

Popcorn also predicts the rise of the vigilante consumer. She sees consumers pressuring, protesting, and politicking against marketplace abuses.

Away from the Office

What will happen beyond your cubicle? Most likely, we'll still be interested in the same areas as in the past: children, family, friends, hobbies. The difference will be what we are dealing with within each of these spheres.

Education. Many people who attended elementary school in the fifties and sixties are shocked by the changes seen in education. American children are moving through school without learning to read, write, add, and subtract. In addition, children cope with problems beyond the imagining of their parents and grandparents. In 1960, major offenses in elementary school consisted of chewing gum in class, talking back to the teacher, cursing, and hitting another student. Today, students pass through metal detectors on their way to kindergarten. They are faced with child pushers trying to turn them on to drugs. Sexual activity begins as early as fifth and sixth grade.

Children spend less time in class learning as teachers spend more time maintaining discipline. Tests are done by "fill-in-the-bubble" with the classic number 2 pencil and graded by a computer. Corporations flood schools with teaching aids, commercializing learning. And corporate gifts come with strings attached. Prediction? Schools will be forced to go back to basics, teachers will have to pass on showing videos and be expected to actually teach. Illiteracy will affect more than 25% of the U.S. population—a figure that will rise with every decade unless measures are taken to teach Johnny to read.

Family. The desire to be on the go all the time will give way to evenings in which the family actually spends time together. With half of all U.S. marriages ending in divorce, the problems of single parents will continue and state governments will expand programs to cut down on deadbeat parents. The classic family of mom, dad, and 2.4 children may fade from existence. Family groups will be formed by people linked together by some other criteria than those of the traditional mold. Prediction? This is more of a prayer than a prediction: Families will start eating dinner together at night.

Retirement. As boomers turn into geezer boomers, Social Security will have far fewer people contributing and far more people withdrawing funds. People will live longer and draw on Social Security and Medicare benefits longer. Already the age at which one can draw Social Security is rising. Within the next decade, personal investment levels will increase as more people realize that retirement will be impossible without prior planning. In addition, elder care will become as important to employees as childcare is today. Many middle-aged employees will have both their children and their parents to plan for. Prediction? The federal government will have to allow people to step away from Social Security in whole or in part, realizing that Social Security cannot bear the weight of supporting the baby boomer generation.

"I wonder if we have really grown to the point where the size of a house in which a person lives will have little interest to his neighbors, but what he contributes in mind and character to the community will bring him respect and admiration."

—Eleanor Roosevelt

Technology

In 1993, 62% of the owners of home computers made over $75,000 a year. But, the massive hi-tech industry is evolving as you read this book. Computers once took up an entire room; today, you can put one in your briefcase. Hi-tech is now more affordable than ever, and tomorrow it will be cheaper still.

As a job opportunity, hi-tech will continue to have more, innovate changes, and demand more of its employees. According to the Bureau of Labor Statistics, computer and electronics industries' employees average 10–28% more hours at work than average U.S. industries.

Schools will become more dependent on technology in the classroom. Laptops, computer workstations, and Internet access will be part of every class, not just the computer lab. Students will have increasing exposure to hi-tech career planning.

Your TV set, once a major space filler in the living room, will hang on your wall like a picture. Your phone, once a rotary dial convenience, will be replaced by a video phone so your boss and your mother-in-law can see you still haven't gotten dressed. And your kids will still program the VCR without ever reading the manual.

The Person Inside

Regardless of the changes in the decades ahead, the basic elements of humanity will not change. Your success will still be based on the person you choose to become. Expand your horizons. Educate yourself. Pursue a dynamic lifestyle. Take responsibility for yourself, your actions, and your success.

Success is romantic, alluring, enticing. Success is hard work, sweat, smiles. Success is choices, paths, helping hands. Success is yours—if you want it.

CHAPTER RECAP

- Focus on environmental issues will sharpen.

- Aging America and pandemic disease will be primary interests in medicine.

SEVEN STEPS TO SELF-FULFILLMENT

- *Know who is responsible.*

- *Believe in something big.*

- *Practice tolerance.*

- *Be brave.*

- *Love someone.*

- *Be ambitious.*

- *Smile.*

(Source: Walter Anderson, The Confidence Course)

- Energy conservation will become essential.

- The workplace will no longer be the focus of American life.

- Family and education will surge to the head of personal priority lists.

- Your success and happiness will depend on YOU.

Recommended Reading

Celente, Gerald. *Trends 2000: How to Prepare for and Profit from the Changes of the 21st Century.* New York: Warner Books, 1997.

Drucker, Peter F. *Managing for the Future.* New York: Truman Talley Books, 1992.

Popcorn, Faith, and Lys Marigold. *Clicking.* New York: HarperCollins, Inc., 1996. Or any other Faith Popcorn book.

Toffler, Alvin. *Powershift: Knowledge, Wealth, and Violence at the Edge of the 21st Century.* New York: Bantam Books, 1991.

Helpful Resources

Business Web Sites

The Better Business Bureau Advisory Service
URL: http://www.bbb.org

Career and Resume Management for the 21st Century!
URL: http://crm21.com

Bureau of Labor Statistics URL: http://stats.bls.gov

Forbes Online URL: http://www.forbes.com

National Business Employment Weekly, from the publishers
of the *Wall Street Journal* URL: http://www.nbew.com

The Monster Board
URL: http://www.monster.com

SmartBiz Resources for Job Seekers and Employers
URL: http://www.smartbiz.com

Career Magazine URL: http://www.careermag.com

Hard@Work URL: http://www.hardatwork.com

careerWEB URL: http://www.cweb.com

Associations for Start-up Businesses

American Association of Professional Consultants
9100 Ward Parkway, Kansas City, MO 64114

American Business Women's Association
9100 Ward Parkway, Kansas City, MO 64114

Equal Employment Advisory Council
1015 15th St. NW, Ste. 1220, Washington, DC 20005

Latin American Management Association
49 New Jersey Avenue, SE, Washington, DC 10003

National Association of the Cottage Industry
P. O. Box 1446, Chicago, IL 60614

National Association of Minority Women in Business
906 Grand Avenue, Ste. 200, Kansas City, MO 64106

National Association of the Self-Employed
P. O. Box 612067, DFW Airport, TX 75261

National Association of Women Business Owners
110 Wayne Avenue, Ste. 830, Silver Springs, MD 20910

National Minority Business Council
235 E. 42nd St., New York, NY 10017

SCORE (Service Corp of Retired Executives)
409 3rd Street, SW, 4th Fl., Washington, DC 20024

Small Business Foundation of America
1155 15th Street, NW, Washington, DC 20005

Glossary

ADA (Americans With Disabilities Act): a federal law that ensures physical access and right-to-work for all Americans. Typical ADA requirements include wheelchair access to buildings, handicapped parking spaces, and Braille menus for the blind.

Affirmative action: offering employment and education to minorities based on their racial status

Age Discrimination in Employment Act (ADEA): a federal law that prevents companies from discriminating against employees for age-based criteria

Amortization: the process of writing off certain expenditures over a period of time

Aptitude test: identifying skills and abilities, usually for employment

Bad debt ratio: the amount of money you believe customers won't pay divided by the total sales, expressed as a percentage

Benchmarking: evaluating your company or product against another company or product noted for excellence in the industry

Buzzword: the jargon or language of a specific business or industry

Chart of accounts: categories used by a business to record financial expenses and assets

Close corporation (C corp): no public investors; stockholders active in daily management of the business

COBRA (Consolidated Omnibus Budget Reconciliation Act): Companies with 20 or more employees must provide maintenance of health insurance for 18 months after employees leave the company

Cost plus pricing: price = sales + profit

Critical shortage occupations: jobs in which there are fewer applicants than positions available

Cross training: learning other jobs in other departments

DBA: doing business as, the alias under which an owner does business. Example: Joe Doe DBA Doe's Deli Delights

Decentralization: moving the main source of business activity and decision making away from headquarters and into branch locations

Depreciation: loss of value, usually on capital investments like desks and computers

EIN: Employer Identification Number. Call the IRS to get your EIN application form. You need an EIN for all IRS business reports unless you are a sole proprietor with no employees

Employee-assistance program (EAP): a mental-health program offered by a company for its employees

Equal Pay Act of 1963: Gender of employee should not be used in determining compensation

Equity financing: obtaining financing (capital) based on collateral in a business or home

ESOP: employee stock option plan, a method of having employees invest in their company

Federal tax deposit coupon: a form submitted with federal tax withholding, Social Security, and Medicare payments

Flexspace/flexplace: working both in and out of the standard workplace, telecommuting, and even sharing a desk with another employee

Gross profit: total profits without deductions or adjustments

IRS form 941: Employer's Quarterly Federal Tax Return, a "must-do" for all corporations and businesses

Just-in-time delivery: receiving materials just prior to need in order to minimize inventory

Liquid assets: cash on hand or readily obtainable

LLC: limited liability corporation

LRP: long-range planning

LTD: long-term disability; insurance against a long-term illness.

Market-based pricing: setting a price based on what the competition is charging for the same or equal products/services

Merit raise or promotion: advancement or salary increases based on performance rather than years of service

Negative personality: an attitude problem, a person who always looks at the downside of every situation

Net profit: the profit remaining after deductions and adjustments have been made

Network: contacts you have through business or social connections

OJT: on-the-job training, learning as you go

Outplacement: placing employees in new jobs or retraining programs once they have been separated from their jobs

P&L: profit and loss, a year-end measurement of sales and expenditures

Partnership: a legal arrangement among two or more people to run a business, assume joint liability, and share profits

PCA: the franchisor for in-store photo studios like those found in Sears or JC Penney

Product penetration: increasing sales through selling more product to an individual customer

Product positioning: placing a product in a high-performance, targeted market

Real time: the here and now

Results-oriented evaluation: being evaluated based on results of a given project(s)

S corp: a domestic corporation with only one class of stock and fewer than 35 stockholders (individuals, estates, trusts only)

Sole proprietorship: a company owned by a single person

SOP: standard operating procedure or standards of performance

Telecommuting: working from home via fax, phone, and e-mail

TQM: Total Quality Management, a comprehensive program designed to maximize productivity and output

WARN: (Worker Adjustment and Retraining Notification Act) Companies with 100 or more employees that pursue a mass lay-off or plant closing must give 60 days notice before the final day of work

Bibliography

"Average Annual Pay for 1994 and 1995 for All Covered Work by Metropolitan Area," Bureau of Labor Statistics, 1995.

"Corporate America's Most Powerful People," *Forbes,* 1996–1997.

"Forbes Four Hundred—Index by Worth, Top 50," *Forbes,* 1996–1997.

"Mass Layoffs Summary," Local Area Unemployment Statistics, USDL 97–154, Bureau of Labor Statistics, May 9, 1997.

"Preparing for Interviews," Career Planning and Placement Center, State University of New York at Buffalo, 1996.

"Rolling Along the Mommy Track," *Time Magazine,* March 27, 1989.

"Women Missing Good Jobs in a Key Growth Industry," USA Today, March 19, 1997.

Allen, Robert. *The Challenge.* New York: Simon & Schuster, 1987.

Anderson, Walter. *The Confidence Course.* New York: HarperCollins, 1997.

Angelou, Maya. *All God's Children Need Traveling Shoes.* New York: Random House, Inc., 1986.

Asheghian, P., and B. Ebrahimi. *International Business.* New York: Harper and Row, 1990.

Baker, Stephen, Gary McWilliams and Manjeet Kripalani. "Forget the Huddled Masses: Send Nerds," *Business Week,* July 21, 1997.

Barker, Robert. "Securing Your Future: A Self-Help Guide," *Business Week,* July 21, 1997.

Bell, Arthur H. *Great Jobs Abroad.* New York: McGraw-Hill, 1997.

Bell, Chip R. *Managers As Mentors.* San Francisco: Berrett-Koehler, 1996.

Berner, Jeff. *The Joy of Working from Home.* San Francisco: Berrett-Koehler Publishers, Inc., 1994.

Bernstein, Albert J., and Sydney Craft Rozen. "The Nice Manager Trap," *Executive Female,* January/February, 1995.

Besson, Tawnee. "Four Typical Job-Search Blunders," *National Business Employment Weekly,* July 1, 1995.

Bick, Julie. *All I Really Need to Know in Business I Learned at Microsoft.* New York: Pocket Books, 1997.

Blair, Gerard M. "Groups That Work," from *Starting to Manage: The Essential Skills.* United Kingdom: Chartwell-Bratt.

Blanchard, Kenneth, Donald Carew, and Eunice Parisi-Carew. *The One-Minute Manager Builds High Performing Teams.* New York: William Morrow and Company, Inc., 1990.

Blanchard, Kenneth, William Oncken Jr., and Hal Burrows. *The One-Minute Manager Meets the Monkey.* New York: William Morrow and Company, Inc., 1989

Bliss, Edwin C. *Getting Things Done.* New York: Charles Scribner's Sons, 1991.

Block, Jay A., and Michael Betrus. *101 Best Resumés.* New York: McGraw-Hill, 1997.

Bly, Amy, and Robert W. Bly. "Improving Your Interpersonal Skills: How to Handle Difficult People." Dumont, New Jersey: Center for Technical Communication.

Brimelow, Peter. "The Glass Floor," *Forbes,* December 16, 1996.

Brinkman, Dr. Rick, and Dr. Rick Kirschner. *Dealing with People You Can't Stand.* New York: McGraw-Hill, Inc., 1994.

Brown, Les. *It's Not Over Until You Win!* New York: Simon & Schuster, 1997.

Byrne, John A. "Commentary: Management Theory—Or Fad of the Month?" *Business Week,* June 23, 1997.

Cairo, Jim. *Motivation and Goal-Setting,* Second Edition. Hawthorne, NJ: Career Press, 1993.

Carey, Patricia M. "Expatriate Games," *Working Woman,* May 1998.

Castro, Janice, and Thomas McCarroll. "How's Your Pay?" *Time Magazine,* April 15, 1991.

Celente, Gerald. *Trends 2000: How to Prepare for and Profit from the Changes of the 21st Century.* New York: Warner Books, 1997.

Church, George, J. "Disconnected," *Time Magazine,* January 15, 1996.

Clemmer, Jim. *Pathways to Performance: A Guide to Transforming Yourself, Your Team and Your Organization.* Toronto: Macmillan Canada, 1996.

Coburn, Jennifer. *Take Back Your Power.* San Francisco: ISM Press, 1995.

Cohen, Herb. *You Can Negotiate Anything.* Los Angeles: Audio Renaissance Tapes, Inc., 1990.

Collins, Nancy W. *Professional Women and Their Mentors.* Englewood Cliffs, NJ: Prentice Hall, 1983.

Corcodilos, Nick A. "The Secret to Finding a Good Headhunter," North Bridge Group, 1995.

Covey, Stephen R. *Seven Habits of Highly Effective People.* New York: Simon & Schuster, 1989.

Covey, Stephen R., A. Roger Merrill, and Rebecca R. Merrill. *First Things First.* New York: Simon & Schuster, 1994.

Covey, Stephen R., and A. Roger Merrill. "New Ways to Get Organized at Work," *USA Weekend*, February 6–8, 1998.

Dauten, Dale. "Ah, the Pitfalls, or Pole Falls, of Team Building," *Greenville News*, July 14, 1997. Op-ed 1.

Davich, Victor. *The Best Guide to Meditation.* Los Angeles: Renaissance Media, 1997.

Davidson, Lance. *The Ultimate Reference Book: The Wit's Thesaurus.* New York: Avon, 1994.

Davidson, Paul. "Plan Revisits Home-Office Tax Deductions," *Greenville News*, July 14, 1997.

Davis, Will. *Start Your Own Business for $1,000 or Less.* Dover, NH: Upstart Publishing Company, Inc., 1995.

DelBuono, Daniele. "Careers 2000 Offers Tips for Co-Op, Post-Grad Jobs," *The Northeastern News*, Northeastern University, April 9, 1997.

Dolan, Kerry A. "When Money Isn't Enough," *Forbes*, November 18, 1996.

Donaldson, Michael C., and Mimi Donaldson. *Negotiating for Dummies.* Foster City, CA: IDG Books Worldwide, 1996.

Drucker, Peter F. *Managing for the Future.* New York: Truman Talley Books, 1992.

Edwards, Paul and Sarah. *The Best Home Businesses for the 90s.* Los Angeles: Jeremy P. Tarcher, Inc., 1991.

Eigen, Barry. *How to Think Like a Boss (Audiotape).* Los Angeles: Audio Renaissance Tapes, Inc., 1991.

Faux, Marian. *The Complete Resumé Guide.* New York: Prentice Hall, 1992.

Feinberg, Mortimer, and John J. Tarrant. "When Smart People Do Dumb Things," *Executive Female*, July/August, 1995.

Ferris, Donna MacCougall. "Don't Let a Job Loss Knock You Off Your Feet," *National Business Employment Weekly*, October 1, 1996.

Fisher, Lionel L. *On Your Own.* Englewood Cliffs, NJ: Prentice Hall, 1995.

Frost, Ted S. *The Second Coming of the Woolly Mammoth.* Berkeley, CA: Ten Speed Press, 1991.

Fulghum, Robert. *All I Really Need to Know I Learned in Kindergarten.* New York: Villard Books, 1986.

Fullerton Jr., Howard N. "Tomorrow's Jobs," *Occupational Outlook Handbook,* Bureau of Labor Statistics, March 7, 1996.

Gabriel, Gail. "Delegating Do's and Don'ts," *Executive Female,* May 1998.

Gaines, Lynne. "Managing People Whose Jobs You Can't Do," *Executive Female,* January/February, 1995.

Geller, Robert E. *How to Survive in the Nonprofit World.* Sacramento: California State Library Foundation, 1990.

Gibbons, Barry. *This Indecision is Final.* Burr Ridge, IL: Irwin Professional Publishing, 1996.

Girard, Joe. *Mastering Your Way to the Top.* New York: Warner Books, Inc., 1995.

Goldstein, Arnold S., PhD. *Starting on a Shoestring.* New York: John Wiley & Sons, 1991.

Gonyea, Wayne M. "Keyword Resumés—Your New Hi-Tech Way to Get a Job!" On-line Solutions, Inc., 1997.

Graham, John R. *203 Ways to Be Supremely Successful in the New World Of Selling.* New York: Macmillan Spectrum, 1996.

Green, Kay. "The Big Hurdle: Contacts and Referrals," *Career Magazine,* 1997.

Greenwald, John, and William McWhirter. "Is Mr. Nice Guy Back?" *Time Magazine,* January 27, 1992.

Greenwald, John, with Bernard Baumohl, Marc Hequet, and Elaine Shannon. "Permanent Pink Slips," *Time Magazine,* September 9, 1991.

Greenwald, John. "Workers: Risks and Rewards," *Time Magazine,* April 15, 1991.

Grove, Andrew S. *Only the Paranoid Survive.* New York: Currency Doubleday, 1996.

Hammonds, Keith H. "Balancing Work and Family," *Business Week,* September 16, 1996.

Hardy, Eric S. "Jobs and Productivity," *Forbes,* April 21, 1997.

Harper, Stephen C. *The McGraw-Hill Guide to Starting Your Own Business.* New York: McGraw-Hill, Inc., 1991.

Harris, Nicole. "A Woman's Place is at the Cash Register," *Business Week,* June 30, 1997.

Hartmann, Stacey. "Job Seekers Face Nontraditional Modes of Screening," *Greenville News,* July 15, 1997.

Hauter, Janet. *The Smart Woman's Guide to Career Success.* Hawthorne, NJ: Career Press, 1993.

Heggy, Pat. "Future Resumés and Diversity in the 21st Century Workplace," Heggy Leadership Enterprises, 1997.

Hendricks, William, ed. *Coaching, Mentoring and Managing.* Franklin Lakes, NJ: Career Press, 1996.

Henze, Geraldine. *Winning Career Moves.* Homewood, IL: Business One Irwin, 1992.

Hiatt, Jeff. "Five Steps for Creating Effective Visions," *BPR Online Learning Center,* 1996.

Hill, Napoleon. *Keys to Success*. New York: Dutton, 1994.

Hochheiser, Robert M. *If You Want Guarantees, Buy a Toaster*. New York: William Morrow, 1991.

Hochheiser, Robert. *How to Work for a Jerk*. New York: Vintage Books, 1987.

Hornstein, Harvey A. *Brutal Bosses and Their Prey*. New York: Riverhead Books, 1996.

Jackson, Maggie. "Telecommuting Taking Hold in America,"*Greenville News*, July 3, 1997.

Jackson, Tom. *The Perfect Resumé*. New York: Doubleday Anchor, 1981.

James, Jennifer. *Thinking in the Future Tense: Leadership Skills for a New Age*. New York: Simon & Schuster, 1996.

James, Peter, and Nick Thorpe. *Ancient Inventions*. New York: Ballantine Books, 1994.

Jeffers, Michelle. "Here Come the Consultants," *Forbes ASAP*, April 7, 1997.

Jordan, Michael. *I Can't Accept Not Trying*. San Francisco: HarperCollins, 1994.

Kaplan, Burton. *Winning People Over*. Englewood Cliffs, NJ: Prentice Hall, 1996.

Kennedy, Marilyn Moats. "The Job-Hunt Club," *Executive Female*, May/June 1997.

Klein, Gary Ethan. "Why You Must Use a Headhunter," Washington, DC: Klein, Landau & Romm, 1996.

Kotter, John P. *Leading Change*. Boston: Harvard Business School Press, 1996.

Larocca, Kay. "A Good Rule On Resumés: Be Concise, to the Point," *Career Magazine,* 1996.

Lee, Tony. "How To Change Careers," *National Business Employment Weekly,* February 1, 1996.

Lee, Tony. "It's Never Too Late to Find Your Perfect Career," *National Business Employment Weekly,* June 1, 1995.

Levine, Michael. *Selling Goodness: The Guerrilla P.R. Guide to Promoting Your Charity, Nonprofit Organization, or Fund-Raising Event.* Los Angeles, CA: Renaissance Books, 1998.

Levine, Michael. *Take It from Me: Practical and Inspiring Career Advice from the Celebrated and Successful.* New York: Perigee Books, 1996.

Levinson, Jay, and Seth Godin. *The Guerrilla Marketing Handbook.* Boston: Houghton Mifflin, 1994.

Levokove, Michael, with Celeste Levokove. *The Selling Edge.* Lakewood, CO: Glenbridge Publishing, Ltd., 1993.

Loeb, Marshall. "What to do When a Headhunter Calls," *Fortune,* August, 1995.

Lovig, Brian. *Bright Business Ideas.* Oroville, WA: Bright Publishing Inc., 1993.

Luthy, David H. "Total Quality Management," Utah Association of Certified Public Accountants, 1997.

Mackay, Harvey. *Swim with the Sharks without Being Eaten Alive.* New York: William Morrow and Company, 1988.

Mahoney, David, with Richard Conarroe. *Confessions of a Street-Smart Manager.* New York: Simon & Schuster, 1988.

Malburg, Chris. *How to Fire Your Boss.* New York: Berkeley, 1971.

Mandino, Og. *The Return of the Ragpicker.* New York: Bantam, 1992.

_____. S*ecrets for Success and Happiness.* New York: Fawcett Columbine, 1995.

March, Robert M. *Working for a Japanese Company.* Tokyo: Kodansha, Inc., 1992.

McCormack, John, with David R. Legge. *Self-Made in America.* Reading, MA: Addison Wesley, 1990.

McCormack, Mark H. *On Negotiating.* Beverly Hills, CA: Dove Books, 1995.

Melcher, Richard A. "Manpower Upgrades Its Resumé," *Business Week,* June 10, 1996.

Myers, Marc. *How to Make Luck: 7 Secrets Lucky People Use to Succeed.* Los Angeles, CA: Renaissance Books, 1999.

Migs Damiani, A. S. "Motivating Employees for Peak Performance," in *AFE Facilities Engineering Journal.*

Miller, Lyle H., Ph.D. *The Stress Solution.* New York: Pocket Books, 1994.

Morris, Dick. *The New Prince,* Los Angeles, CA: Renaissance Books, 1999.

Munk, Nina, and Suzanne Oliver. "Think Fast!" *Forbes,* March 24, 1997.

Munro, Barry Graham. S*mart Salespeople Sometimes Wear Plaid.* Rocklin, CA: Prima Publishing, 1994.

Noer, David M. "After The Pink Slips." *Executive Female,* July/August 1995.

Oakley, Ed, and Doug Krug. *Enlightened Leadership.* New York: Simon & Schuster, 1991.

Ogilvy, David. *Confessions of an Advertising Man.* New York: Atheneum, 1988.

Orsburn, Jack, Linda Morgan, Ed Musselwhite, and Jack Zenger. *Self-Directed Work Teams: The New American Challenge.* Business One Irwin, 1990.

Parkinson, J. Robert. *How to Get People to Do Things Your Way.* Lincolnwood, IL: NTC Publishing Group, 1995.

Pascale, Richard Tanner. *Managing on the Edge.* New York: Simon & Schuster, 1990.

Paulson, Edward, with Marcia Layton. *The Complete Idiot's Guide to Starting Your Own Business.* New York: Alpha Books, 1995.

Peale, Norman Vincent. *The True Joy of Positive Living.* New York: William Morrow and Company, Inc., 1984.

Pell, Dr. Arthur R., *The Complete Idiot's Guide to Managing People.* New York: Alpha Books, 1995.

Perrault, Michael R., and Janet K. Irwin. "Women in Power." Agoura Hills, CA: Advanced Teamware, 1996.

Peters, Tom, and Nancy Austin. *A Passion for Excellence.* New York: Random House, 1985.

Peters, Tom. "Opportunity Knocks," *Forbes ASAP,* June 2, 1997.

Popcorn, Faith, and Lys Marigold. *Clicking.* New York: HarperCollins, Inc., 1996.

Powell, Colin, with Joseph E. Persico. *My American Journey.* New York: Random House, Inc., 1995.

Rancourt, Karen. *The Empowered Professional: How to Succeed in the 90's.* Harvard, MA: 1996.

Randall, Karen. *The Twelve Truths about Surviving and Succeeding in the Office.* New York: Berkeley Books, 1997.

Reilly, Tom. *Value-Added Selling Techniques.* Chicago: Congdon & Weed, 1989.

Reinhold, Barbara Bailey. *Toxic Work.* New York: Dutton, 1996.

Ricks, David A. *Blunders in International Business.* Cambridge, MA: Blackwell Publishers, 1993.

Riley, Pat. *The Winner Within.* New York: G.P. Putnam's Sons, 1993.

Rincover, Arnie. "Type A Personalities," CareerWeb, 1994.

Robbins, Anthony, and Joseph McClendon, III. *Unlimited Power, A Black Choice.* New York: Simon & Schuster, 1997.

Roth, Charles B., and Roy Alexander. *Secrets of Closing Sales.* Englewood Cliffs, NJ: Prentice Hall, 1993.

Rudolph, Barbara, and William McWhirter. "Why Can't a Woman Manage more Like . . . a Woman?" *Time Magazine,* November 8, 1990.

Schweitzer, Albert. *Out of My Life and Thought.* New York: Holt Rinehart Winston, 1949.

Searing, Jill A., and Anne B. Lovett. "Five Big Career Crises: Overcome and Conquer Them," *Executive Female,* May/June 1997.

Silverstein, Stuart. "Job Prospects Look Hot for 'Geezer Boomers' in 2020," *Los Angeles Times,* April 26, 1997.

Silverstein, Stuart. "More Big Firms Cut Jobs Despite Economy's Rise," *Los Angeles Times,* September 9, 1994.

Simms, Darrell. *Black Experience Strategies and Tactics in the Business World.* Beaverton, OR: Management Aspects Inc., 1991.

Smith, Leslie. "Connecting with Other Women," *Executive Female,* May/June 1997.

Society of Human Resource Management and Aon Consulting, *1997 Survey of Human Resource Trends.*

Sotkin, Joan. *Starting Your Own Business.* Laguna Hills, CA: Build Your Business, Inc., 1993.

Taggart, James H., and Michael C. McDermott. *The Essence of International Business.* Hemel, England: Prentice Hall International, Inc., 1993.

Thomas, Dave. *Well Done!* Grand Rapids, MI: Zondervan Publishing House, 1994.

Tien, Ellen, and Valerie Frankel. *The I Hate My Job Handbook.* New York: Fawcett Columbine, 1996.

Toffler, Alvin. *Powershift: Knowledge, Wealth, and Violence at the Edge of the 21st Century.* New York: Bantam Books, 1991.

Tulgan, Bruce. *Managing Generation X.* Santa Monica: Merritt Publishing, 1995.

Tunick, George. "Re-Educating Chauvinists," *Executive Female,* January/February, 1995.

Wallis, Claudia. "Onward, Women!" *Time Magazine,* December 24, 1989.

Weisbord, Marvin R. *Productive Workplaces: Organizing and Managing for Dignity, Meaning and Community.* San Francisco: Jossey-Bass, 1991.

Wheeler, Carol. "Just (Don't) Do It," *Executive Female,* May/June, 1997.

Woodring, Susan Fowler. *Mentoring: How to Foster Your Career's Most Crucial Relationships* (audiotape). Boulder, CO: Career Track, Inc., 1992.

Yate, Martin. "The Seven Secrets of Long-Term Career Survival," Adams Online. Adams Media Corporation, 1997.

Audiobooks on Success from
Audio Renaissance

Bloomfield, M.D., Harold H., and Robert K. Cooper.
The Power of 5

Buskirk, Richard H. *The Entrepreneur's Audio Handbook*

Buzan, Tony. *Super-Creativity*

Canfield, Jack, and Mark Victor Hansen. *The Aladdin Factor:
How to Ask For and Get Everything You Want*

Carter-Scott, Chérie. *If Life Is a Game, These Are the Rules*

Cohen, Herb. *You Can Negotiate Anything*

Cypert, Samuel A. *Believe and Achieve*

De Bono, Edward. *Edward De Bono's Smart Thinking*

Decker, Bert. *You've Got to Be Believed to Be Heard*

DeJong, Hans. *How to Use the Silva Method™*

_____. *How to Use the Silva Method™ For Prosperity
and Abundance*

_____. *Silva Mind Control® For Success and
Self-Confidence*

_____. *Silva Mind Control® For Super Memory and
Speed Learning*

Fensterheim, Herbert, and Jean Baer. *Don't Say Yes When You
Want to Say No*

Fox, Jeffrey J. *How to Become CEO: The Rules for Rising to the Top
of Any Organization*

Goleman, Daniel. *Emotional Intelligence*

_____. *Working with Emotional Intelligence*

Gross, Ron. *Peak Learning*

Hansen, Mark Victor, and Jack Canfield. *Dare to Win*

Heider, John. *The Tao of Leadership*

Hill, Napoleon. *Napoleon Hill's Keys to Success: The 17 Principles of Personal Achievement*

————. *Selling You!*

————. *Think and Grow Rich*

Little, Tony, with Jesse James. *Tony Little's Conceive, Believe and Achieve*

————. *Tony Little's There's Always a Way*

Maltz, M.D., Maxwell. *Psycho-Cybernetics*

McLaughlin, Peter, with Peter McLaughlin Jr. *Catchfire!*

Messing, Bob. *The Tao of Management*

Morris, Tom. *If Aristotle Ran General Motors*

Musashi, Miyamoto. *The Book of Five Rings: Samurai Strategies for Modern Business Success*

Pickens, James W. *The Art of Closing Any Deal*

RoAne, Susan. *How to Work a Room: Networking Strategies and Beyond*

————. *The Secrets of Savvy Networking*

Robbins, Anthony. *Introduction to Anthony Robbins' Personal Power II*

Robbins, Anthony, with Coach John Wooden. *Powertalk!* ™: *The Decision that Ensures Your Success*

Robbins, Anthony, with Dr. Barbara De Angelis. *Powertalk!* ™: *Learn to Use the Power of Questions*

Robbins, Anthony, with Dr. Wayne Dyer. *Powertalk!* ™: *The Master Key to Personal Transformation*

Robbins, Anthony, with Dr. John Gray. *Powertalk!* ™: *On Creating Extraordinary Relationships*

Robbins, Anthony, with Dr. Stephen R. Covey. *Powertalk!* ™: *The Power of Anticipation*

Robbins, Anthony, with Deepak Chopra. *Powertalk!* ™: *The Power of the Human Paradox*

Robbins, Anthony, with Paul Zane Pilzer. *Powertalk!* ™: *The Power to Create, the Power to Destroy*

Robbins, Anthony, with Bernie Siegel. *Powertalk!* ™: *References, the Fabric of Our Lives*

Robbins, Anthony, with Mark McCormack. *Powertalk!* ™: *The Six Master Steps to Change*

Robbins, Anthony, with Dr. Leo Buscaglia. *Powertalk!* ™: *Where Love Begins*

Robbins, Anthony, with Dr. Leo Buscaglia, Dr. Barbara De Angelis, and Dr. Wayne Dyer. *Powertalk!* ™: *Personal Series*

Robbins, Anthony, with Dr. Stephen R. Covey, Paul Zane Pilzer, and Coach John Wooden. *Powertalk!* ™: *Professional Series*

Sher, Barbara. *Wishcraft: How to Get What You Really Want*

Spence, Gerry. *How to Argue and Win Every Time*

Tartaglia, M.D., Louis A. *Flawless: Your Top Ten Character Defects and What to Do About Them*

Templeton, John Marks. *The Templeton Plan*

_____. *Worldwide Laws of Life*

Index

About the Author

Barbara Somervill has been involved in business of all sizes for most of her adult life. Family business, corporate communications, trade journalism, and advertising have given her a chance to look at business opportunities from many sides. Today she runs a corporation of one, serving as ceo, president, writer and editor, secretrial staff, and chief custodian. She lives in Simpsonville, South Carolina, and may be contacted via e-mail at someriter@aol.com.